Narrative Strategies for Participation in
Dante's *Divine Comedy*

LEGENDA

LEGENDA is the Modern Humanities Research Association's book imprint for new research in the Humanities. Founded in 1995 by Malcolm Bowie and others within the University of Oxford, Legenda has always been a collaborative publishing enterprise, directly governed by scholars. The Modern Humanities Research Association (MHRA) joined this collaboration in 1998, became half-owner in 2004, in partnership with Maney Publishing and then Routledge, and has since 2016 been sole owner. Titles range from medieval texts to contemporary cinema and form a widely comparative view of the modern humanities, including works on Arabic, Catalan, English, French, German, Greek, Italian, Portuguese, Russian, Spanish, and Yiddish literature. Editorial boards and committees of more than 60 leading academic specialists work in collaboration with bodies such as the Society for French Studies, the British Comparative Literature Association and the Association of Hispanists of Great Britain & Ireland.

The MHRA encourages and promotes advanced study and research in the field of the modern humanities, especially modern European languages and literature, including English, and also cinema. It aims to break down the barriers between scholars working in different disciplines and to maintain the unity of humanistic scholarship. The Association fulfils this purpose through the publication of journals, bibliographies, monographs, critical editions, and the MHRA Style Guide, and by making grants in support of research. Membership is open to all who work in the Humanities, whether independent or in a University post, and the participation of younger colleagues entering the field is especially welcomed.

ALSO PUBLISHED BY THE ASSOCIATION

Critical Texts
Tudor and Stuart Translations • *New Translations* • *European Translations*
MHRA Library of Medieval Welsh Literature

MHRA Bibliographies
Publications of the Modern Humanities Research Association

The Annual Bibliography of English Language & Literature
Austrian Studies
Modern Language Review
Portuguese Studies
The Slavonic and East European Review
Working Papers in the Humanities
The Yearbook of English Studies

www.mhra.org.uk
www.legendabooks.com

ITALIAN PERSPECTIVES

In the light of growing academic interest in Italy and the reorganization of many university courses in Italian along interdisciplinary lines, this book series, founded by Maney Publishing under the imprint of the Northern Universities Press and now continuing under the Legenda imprint, aims to bring together different scholarly perspectives on Italy and its culture. *Italian Perspectives* publishes books and collections of essays on any period of Italian literature, language, history, culture, politics, art, and media, as well as studies which take an interdisciplinary approach and are methodologically innovative.

APPEARING IN THIS SERIES

Managing Editor
Dr Graham Nelson, 41 Wellington Square, Oxford OX1 2JF, UK
www.legendabooks.com

Narrative Strategies for Participation in Dante's *Divine Comedy*

❖

KATHERINE POWLESLAND

l

LEGENDA

Italian Perspectives 53
Modern Humanities Research Association
2022

Published by Legenda
an imprint of the Modern Humanities Research Association
Salisbury House, Station Road, Cambridge CB1 2LA

ISBN 978-1-83954-037-0 (HB)
ISBN 978-1-83954-038-7 (PB)

First published 2022

Copy-Editor: Dr Amanda Wrigley

CONTENTS

❖

ACKNOWLEDGEMENTS

❖

More than any institution I've known, the University of Cambridge seems to inspire goodwill and generosity both among those who study and work there and the people of its city. I am indebted to the many who lent time, resources, and expertise in their own fields to this project, including Alan Blackwell, Martin Bond, Julia Dale, Paul Fletcher, Jill Fordham, Penelope Hayes, Robin Kirkpatrick, Jenny Kirner, Bill Marshall, Emma Pierce, Anna Reali, David Richardson, Alan Rogerson, and Keith Sykes. I thank, with great affection, my dear Italian Section medievalist friends and fellow researchers: Valentina Mele, Nico Morelli, and Helena Phillips-Robins. Above all, I am grateful to Heather Webb, whose breadth of vision, guidance, and willingness to play has made the production of this book a joy.

K.P., June 2022

TRANSLATIONS, ABBREVIATIONS, EDITIONS

❖

Dante's poetry in the original is cited from Petrocchi; the abbreviations *Inf.*, *Purg.* and *Par.* are used for *Inferno*, *Purgatorio* and *Paradiso*. Translations of the *Divine Comedy* are from Robin Kirkpatrick's translation for Penguin (2006–07). Translations of other authors are my own unless otherwise noted.

The following commentaries on the *Divine Comedy* are cited according to the *Dartmouth Dante Project* <http://dantelab.dartmouth.edu>:

Jacopo Alighieri (1322)
L'Ottimo Commento (1333)
Benvenuto da Imola (1375–80)
Francesco da Buti (1385–95)
Anonimo Fiorentino (circa 1400)
Ernesto Trucchi (1936)
Natalino Sapegno (1955–57)
Umberto Bosco and Giovanni Reggio (1979)
Anna Maria Chiavacci Leonardi (1991–97)
Robert Hollander (2000–07)
Nicola Fosca (2003–15)

The following commentary is cited according to the Project Gutenberg e-book <http://www.gutenberg.org/files/30766/30766-h/30766-h.htm>:

Jacopo Alighieri, *Chiose alla cantica dell'Inferno di Dante Alighieri*

The following commentary is cited according to the digital resource <https://digitaldante.columbia.edu>:

Teodolinda Barolini, *Digital Dante Edition with Commento Baroliniano*

The following commentaries are cited from the printed editions below:

The Divine Comedy, trans. by Robert M. Durling, introduction and notes by Ronald L. Martínez and Robert M. Durling, 3 vols (New York: Oxford University Press, 1996–2011)

The Divine Comedy, trans. and ed. by Robin Kirkpatrick, 3 vols (London: Penguin, 2006–07)

The Divine Comedy, trans. with commentary by Charles S. Singleton, 3 vols (Princeton: Princeton University Press, 1980)

Verses from the *Holy Bible* (Douay/Rheims Version) are cited according to the following digital resource:

<http://www.drbo.org/>

INTRODUCTION

❖

Reading Interactively[1]

This book sets out a new model for reader participation in a printed text, taking as its subject Dante's *Divine Comedy,* and exploring how participation may be invited through mechanisms of narrative transmission. These include instruments of immersion, world creation, narrative perspective, narrative mediation, and narrative indeterminacy, or the similes, ellipses and other 'gaps' in the fabric of a narrative text that, in the words of reader response theorist Wolfgang Iser, give us 'the opportunity to picture things; indeed, without the elements of indeterminacy, the gaps in the text, we should not be able to use our imagination' (1974: 283). That the poem, in Simone Marchesi's phrase, 'invites an active hermeneutic engagement on the part of its readers' (2011: 4) is an established component in contemporary critical discourse on Dante. My interest in this book lies in extending this discussion through identifying the central narrative mechanisms by which such active engagement may be invited. Underlying my approach is the proposal that recent advances in two academic fields that both foreground the role of the body in constructing meaning — namely, cognitive neuroscience and video game critical theory — offer new tools to consider in textual literary theory, inviting fresh perspectives on the centrally important question of how to read the *Divine Comedy.*

Gianfranco Contini frames precisely this issue of different ways of reading Dante's narrative poem in his 1965 essay, 'Un'interpretazione di Dante', published in the collection *Un'idea di Dante* (1976), in which he raises the 'simple but radical' question [semplice e drastica domanda], of whether anyone, today, actually 'reads' the poem, 'se si legga ancora la *Divina Commedia*':

> What follows is a sincere examination of conscience of one to whom some responsibility for, or perhaps custodianship of, things Dantean has been entrusted. Such an examination must begin with the simple but radical question: whether anyone still reads the *Divina Commedia.* Not because one must at school, or from a sense of cultural obligation, but for the sheer pleasure of ranging, time and again, across the length of its narrative, one end to the other — yielding to its narrator, playing its game, letting its surprises do their work, just as we do every day with Homer and the *Aeneid, Orlando Furioso* and *Don Quixote,* with the *Promessi sposi* and all the other great novels of the nineteenth century, with the *Recherche du temps perdu,* with *Ulysses.*[2] (Contini 1976: 69)

'Reading' the poem, it becomes clear, means from end to end, 'da un capo all'altro'; respecting its mechanisms, yielding to the structures — literally, the game, the *gioco*

— of its narration, precisely as one would with any other of the great European literary narratives. Narrative theory has traditionally described such a mode of reading as *immersive* (although there are important differences between types of immersion):[3] an experience of such deep absorption in an alternative reality that the 'real' or physical world fades from conscious awareness — an experience Dante himself describes in *Purgatorio* XVII, writing of our deafness to even 'a thousand trumpets' [mille tube], in the midst of an imaginative transportation:[4]

> O imaginativa, che ne rube
> talvolta sì di fuor ch'om non s'accorge
> perché dintorno suonin mille tube,
>   chi move te, se 'l senso non ti porge? (13–16)

> Imagination, you at times will steal
> the outer world from us so we can't tell
> (even if horns in thousands blare around)
>   who makes you move when sense does not provide.[5]

In video game critical theory, a new model of immersion known as *presence* is gaining traction, as I explore later in this Introduction. Widely understood as 'the experiential counterpart of immersion', a definition attributed to cognitive neuropsychologist and digital media theorist Wijnand IJsselsteijn (2004: 136), presence describes an experience of a perceptual illusion of realistic embodied interaction in a virtual world, not simply as spectator but as a participant with agency. Contini's own metaphor of a physical roaming back and forth across the narrative's contours — literally, a 'running across', 'ripercorrerne il racconto' — invites precisely the conceptualisation of such an embodied, present, entering-in to the virtual space of the narrative, rather than a critically evaluative position of external observation. And whilst I have foregrounded here the digital, this lexicon of active physicality may also evoke for the medievalist the deeply personal and bodily modes of interaction with devotional texts associated with medieval practices of affective piety, to which I shall turn in the next chapter.

Certainly, a mode of experiential learning — learning by actively doing — lies at the very heart of the *Divine Comedy* (henceforth *Comedy*), motivating Dante's own journey, as Beatrice explains in *Purgatorio* XXX:

> 'Tanto giù cadde, che tutti argomenti
> a la salute sua eran già corti,
> fuor che mostrarli le perdute genti.' (136–38)[6]

> 'He fell so far that every other means
> to save this man, by now, came short, unless
> he saw, himself, those people who are lost.'

All attempts to *tell* Dante what he needed to understand, all 'argomenti', says Beatrice, had failed; and this is why Dante had to be sent to encounter — that is, directly experience through personal interaction — the 'perdute genti' for himself. As Christian Moevs observes: 'The point of the *Comedy* is that understanding *is* practical' (2005: 171; emphasis in original).[7]

However, it is rather, I suggest, into a critically evaluative mode of external objectivity — undeniably a position of 'great intellectual pleasure', as Zygmunt Barański has written (1989: 11) — that the discursive commentary tradition has tended to invite the Dante scholar, from its earliest days when, in 1322, Dante's son Jacopo Alighieri stated his intention to explicate the poem's 'profound and authentic meaning' [profondo e autentico intendimento] (Proemio, Libro Primo, 43). Such a tendency to privilege an elucidation of 'meaning', I suggest, has led to a lack of focus on individual participatory experience as an important and complementary mode of reading the poem.[8] But the *Comedy*, I shall propose, is an exceptionally participatory text (within what may be a relatively limited canon of such texts) as a result of Dante's deployment of a range of particular narrative strategies, and my position is that this is an important feature of the poem that has been neglected in Dante scholarship.

My interest is in technical narrative strategy: the narratological mechanisms in the poem that can serve as observable cues — and therefore open to analysis, whether the reader interacts with them or not — to reader presence and 'participation' in the *Comedy*. My aim is to describe what constitutes such a participatory mode of reading; to identify the mechanisms in the text that invite it; and through replicable and quantified evidence, to demonstrate that such a mode of reading is strategically invited throughout the poem.

Narratological approaches to the *Comedy*

With a few significant exceptions, the narrative mechanisms of Dante's text have remained relatively under-examined. In the 1950s, three separate essays by Hermann Gmelin (1951), Erich Auerbach (1953), and Leo Spitzer (1955) took up the question of the device of the so-called 'direct address' to the reader, noting its potential to mediate a 'new relationship' between poet and reader (although the nature of this new relationship remains undefined in their essays).[9] However, in focusing on only 'the most accessible' (to appropriate Barański's phrase) of the poem's invitations to participate — those that serve to invite the reader out of the narrated space in order to exercise her cognitive faculties at a conscious level ('pensa', 'ricorditi', 'imagini': think, remember, imagine) — none of the essays takes account of the several ways in which a text can beckon a reader agentially further *in* by recruiting her cognitions at a pre-rational or unconscious level: by varying her depth and modality of immersion, her sense of location, her perceptual frame or line of sight, and her sense of personal agency in the narrated space.[10]

Yet the question of some kind of unbidden reader identification with the mobile, mutable 'io', the 'I' of the Dantean protagonist, with this 'figure that we see here now, *standing in the body* on this shore', in Charles S. Singleton's terms (1954: 11–12; my emphasis), is observable in the work of a large number of scholars, including in the early commentaries.[11] William Franke's return to the question of the direct addresses indeed asks whether in fact 'it is possible to read the whole poem as leveraged from [the direct addresses] [...], and to hear an implicit address to readers right from the reference to "*our* life" in the very first line of the work' (2000: 119).

Certainly, Robin Kirkpatrick's work, beginning in the 1970s and continuing into the 2020s, on reader agency and intellectually informed creative interaction suggests precisely such a response to a call within the text, consistently according due emphasis to engaging both from within and without the narrative.[12] From the 1990s, Teodolinda Barolini's work on narrative form has — crucially, as far as a narrative poetics is concerned — kept the question of the poem's so-called 'truth claims' on the table, and more recently has opened important new discussions on reality and realism.[13] To my mind, however, the overtly narratological strand of scholarship established in the 1990s created something of an 'anti-collaborative' detour in the application of narrative theory to the poem, detecting in Dante's narrative strategies artful persuasion of a credulous reader,[14] and an author occupied with his own authority;[15] and advocating instead, to quote Barolini, that 'we' '[stand] resolutely outside of the fiction's mirror games [...], the formal structures that manipulate the reader so successfully' (1992: 16).[16]

It is this stance of locating oneself 'resolutely outside', of not entering in at all, that I query. Whilst I am not sure that it is possible for even the best-intentioned scholar to resist wholly some capitulation to mechanisms of immersion, on the one hand Barolini of course is absolutely right: the scholar, it may be argued, is a particular kind of reader, one with a responsibility to perspicacity both in interpreting the meaning of the text and identifying the methods by which such a meaning is constructed. And deep immersion, it has long been held, can impede critical consciousness; a condition referred to as semiotic or inattentional blindness.[17] But without immersing, without yielding to the narrator, without conceding 'la sua fiducia al narratore', in Contini's terms, how does the reader trip those mechanisms in the text that, I shall propose, have been designed to invite participation?

My interest is in identifying and examining such narratological triggers to certain processes of embodied cognition, or what I refer to as reader or cognitive participation. A key criterion for the scholar in recognising these triggers at all is, I propose, a sensitivity to the possibilities of such a participatory mode of reading. The mechanisms that invite participation are subtle, complex, and largely invisible to the external observer seeking a recognisable narratological device — completely different to the self-heralding direct addresses. Instead, mechanisms of participation typically generate their effect through a juxtaposition or sequence of narratological devices that in isolation would be unremarkable (a run of focal view shifts, for example, as I will explore later in this chapter), but which cumulatively, or in combination, produce their effect (a single dissonant shift in the sequence, say). As such, the reader will very often discover that something is at work in the text only once she has triggered its mechanism and is rewarded with a visceral, somatosensory, or affective response.[18] In the *Comedy*, I shall propose, such narratological events run into the thousands of instances, and a progression is often visible in their deployment across the canticles, lending weight to an argument that they are the product of a strategy rather than a simple accident of literary production.

Second, I would propose that unilateral reader resistance to the formal structures of the narrative is unnecessary. Dante, I will suggest, deploys his narrative strategies in pursuit of working *with*, not against, the reader — to facilitate, not to manipulate; beckoning her in when experiential understanding will deepen her grasp of the journey to revelation; encouraging her out again when agential cognitive work (judging and reasoning, but also frame-by-frame remembering and imaginative construction) is required.

As Paola Nasti and Claudia Rossignoli observe, the commentary tradition has accommodated a plurality of exegetical practices and constant evolution, including what they refer to as 'methodological osmosis' (2013: 5), or the integration of tools from other disciplines.[19] My approach borrows from emerging theories in video game criticism of embodied interaction in a virtual space, which I propose offer to textual literary theory the possibility of a substantial new lexicon of narrative mechanisms rooted in invitations to different types of presence and in the device of the avatar.[20]

Such a reverse-engineered approach — reading video game critical concepts back into textual narrative theory — at the time of writing, is new: to my knowledge, this published work is the first of its kind. As yet, there is also only a very small body of published work by scholars with a formation in Dante that engages with video game criticism in relation to the poem.[21] There is, however, a growing body of work in Dante scholarship in areas that intersect with my approach: particularly, in embodied cognition or the virtual body (including work by Heather Webb, David Gary Shaw, Daniel T. Kline),[22] and on spatiality (including Bill Brown, Aarati Kanekar, John Kleiner, Michael Sinding).[23]

In this chapter, then, I will set out one example of what I propose to be such an invitation to reader participation, in the instance of Bernard's sign — ostensibly for the journeying Dante — in *Paradiso* XXXIII. In exposing the mechanisms of such an invitation, its near invisibility from a perspective of external observation, and its range of effects, I hope to demonstrate the benefits to the scholar of this proposed mode of participatory reading or, to borrow Contini's terms, of a freely chosen entry into Dante's narratological 'game'.

Bernard's interaction *manqué*

The final dramatised interaction between characters in the *Comedy,* Bernard's signal to Dante to look upwards in *Paradiso* XXXIII, might be described as an interaction *manqué*:

> Bernardo m'accennava, e sorridea,
> perch'io guardassi suso; ma io era
> già per me stesso tal qual ei volca:
> che la mia vista, venendo sincera
> e più e più intrava per lo raggio
> de l'alta luce che da sé è vera. (49–54)[24]

> Now Bernard, smiling, made a sign to me
> that I look up. Already, though, I was,
> by my own will, as he desired I be.

> My sight, becoming pure and wholly free,
> entered still more, then more, along the ray
> of that one light which, of itself, is true.

Bernard and the journeying Dante protagonist are in the Empyrean and are, we can assume (allowing for the complexities of spatial representation there), near one another with the celestial Rose encircling them. Bernard gestures and smiles at Dante, but Dante is already doing what Bernard wants — looking upwards — even as Bernard signals his desire, 'ma io era | già per me stesso tal qual ei volea' (50–51).[25]

For the reader who is moved to stop and consider this, it may come as something of a surprise to find that for a split second she seems to be looking the wrong way — at Bernard — at the very moment at which Dante first turns his gaze on the divine image. Can her gaze really have lagged his, however minutely, at such a key point in the narrative, the moment at which the journeying protagonist finally begins his encounter with the divine? She may wonder if she has misread, but there seems no doubt: her attention is clearly directed first to the gesturing Bernard: 'Bernardo m'accennava, e sorridea' (49), then to the journeying Dante, only to find that whilst she was looking at Bernard, Dante was looking elsewhere. And not looking just anywhere, but melding his gaze with the holy ray, 'ma io era | già per me stesso tal qual ei volea' (50–51), beginning his 'breakthrough', as Robert Hollander puts it, his own unmediated encounter with God.[26]

By bringing to conscious awareness the sequential mental models invited in the sequence, this type of frame-by-frame analysis highlights an effect of cognitive dissonance, or 'the existence of non-fitting relations among cognitions' in social psychologist Leon Festinger's definition (1962: 3).[27] Whilst most readers, I propose, will have no conscious awareness of such dissonance, this sequence troubled Charles Singleton (1980) to such an extent that he was led to conclude that Dante had actually made a mistake in his handling of narrative perspective (one, he says, of just two in the poem), writing in his commentary that:

> Strictly-speaking, the poet is [...] guilty of a momentary slip in maintaining the point of view [...], for if, as is affirmed, he was 'already such as Bernard desired', he was indeed already completely intent on gazing into the light, and therefore could not have seen that Bernard was gesturing and smiling to urge that he do so. (Gloss on ll. 49–51)[28]

Accepting Singleton's conclusion might throw Dante's poetic authority into question: if the Dante who is present at that moment in the Empyrean didn't see Bernard's sign, having already turned his eyes towards God, then how can the returned poet, back on earth, narrate the event, other than by retrospective inference — that is, by making it up? Of course 'artifice', to borrow Christian Moevs's term (2005: 183), is inherent in any compelling and convincing retrospectively reconstructed textual narrative account.[29] However, when the narrative mechanisms that underpin such reconstruction become perceptible, there is a risk to reader immersion, and in this case, Singleton's urge in response has been to dismantle the text to locate a reason for his discomfort, identifying — correctly — an anomaly in its construction, and concluding — incorrectly, in my view — that this anomaly is a mistake of narrative technique.

So, what has happened? We might characterise the process as follows. Mentally modelling the first-person perspective of the narration, Singleton has 'felt' something in the text — the dissonance of the lag in modelling turning his eyes to God. This apparently unconscious experience of cognitive dissonance has triggered an instinct to interrogate the sequence: critically or intellectually, in Singleton's case. He has sought a mechanism to explain what has drawn his attention but has not been able to identify a recognisable one. (In fact, the mechanism is a dissonant switch in focal view, one that narratologist Gérard Genette's work on 'mood' helps us identify, as I will show in the next section.)[30] Instead, Singleton concludes that Dante has made a mistake, one that — with no obvious mitigation for such visible artifice — exposes the 'made' (*fictio*) nature of the poem, not only potentially undermining its alleged claims to truth, but fully rupturing Singleton's immersion in the narrative.

That Singleton experienced the sequence as cognitively dissonant seems clear. But not all readers, I suggest, will have a similar experience of dissonance in response to the same mechanism in the text, particularly those who are too far 'in', or too far 'out', of the text — that is, engaging with the text at an extreme of immersion. To borrow Marie-Laure Ryan's classifications of immersion (see n. 3), the 'epistemically immersed' are most likely to be too far 'in' — too immersed — to notice any dissonance. Epistemic, or plot-driven, immersion — the desire to know what comes next, and the characteristic mode, I shall suggest, of the 'desiderosi d'ascoltar' (those 'listening hard', in Kirkpatrick's translation) (*Par.*, II. 2) — can make the reader feel profoundly gripped in the narrated events, but it does not require that she imaginatively enter in to the narrated space on her own account. Essentially, the reader is watching events happen to other people, without any meaningful transfer of virtual experience from protagonist to reader. This leaves her dependent on narrative mediation — being told what happens next — rather than collaborating in her own production of meaning. This is the type of immersion that can leave the reader at risk of semiotic blindness, or an obliviousness to signs in the text. Festinger accounts for this in his theory of cognitive dissonance by suggesting that since the brain experiences mild cognitive dissonance as 'uncomfortable', its automatic response is 'to try to reduce the dissonance and achieve consonance' (1962: 3), a phenomenon referred to in cognitive science as 'autocorrection'.[31] So, the epistemically immersed reader is unlikely to register any dissonance because her brain automatically compensates for it at a pre-rational level, without troubling her immersion in the narrative.

The second group is composed of those readers who are standing 'resolutely outside' the formal mechanisms of the poem, reading analytically, effectively disabling the poem's formal mechanisms — a bit like repeatedly pressing the pause button when watching a film or playing a video game. Without entering in to the narrative space to trigger the mechanism of the dissonant focal view switch, such a reader is very unlikely to register its existence and, since it is an almost invisible device, she would have to systematically examine each of the five thousand or so (mostly consonant) focal view switches in the poem in order to detect from outside the presence of one dissonant switch. However, as suggested earlier, in practice this is likely to be an unusual position since even the most self-consciously resistant reader will almost certainly yield to Dante's mechanics of immersion at some point. Most scholars will find themselves, I suggest, shifting somewhere on a continuum between these two extremes, the dissonance of the mechanism inviting, at the very least, a brief pause or hiatus in narrative processing. Of more significance, perhaps, then, are the differences in how those readers *respond* to the experience of dissonance. My suggestion is that there are two main classes of response: the critically evaluative or intellectual response (as I shall suggest Singleton's to be); and the participatory.

In the processing of cognitive dissonance, cognitive science allows for an alternative response to autocorrection, namely 'intrinsic motivation', or a response of agential curiosity.[32] In such cases, the dissonance serves to introduce a small gap into the immersive tissue of the text, inviting a momentary surfacing into critical consciousness or pre-consciousness. Sensing the dissonance, then, Singleton may have experienced a piquing of his curiosity — 'what's going on here?' — and an instinct to pause, to step outside the narrative, and to deploy his curiosity in dismantling the text to locate a reason for his discomfort, a technical cause for the pull on his attention. By contrast, the reader whose habit is to read in participatory mode has, I propose, a different instinct: she unconsciously deploys her curiosity to redouble her engagement *within* the narrated world, engaging with the sign in the text itself — Bernard's sign — and redoubling her own *imaginative* work: a response of, 'wait a minute, what do you want me to look at? Oh, up there!'[33] This is an instance of narrative indeterminacy — a gap — that invites the reader in participatory mode to directly reproduce, or simulate, the protagonist's experience for herself, bridging the gap that the narration has opened up by the dissonant focal view shift, imaginatively 'standing in the [protagonist's] body' herself (Singleton 1954: 11).

To respond in such a participatory mode is not easy, but I contend that the poem as a whole functions strategically to invite the progressive refinement of the requisite cognitive skills in the responsive reader, so that by the time the reader reaches Bernard, such a habit of cognitive 'curiosity' rather than 'autocorrection' may have become naturalised.[34] Before proceeding further, however, it may be helpful to establish precisely how the technical mechanism at play in Bernard's sequence functions, and how it serves as an *invitation* to a response of some kind.

Focal view switching

The device responsible for triggering a potential experience of cognitive dissonance in Bernard's interaction *manqué* is, as mentioned above, an unexpected switch in focal view.[35] Focal view ('mood', in Genette's terms), is one of the two main components of narrative perspective ('voice' being the other).[36]

For the purposes of analysing Bernard's gesture — and without wanting to oversimplify a sophisticated narratological device — it is sufficient to understand focal view as the visual or perceptual frame through which the reader perceives the events of the narrative. In the case of the *Comedy*, the two main focal characters through whose eyes events are usually framed are the *journeying Dante* protagonist (familiar as the 'Pilgrim' in the 'Pilgrim–Poet' binary that took hold in Dante scholarship in the second half of the twentieth century), and the returned narrating poet, the *narrating Dante* ('Poet'). These two focal characters, the journeying Dante and the narrating Dante, have different sight and knowledge privileges, and they occupy different locations: an inner story world, in which the younger journeying Dante travels through the three realms of the afterlife, framed by an outer story world in which the returned poet ostensibly performs the writing of his poem concurrent with the reader's reception of it.[37] This bi-location construction, twin protagonists, and past and ostensibly present time zones gives the author the device of a *frame narrative*. I return to the implications of this more fully in Chapter 4.

Focal view affects where the reader feels herself to be located in relation to the protagonist: looking *with* him or through his eyes (internal focal view, typical in first-person narratives), or looking *at* him from a position of outside observation (external focal view, third-person narratives). The narrating Dante — back on earth and already 'knowing the end', as Singleton puts it (1977: 25) — observes events in the inner story world from an external viewpoint, and has access to omniscience: he can show the reader what is going on behind the journeying Dante's back, as he does in Singleton's other noted 'slip', the arrival of Statius in *Purgatorio* XXI, or outside his line of sight, in the case of Bernard.[38] By contrast, the journeying Dante has restricted and highly subjective sight, able to see or experience only what his mortal perceptual faculties allow: he cannot see in the dark (on the thick black smoke-enveloped terrace of Wrath, for example, in *Purgatorio* XVI), nor can he see events that happen beyond his visual field.[39] But when the reader looks through his eyes, she sees precisely what he does at that particular point in his physical, spiritual, emotional and cognitive journey.

Dante's narrative frame device gives him the flexibility to switch between an external, omniscient mode and an internal, subjective mode, thereby inviting the reader to feel sometimes as if she is watching the journeying Dante from the outside, inferring his experience from what he says (although he speaks rarely, as I discuss in Chapter 4) and from his narrated body states; and at other times as if she is located inside his head, with direct access to his inner perceptual experience. Dante deploys such switches constantly throughout the poem, typically locating them at the junction of tercets, which allows the brain to assimilate them largely unconsciously without much threat to immersion. In the sequence with Bernard, however, one of these focal view switches is rendered perceptible (at a pre-rational rather than a conscious level, as I have argued), and it is this perceptibility that creates the instance of cognitive dissonance. Expanding the sequence slightly for context, I will try to explain how and why.

The first tercet recounts the journeying Dante's condition in the moments just before Bernard's gesture:

> E io ch'al fine di tutt' i disii
> appropinquava, sì com' io dovea,
> l'ardor del desiderio in me finii.

> And drawing nearer, as I had to now,
> the end of all desires, in my own self
> I ended all the ardour of desire.

This tercet is focalised through the journeying Dante. The reader is effectively located inside the journeying Dante's head as the narration evokes an internal state (the feeling of approaching and then reaching the end of all desire) that the reader could not deduce through external observation. The personal tone and reference to subjective experience is further characteristic of the journeying Dante's perceptual frame.

Next comes the half-tercet account of Bernard's sign:

> Bernardo m'accennava, e sorridea,
> perch' io guardassi suso;

> Now Bernard, smiling, made a sign to me
> that I look up.

This is technically focalised through the narrating Dante.[40] Bernard's gesture is presented as an action that anyone present could have seen, with none of the internal markers characteristic of the journeying Dante's focal view. However, because narrated events in the immediately preceding tercet were strongly focalised through the journeying Dante, and because of the very light touch of the external focal view that here facilitates an ambiguity in focalisation, the reader may quite naturally feel as if she continues to see the action through the journeying Dante's eyes — and my contention is that the narrative invites precisely this — thereby reasonably inferring that she is looking with the journeying Dante directly at Bernard.

However, the second half of the tercet, relating how Dante feels his vision gradually align with the holy ray, powerfully challenges such an inference:

> [...] ma io era
> già per me stesso tal qual ei volea.

> Already, though, I was,
> by my own will, as he desired I be.

The reader might feel a jolt of surprise. The journeying Dante is apparently looking elsewhere, and has been all along; and, indeed, if we trace back his line of sight in the text, we realise that his eyes have been directed upwards without interruption since the last part of *Paradiso* XXXI, 'Io levai li occhi' [I raised my eyes] (118). But now, the reader may sequentially infer, she really *is* looking with the journeying Dante, experiencing an unmediated vision of God with him. In technical terms, then, this feels like the journeying Dante focal view. In reality, however, this half-tercet is one of the rare instances when either focal view can technically be inferred, thanks to the contextualising data of the reader already knowing what 'tal qual ei volea' (51) means. The ambiguity opens up a gap in the text that accommodates the reader who is inclined to pause in her consumption of the narrative.

Finally, the reader is returned unequivocally to the journeying Dante's focal view as his sight progressively intertwines with the divine light, becoming 'sincera' (52), a subjective personal experience that could not be known from the outside:

> ché la mia vista, venendo sincera,
> e più e più intrava per lo raggio

> My sight, becoming pure and wholly free,
> entered still more, then more, along the ray

and in the last line (and not material for my argument here but included for completeness), focal view switches back to the narrating Dante, marked by a change in tone from the personal to the authoritative:[41] 'de l'alta luce che da sé è vera' [of that one light which, of itself, is true].

To summarise:

E io ch'al fine di tutt' i disii appropinquava, sì com' io dovea, l'ardor del desiderio in me finii.	— *journeying Dante*
Bernardo m'accennava, e sorridea, perch' io guardassi suso;	— feels like *journeying Dante,* but technically *narrating Dante*
ma io era già per me stesso tal qual ei volea:	— feels like *journeying Dante,* but technically either
ché la mia vista, venendo sincera, e più e più intrava per lo raggio	— *journeying Dante*
de l'alta luce che da sé è vera.	— *narrating Dante*

The switch of particular interest, then, occurs between the first and the second tercets, but only becomes apparent midway through the second, heralded by the narratively pugnacious 'ma' [but] at the caesura (50).[42] It is this lag that creates the dissonance. The reader may quite justifiably feel herself invited to look directly at Bernard through the journeying Dante's eyes, but the contextualising information that follows — that Dante is already looking elsewhere — alerts the reader to an error in the construction of her mental model. As the second half of the tercet unfolds, the reader might begin to sense that something odd has happened: the 'già' [already] (51) that follows inverts the order of action, meaning that she misses the journeying Dante's crucial visual action (shifting his gaze from Mary to the divine light), until a split second afterwards when the narrating Dante supplies the information from an external focal view.

But if Dante's focal view switch really is not the mistake Singleton suggests, then this raises two further questions. First, as mentioned earlier in relation to the poet's authority, how does Dante know what Bernard is doing if he doesn't actually look at him? And, second, why might the reader need to look at Bernard if Dante does not?

Bernard's object

Singleton, as we saw earlier, was exercised by the practical difficulty of the journeying Dante being able to look in two directions simultaneously. Whilst there may be other interpretations for Dante's perceptual capacity that Singleton has perhaps not explored, my interest is in mechanisms of narrative mediation, so I focus here only on the narrative data provided in the text.[43] Some modern commentators resolve the question by simply making Bernard vanish, inferring that the sequence enacts the journeying Dante's mental separation from tutelage. In their respective glosses, Anna Maria Chiavacci Leonardi and Nicola Fosca conclude that Dante now stands alone in his encounter with God: 'Dante is alone on the stage before that God to whom he has turned', writes Chiavacci Leonardi (gloss on ll. 50–51); and Fosca, that 'Dante is alone before God' (ll. 49–54). However, Dante has given no suggestion that the Empyrean is a space in which interlocutors might just disappear. Robert Hollander, more productively as far as my position is concerned, finds Bernard still present but held within the protagonist's inner world: 'He has not outrun his need for guidance so much as he has internalised his guide' (ll. 50–51).

There is considerable narratological work to do here to excavate more fully the question of the poem's 'fiction' that lies beyond the current scope of this book, but with which I propose premises of embodied cognition and Virtual Reality (VR) can further productively assist. There is, for example, the question of the virtual and the material real: the journeying Dante may not have 'seen' (in any concrete terms) Bernard's sign, but may have 'sensed' it as a 'subjective inner reality', as Singleton writes of the visions in *Purgatorio* XV (gloss on ll. 115–17). Further, whilst inference as a mechanism of production might point to the 'made' (*fictio*) quality of the poem, we need not conflate something that is 'made' with something that is 'made up' or invented.

But if the journeying Dante does not need to see Bernard's sign, why does Dante choose to include the information of the sign at all? The sign makes no difference to the journeying Dante's actions and so, in terms of narrative understanding, it is redundant. But Dante *does* include it, and this inclusion *does* invite the reader to look directly at Bernard on her own account, acting independently of the protagonist. I have suggested that the dislocation of focal view creates a gap into which the reader is invited to unconsciously 'insert' herself in a mode of imaginative participation. The dissonant focal view switch, then, is 'made' in service of reader participation: it is not an *error*, but an *invitation*. This is the mitigation for Dante's narratorial inference that Singleton missed and that forced him into his conclusion of Dante's 'slip' of perspective. And this invitation, I would propose, is a radical one. Is it possible, reader, that every time you read this sequence, Bernard is signalling directly to *you*?

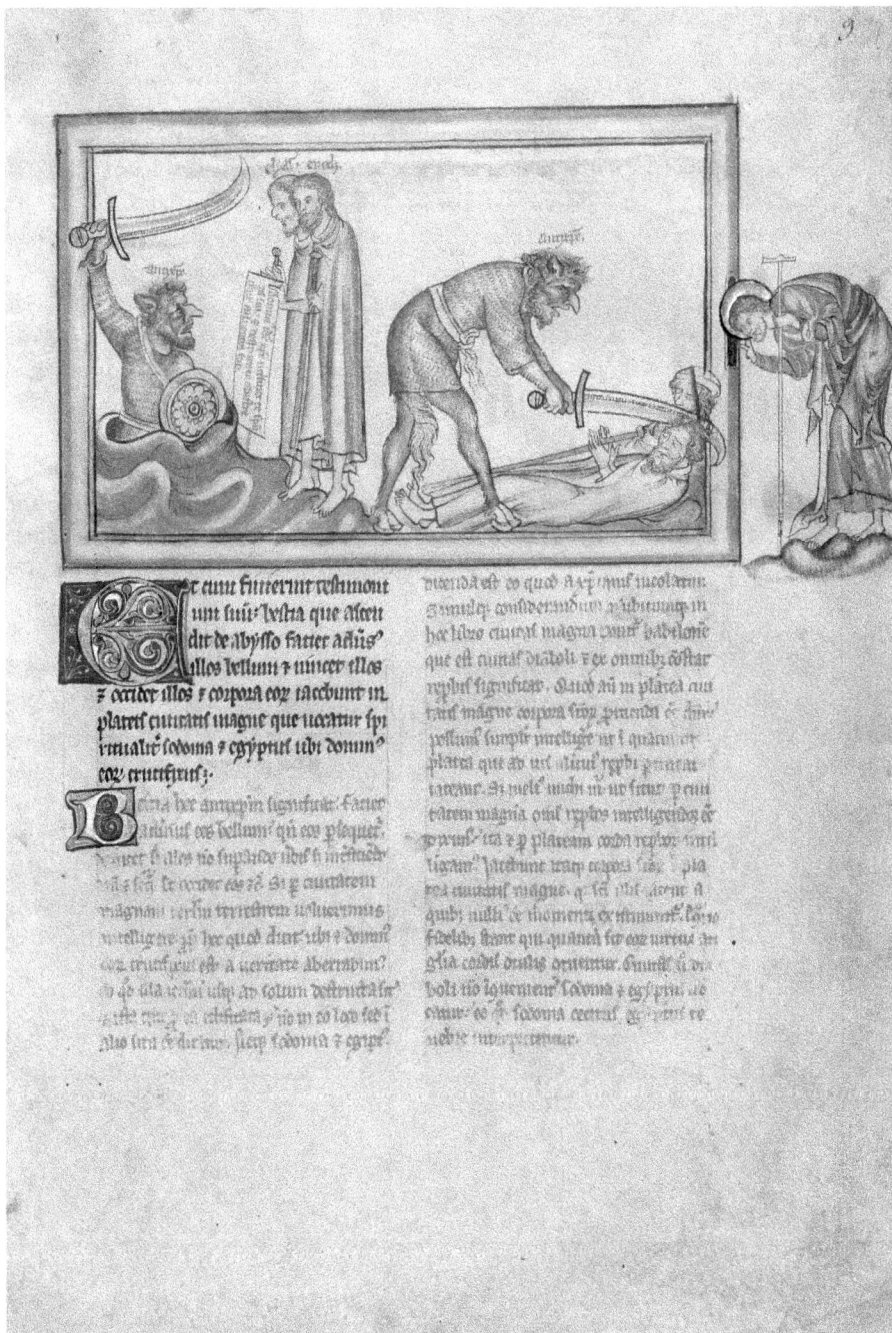

FIG. I.I. Unknown illuminator, *The Massacre of the Two Witnesses by the Beast*, about 1255–60. Tempera colours, gold leaf, coloured washes, pen and ink. Leaf: 31.9 × 22.5 cm, Ms. Ludwig III 1 (83.MC.72), fol. 17. The J. Paul Getty Museum, Los Angeles. Digital image courtesy of the Getty's Open Content Program.

Bernard's double frame violation

Such a possibility would require that Bernard commit a narrative frame violation — indeed, a double frame violation: stepping out of the inner story world and gesturing transparently through the medium of the outer story world to engage the attention of the reader directly in her own world.[44] This might seem far-fetched to the twentieth- and early twenty-first-century reader, habituated as she is to the notion of the text as closed artefact.[45] However, I would argue that it is a less novel idea for the twenty-first-century video gamer — although admittedly she might expect her interlocutor to try to shoot her rather than to smile or wave at her.

But there are certainly precedents for such an idea in medieval narrative artefacts. The second-person narration model of the medieval gospel meditation, for example, is characterised by repeated metalepses wherein the narrator or authorial voice addresses the reader directly ('imagine this', 'think that', and so on), as I shall set out in the next chapter. Further, visual metalepses were not uncommon in manuscript illuminations. 'As a container, the medieval [picture] frame often seems rather leaky', writes art historian Stuart Whatling (2010: 84), as illustrated in the illumination above (Fig. I.1) from the Book of Revelation in the Getty Apocalypse manuscript (1255–60).

From a position external to the frame, St John witnesses the visions represented within it. Such a form of inward-looking metalepsis might remind us of the *visibile parlare* [visible speech] in Dante's Purgatory, the marble bas reliefs on the terraces of the mountain. Of the first, Dante relates in *Purgatorio* X that he recognises ('conobbi', 29) the event of the Annunciation, experiencing the Archangel as vividly as though he were present at the scene: 'dinanzi a noi pareva sì verace | quivi intagliato in un atto soave, | che non sembiava imagine che tace' [[the angel] appeared so truthfully before us now, | carved in a gesture of pure gentleness, | he did not seem an image keeping silence] (37–39). By *Paradiso* XXXII — and raising interesting questions for the reader's own sense of location or movement across frames at that point — the journeying Dante will have breached this 'frame', recognising himself as directly present at an eternal simulation of the Annunciation as he gazes at Gabriel descending once again to Mary: 'e quello amor che primo lì discese, | cantando "Ave, Maria, gratïa plena," | dinanzi a lei le sue ali distese' [And that first angel-love, descending there, | was singing — wings extended in her sight — | "Ave, Maria, gratïa plena"] (94–96).

There are also examples in narrative art of characters stepping *out* from narrative frames. The Ashburnham Pentateuch's illustration of Jacob's dream of the ladder, for example (in Fig. I.2, below), shows how on awakening, Jacob, in Whatling's words, 'steps right out of the picture frame and into the border, ready to walk off in the way of the Lord' (86).

And for most of the *Comedy* (until the ascent of the celestial ladder in *Paradiso* XXII is completed), the reader experiences the narrating Dante repeatedly 'gesturing' verbally out of the text at her through the device of the direct address, inviting her to import her own memories, judgments and imaginings into his narrative system in a collaborative approach to the construction of meaning (I set

FIG. I.2. Unknown illuminator, Jacob's dream of the ladder, Ashburnham Pentateuch, late sixth–early seventh century, Paris, Bibliothèque Nationale, MS nouv. acq. lat. 2334, fol. 25r. Sourced from gallica.bnf.fr / BnF.

this out systematically in Chapter 4). Might we then similarly conceive of Bernard's externally directed metalepsis as a gesture *out* of the text, at the reader? Is it possible to read this as a collapsing down of narrative layers to a single point, a *punto*, a direct interaction between inner story world character and reader?[46]

My proposal is that this dissonant shift in focal view can invite the reader to switch momentarily in her mental modelling from a mode of spectatorship focused on the journeying Dante protagonist into a mode of agential participation, acting independently to mentally turn her eyes to God, and thereby briefly, I shall suggest, electively identifying as the first-person 'I' of the text herself. The temporary dislocation of her line of sight from the journeying Dante's opens a *gap* in the narrative that the reader herself must bridge. The encounter with God, as the narrating Dante repeatedly reminds us, defies narrative: it is unsayable. What happens at the point of the divine encounter remains an open question both in theological terms (as Barański set out in 'Dottrina degli affetti e teologia (2018)) and also, importantly, I would suggest, in terms of the narrative mechanisms that support it. Whilst guided by the former, my particular focus in this book is the latter: indicating the existence of this gap in narratological terms, identifying the web of invitations to reader participation upon which it depends, and setting out as a result my proposal for a reading mode I shall describe as *first-person participation*.

From immersion to presence: a new framework for reader response criticism

The end point of this book is a definition of this new concept of 'first-person participation' — a provisional term I offer in the seeming absence of any existing notion in reader response theory — built upon a systematic uncovering of the narratological mechanisms through which I propose this mode of reading to be invited in the *Comedy*.

First-person participation is a mode of interaction with a narrative artefact that may be triggered through a sustained experience of a particular form of embodied immersion known as *presence*, defined in the field of video game criticism as 'the experiential counterpart of immersion' (IJsselsteijn 2004: 136). Immersion is a subjective feeling of deep absorption that need not involve the sensorimotor system, but instead can be triggered by a desire to *know* an outcome (as with a page-turner book) — that is, a spectatorial experience in which the reader can feel lost to the outside world for the duration of her reading, but after which she ultimately does not herself experience any residual sensation of personal transformation. Being primarily a mental phenomenon, the experience of immersion is difficult to analyse or discuss other than retrospectively and subjectively by self-report. The physically rooted responses inherent in presence, by contrast, as I shall set out in the three central technical chapters of this book, can be linked to particular observable triggers, or mechanisms, in the text. Presence is *embodied* and *experiential* because it requires the involvement of bodily systems in re-presenting, within the reader, the body states narrated in the text; and the involvement of these systems is triggered, or strategically invited, by specific mechanisms in the text. So, whether one reader consciously feels or experiences something and another does not — as discussed above in relation to Singleton's perceptible experience of dissonance in response to the narration of Bernard's sign — the *existence* of such textual triggers can be objectively identified in particular narratological mechanisms in the physical body of the text. This is the root of the notion in this book of *invitations to participate*.

Textual literary theory does not yet have a full lexicon to describe the phenomenon of embodied interaction in a virtual environment. This is why I propose that we turn to critical theory in an alternative narrative medium that foregrounds the involvement of the human body in constructing a meaningful interpretation of a virtual world: video games.

A necessary preliminary question is whether there is any merit in trying to compare a narrative text with a video game since each is based in a different semiotic system. My stance in this book is one of informed experiment. I do not seek to make any general claims in relation to cross-media narrative theory. Instead, taking the *Comedy* as my model for exploration, I follow W. J. T. Mitchell on the principle of careful analytical experimentation at 'the borders between "textual" and "visual" disciplines': namely, that this 'ought to be a subject of investigation and analysis, collaboration and dialogue, not defensive reflexes' (1996: 53).

My reasons for suggesting this experiment are three-fold. First, cognitive neuro-science increasingly offers evidence that the brain does not distinguish between the so-called 'real' (that is, physical, material, or real-world cues) and the 'imagined' (virtual) at a neural level, *provided that the imagined or virtual data is sufficiently realistic*. Specific models in support of this notion include Gallese et al.'s 1996 'mirror' system (1996: 131) (discussed in Chapter 1 of this book); Revonsuo's 2006 'world-simulation metaphor' (2006: 109), which proposes that we do not experience the physical world directly but instead via a simulation, precisely as we experience a dream; and Jeannerod's 'S-states' model or neural simulation of action (2001: 103). Different theories of embodied cognition have converged on an understanding that so-called 'off-line cognition' — the kind of cognising we do in imagining, daydreaming, dreaming, reading, and in virtual reality — involves the same neural mechanisms we use in cognising the physical world (as I further explore in Chapter 2).[47]

Second, and directly related to this new neurobiological understanding, VR gives us tangible, observable evidence of this phenomenon when we observe a player wearing a VR headset making dissonant movements — such as falling over — that are inappropriate in the player's real-world physical situation and instead mirror her avatar's experience in the virtual space.[48] According to Jeremy Bailenson, director of the Virtual Human Interaction Lab at Stanford University, this is because 'VR can be stored in the brain's memory center in ways that are strikingly similar to real-world physical experiences [...]. When VR is done well, the brain believes it is real.'[49] When the player experiences presence in the virtual world, the virtual data 'over-rides' proprioceptive data from the real world: your body still falls, even though you 'know' you are physically located in the real world. In relation to printed texts, I am not proposing that the reader responds through externally observable motor reflexes, but rather through the internal systems of the body including the visceral and the neural.

Third, I suggest that Biocca's 'Book Problem' indirectly invites us to explore in important ways the mechanisms by which written texts create their effects in readers. In 2003, in a paper entitled 'Can We Resolve the Book, the Physical Reality, and the Dream State Problems?', presented at an EU Future and Emerging Technologies conference, leading communications theorist and cognitive scientist Frank Biocca asked a key question for presence theorists. He had observed in empirical research that books could be as immersive as the real world; but, he asked, how could this be so, given the freshly emerging understanding that an experience of presence is rooted in sensorimotor data, and that books — in his assumption — cannot cue such sensorimotor data? In the published version of his conference paper, he writes:

> If sensorimotor immersion is the key variable that causes presence, then how do we explain the high levels of presence people report when reading books [...]? Books are very low fidelity, non-iconic media and are extremely low on all sensorimotor variables identified as causing presence: extent of sensory data, control of sensors, and ability to modify the environment. (2003: 4)

My suggestion is that Biocca's assumption about the 'low fidelity' nature of books is wrong, in the case of the *Comedy* at least. Medieval scholars in the field of affective devotion have long discussed the ability of texts to invite powerful and even directly observable responses in readers. We might perhaps uncritically assume this to be somehow linked to the mental constitution of the medieval reader rather than any particular mechanism in the text itself. But as Bailenson has pointed out, virtual data '*done well*' (my emphasis) is extraordinarily powerful in VR; that is, when it deploys mechanics designed to invite a sustained experience of reality.

My proposal is that we simply have not yet looked for the particular mechanisms — deployed in such an expert, unusual, or innovative way that the effect really is 'done well' — that might invite the same such 'realistic' experience in a textual narrative like the *Comedy*. Video game criticism focuses strongly on mechanisms of embodied experience and presence, so my suggestion is that, with caution and respect for working assumptions and terminology differences across the two fields, we borrow certain ideas and theoretical approaches from video game criticism as models for thinking in relation to written texts, and start exploring some of its mechanisms for potential textual analogues to see whether there may be invitations not just to immersion but to embodied presence in Dante's poem.

My interest is particularly in the mechanics that support the experience of player participation in games that are played in first-person mode, a mode of play found across video game genres, from action–adventure games like *Mirror's Edge: Catalyst*, to puzzle-platform games like *Portal 2*, and the more widely recognised first-person shooter genre including *Half Life 2*, in which the player typically controls an avatar.[50] As I discuss in Chapter 4, the avatar, the game's protagonist, furnishes the player with what video game critic and discourse analyst James Paul Gee refers to as a 'surrogate body' (2015: 17) in the virtual space of the game, through which the player experiences the virtual environment of the game in an embodied way.[51]

In a well-designed game played by an attentive player, two transformations take place in the player's participation in the game world. The first is that the player's cognitive functions begin to respond in the virtual world in the same way that they respond in the real world, because the well-designed game world is programmed to provide perceptually identical reciprocal feedback to her neural system to that which the real world provides. This invites the reader to move beyond epistemic immersion and into a mode of present participation, specifically, I propose in this book, through *spatial* and *social presence*.[52]

The second transformation is that the gap between avatar identity and player lessens as the player progressively naturalises the skills she has learned through the medium of the avatar; this is the basis of what I shall describe as *self-presence*. As a result, the reader becomes more cognitively adept, I shall suggest, in switching between the two identities, experiences and worlds.[53] Gee names this phenomenon 'projective identity' (94), describing it as when 'players [...] create, by their play, a mesh among the character (avatar), the character's goals and now their own, too, and the virtual world'.[54] Gordon Calleja's 'alterbiography of self', 'where players interpret the events in the game as happening to *them* specifically, rather than to an external character' (2011: 124–25), describes a very similar phenomenon.[55]

In Gee's terms, this 'gives rise to a new sort of being' (2015: 94), one that is not boundaried by its own perceptual, cognitive, and social habits but that, instead, through the prosthetic medium of the avatar–protagonist, has been able to explore and try out new cognitive and perceptual habits in the safe space of the game world, '[inserting] themselves — their own desires, values and goals — into the [designed] mesh' of the game (94). It is an outcome that media scholar Bob Rehak describes as '[merging] spectatorship and participation in ways that fundamentally transform both activities' (2003: 103).

This is why I propose a participatory mode of reading the *Comedy* to be so important as a generative companion mode to the critically evaluative mode more commonly associated with scholarship. It is, I propose, the essential key to revealing important invitations to the reader that might otherwise remain unexperienced, undetected, and under-discussed in Dante scholarship. In the case of Bernard's sign, the instance of dissonance thins the immersive tissue just sufficiently to trigger a change in cognitive mode, inviting a highly agential deployment of the imaginative faculty, stretching the reader's cognitive capabilities beyond epistemic immersion in the plot or a primarily intellectual engagement with the text's meaning, and instead engaging in a sustained act of imaginative elaboration. My suggestion is that Dante has programmed such a development path for the cognitions into the narrative mechanics of the *Comedy* so that the poem functions not only as a single enunciation — a truthful account of one man's experience of the journey, real or virtual, to revelation — but also as a *system* that invites others to mentally simulate their own journey. Bernard's redundant sign to the protagonist to look up completes, I propose, Dante's poem-long invitation to the reader to look for God on her own account.

Structure of the book

Following on from the discussion in this Introduction of the dissonant focal view switch detectable in the narration of Bernard's sign, in Chapter 1 I shall claim that, notwithstanding my recourse to VR technology to illuminate its mechanisms, the participatory mode of reading I set out here in fact returns us to original medieval modes of interaction with a text, inviting us to overturn habits of reading that became established with the print revolution and with the Cartesian separation of mind and body. I shall explore the role of embodied cognition in medieval theory of mind and in relation to rhetoric, gesture, and memory, and to the reading practices of medieval affective piety. I also survey evidence of an 'embodied reader' in the text of the *Comedy* itself — a body that can sit on a bench, for example, that has a voice, ears, eyes, a finger that can be pulled almost instantaneously from a fire. I invoke the crucial theoretical matter of personal response and subjectivity: its importance as a dimension of working with the poem and its reader, its 'slipperiness' in analytical terms, and how focusing not on individual affect but on perceptible narrative mechanics in the text — regardless of whether any particular reader responds to such an invitation — offers to literary theory a new and robust basis for replicable, objective analysis of personal interaction with a text in a way that can be brought into proper scholarly debate.

The main, technical, corpus of the book follows, focusing on three types of reader 'presence', or forms of experiential immersion, together with the narrative mechanisms that invite the perceptual illusion of each in the responsive reader (that is, the reader who reads as directed by the mechanisms of the text). These are *spatial presence*, *social presence*, and *self-presence*, and I discuss each of these in turn.

Chapter 2 sets out a model of *spatial presence*, defined as the realistic perceptual illusion of 'being there'. I seek to describe in this chapter how the poem uses specific narrative mechanics of world creation to invite in the reader an experience of embodied transportation, identifying how this differs from traditional development of 'setting' in textual literary theory. I explore certain mechanics of spatial presence in highly immersive video games to identify analogues with particular spatialising effects invited by the text of the *Comedy*, such as vection, illustrating my argument with the episodes of Dante's descent on the monster Geryon in *Inferno* XVII and the ascent of the celestial ladder in *Paradiso* XXII. I set out in conclusion the narrative strategy I term 'narration through situated body states', demonstrating how Dante deploys and develops this strategy longitudinally across the poem to invite the reader to feel present in the three realms of the afterlife.

In Chapter 3, I develop a model of *social presence* in relation to the *Comedy*, defining this as the realistic perceptual illusion of being physically in relation with others, and analysing the role of gesture, posture, and facial expression in Dante's poem through a lens of kinesic intelligence (that is, intuitive or 'direct' reading of body language) rooted in recent theories of embodied cognition and simulation theory. Through a close reading of two episodes — the snapping of Pier's twig in *Inferno* XIII and St Peter's contagious flush in *Paradiso* XXVII — I identify the narrative mechanisms that underpin a strategy I shall term 'narration through kinaesthetic empathy', exploring how this narrative mode changes and develops between and beyond the two episodes and taking in the mortal journeying Dante protagonist's body, the narrating Dante's body, and the virtual bodies of the souls of the afterlife. The chapter ends with a note on the vexed question of reciprocity in virtual social interaction and its clear and necessary practical limitations in the medium of a 'closed' text. I propose that Dante finds an extraordinary and innovative solution to even this contemporary problem through the device of the language of praise in the Empyrean.

In Chapter 4, I explore how the poem makes available to the reader a truly personal version of the extended mental model of the narrated journey. I set out a series of five narrative strategies in the poem that, in combination, invite an experience of 'self-presence', or the realistic perceptual illusion that 'something is happening to me'. I begin by assessing strategies for the handling of *narrative perspective* in the poem, identifying four 'faces' of the Dantean 'I', in a new model of *narrating instances*, and exploring Dante's innovative handling of line of sight through a strategy I term 'narration through mobile camera view'. Then, I examine the poem's mechanics of *narrative mediation*, identifying a continuum of invitations to the reader with, at one end, the explicit, immersion-rupturing *direct addresses* and, at the other, a vast and systematic programme of largely imperceptible invitations to cognitive participation invited through 'gaps' in the text. Specifically, I explore the mechanism of the narrative *ellipsis* whose some three hundred instances in the poem invite the same process of unconscious inference-making that characterises human cognitive processing; and the invitations to enactive mental modelling repeatedly put forward in the *similes* that together account for one fifth of the poem's narration. Illustrating each mechanism with examples taken from longitudinal analysis across the *Comedy*, I seek to show how each of the mechanisms of self-presence in the poem contributes to the famously and exceptionally participatory nature of the poem.

In the final chapter of the book, I shall, in conclusion, propose that systematic and sustained responsiveness to these invitations to individual reader presence in the poem constitutes a mode of reading I term *first-person participation*, setting out a formal definition and indicating how to read in that mode. It is a mode of reading, I shall argue, in which the reader responds to invitations to a particular form of embodied imaginative elaboration that can lead, in the responsive reader, to an unusually 'realistic' experience of the virtual world, one that can bring about a transformation in perception or understanding. The ability to read in this mode can be learned over time: indeed, I shall suggest, the poem is designed precisely in its narrative mechanics to function as a framework for burnishing the cognitive skills that underpin such learning. Finally, we return to Bernard's interaction *manqué* in *Paradiso* XXXIII where, in a simulation of first-person participation, I shall seek to demonstrate how two distinct 'io's become momentarily perceptible to the reader in the text. Once experienced by the reader, such a perceptual recognition, I shall suggest, invites a radical re-reading of the poem, instantiating a new sensitivity to electively identify as one of a kaleidoscope of 'io's that constitutes the agency of the first-person subject in Dante's poem.

Notes to the Introduction

1. An earlier version of this chapter was published in *Le tre corone* as 'Invitations to Participate: Bernard's Sign' (Powlesland 2017).
2. Contini's essential shift of focus, importantly, is away from Benedetto Croce's famous formulation of two elements that are both within authorial production — 'the Crocean problematisation of "structure" and "poetry"' (Contini 1976: 71) — and instead towards the responsibility of the reader to read as directed by the text, asking 'if therefore the opposition, rather than that of poetic form and poetic object [supporto e oggetto poetico], is instead between one mode of reading and another [tra modo e modo di leggere]' (72) — a binary not within artistic production alone, but that integrates production and reader reception. I am grateful to Helena Phillips-Robins for discussion on translating Contini.
3. Digital media theorist Marie-Laure Ryan offers a discussion of different types of immersion: spatial, epistemic, temporal, emotional. The differences between her four categories of immersion might be summarised as follows: spatial immersion depends on 'sense of place'; epistemic immersion on 'the desire to know'; temporal immersion on 'curiosity, surprise, and suspense'; and emotional immersion on 'empathy' (2009: 54–55).
4. In the long history of glossed readings of the *Divine Comedy*, commentators have largely neglected the question of immersion in this passage and of what Dante may be inviting us to consider or be alert to in metaliterary terms, focusing instead on the question of divine intervention in this process. For a more typical reading see, for example, Dino Cervigni's essay 'Dante's Poetry of Dreams' (1982: 25).
5. All translations of the *Divine Comedy* are reproduced from Robin Kirkpatrick's translation for Penguin (2006–07). For a discussion by Kirkpatrick of the nature of translation in relation to the *Comedy*, see his essay 'Dante Translating' in which he observes that Penguin's subsequent 2012 publication of a single-language version free of notes 'helps to emphasise that Dante is a great narrative writer, or even a page-turner, who needs to be read through without intrusive footnotes or commentaries' (2019: 133).
6. As will often be the case in this book, my interest in modes of interaction here provides an alternative reading to established interpretations in commentaries on the *Comedy*. In this instance, the traditional focus is on Beatrice's words as an invitation to the journeying Dante protagonist to dwell on the consequences of sin in terms of it's 'awful punishments' in Trucchi's words (gloss on ll. 136–38). Fosca, for example, suggests the intention is to 'arouse in him that fear of punishment' (gloss on ll. 136–41); Chiavacci Leonardi, that seeing the damned will 'shake him [riscuoterlo] from his errancy' (gloss on l. 38). My reading additionally perceives an invitation to the reader to similarly make it possible for her to 'be shown' the lost people, to find a way to make herself present at the interactions in the afterlife, through a particular form of imaginative reconstruction of this journey.
7. This question of experiential understanding in relation to Dante's works has been raised by others. Denys Turner writes that 'the language of the *Comedy* [...] enacts that of which it speaks' (2010: 286). John Took proposes of the *Convivio* that 'Dante sets out, not merely to *in*form [...], but to *trans*form, to bring home to his readers the fullness and incontrovertibility of their presence in the world as creatures of orderly intellection and of moral determination' (2013: 199; emphasis in original). Jeremy Tambling (1988: 7) proposes that the model of active readership invited in the *Comedy* differs from that of the arguably passive reader of the *Vita nuova*.
8. This notwithstanding, there are certainly instances of what might be considered immersive experiential commentary in the Trecento tradition, including, for example, Benvenuto da Imola's observations of his own growing thin, 'mihi simile accidit', in response to the poet's wasting over the years in writing his poem (*Par.*, XXV: gloss on 1–9). An analysis of the extent of such commentary would be very instructive but lies beyond the scope of this particular book. For an introduction to the commentary tradition in Dante studies see, for example, Deborah Parker (1997); Paola Nasti and Claudia Rossignoli's 2013 edited volume; and, particularly on the early tradition, Saverio Bellomo (2004). Contini suggested that this scholarly tradition has yielded 'oceans of exegesis', identifying 'the vexation of anyone who, undertaking to read Dante's great poem, is obliged to cope with the inescapable preliminary task of technically

ascertaining the exact meaning of the text' (1969: 1–2). More recently, Barański has observed that the *Comedy* is a text 'overwhelm[ed]' by its own scholarship (2017: 2).

9. Spitzer (1955: 144) and Auerbach (1953: 268) both use the phrase 'a new relationship'. The essays focus on description of the addresses rather than analysis of its narratological mechanisms. The use of the term 'appelli' [addresses] in this context is usually attributed to Giuseppe Petronio (1965: 98).

10. Barański's focus — invitations to exegesis — is the intellectually interpretative foil to my participatory one, but the notion of the addresses as the visible face of a larger strategy is the same: '[Dante's] addresses to the ubiquitous *lettor* are simply the most accessible examples of this design [that of '[working] at deciphering his poem']' (1989: 7).

11. Here Singleton is writing on the line 'Poi ch'ei posato un poco il corpo lasso' (*Inf.*, I. 28). There is considerable evidence in scholarship that Dante's 'io' has been experienced as disruptive by readers, and difficult to understand in analytical terms. Took, for example, talks of 'the anxious "I"' (2013: 202). On the protagonist's putative 'transmutability', Pertile (2010: 167) concludes: 'During the weeklong journey, the character Dante does *not* change, except superficially and temporarily as required by the circumstances in which he happens to find himself. He may show joy and sadness, pity and cruelty, curiosity, fear and rage, but these are passing feelings and emotions, which attest to his "transmutability" but do not transform him in any permanent way'. I partially agree with Pertile as will become evident in my analysis of the journeying Dante protagonist as fulfilling an avatar function for the reader, a mediating body through which she may experience the virtual world and encounters of the poem; but I also disagree with his conclusion, in that I think the journeying Dante protagonist *is* transformed, as part of this function. I explore this in Chapter 4, in which I seek to offer a fresh way to think about the Dante protagonist(s) as a combination of strategic functions mediating the reader's experience. Tambling suggests that 'the unity of the subject [across Dante's works] is a fictional one' (1988: 165), suggesting we can therefore read Dante as standing in opposition to the Cartesian *cogito* and the belief in a stable, single identity. This stands in interesting relation to Pertile's suggestion of a transmutable self that is 'inconstant, uncertain, capricious, subject to the fluctuations of desire and to the changes of time and place' (2010: 165).

12. See the opening of Chapter 4 in Kirkpatrick (1978), particularly pp. 108–14. Elsewhere, he writes: 'I shall argue that only an active — even "creative" — reading of the *Comedy* can do justice to the work as Dante has written it' (1987: 3). In the Introduction to his translation of *Paradiso*, he proposes that: 'In a certain sense, the *Paradiso* may best be read as a pure exercise in imagination and intellect or, in other words, as a game' (2007: lxii). On a related notion of a dynamic model of characterisation in the *Comedy*, see Hooper 2019.

13. Barolini opens her argument in *The Undivine Comedy* by citing Bruno Nardi's *Dante profeta*: 'Those who consider the Dantean vision and the rapturous ascent of the prophet to heaven to be literary fictions mistake the poem's meaning' (1992: 3) See, more recently, Barolini 2013 and, also, Moevs (2005: 178), particularly, 'One thing is clear: one cannot reduce such claims [to truth] to some notion of objectively reporting prior spatiotemporal events'.

14. Barolini characterises the writer as 'exploiting his poetic genius' (1992: 13), deploying 'poetic cunning' (13); she cautions sensitivity to 'our narrative credulity' (16); and writes of 'the formal structures that manipulate the reader so successfully' (16). Later, Geryon is described as a 'weapon in a massive and unrelenting campaign to coerce our suspension of disbelief' (61).

15. See specifically Albert Russell Ascoli, *Dante and the Making of a Modern Author*, in which he sets himself the task of understanding 'why Dante might find it difficult to attribute the role of *auctor* and the quality of *auctoritas* to himself and his works, despite his evident valorisation of, and desire for, them' (2008: 9). I discuss further the question of *auctoritas* in Chapter 4, n. 7. See also Ascoli (2019); as this book sets out, I cannot agree with Ascoli's conclusion in that essay that Dante 'assume[s] the starring role' (2019: 14) in his poem, but contest rather that this is a role into which he systematically invites the reader.

16. Further: 'Detheologising [...] signifies releasing our reading of the *Comedy* from the author's grip, finding a way out of Dante's hall of mirrors' (17). Tracing back Barolini's 'we' to its source in the chapter, I take it to refer to 'all readers of Dante's poem' (4).

17. Ryan (2015: 6) discusses semiotic blindness. On inattentional blindness, see Mack and Rock (1998).

18. I clarify, in case of any doubt, that under my terms a participatory reading necessitates a generative relationship between the rational and the pre-rational cognitions, the imagination, affect, and the intellect. As I hope to make clear in my analysis of the functioning of these mechanics in the narrative, I fully support Kirkpatrick's observation that '[c]ertainly, the story which Dante is telling will call into play an extremely wide range of emotions and an even wider range of imaginings. And all of these will have their value: but only if guided by intelligent discrimination and an eye for the analysis of fact' (2004: 14).

19. They cite specifically Iacomo della Lana's importing of tools from the sciences (2013: 5) and conclude: 'The focus of Dante readers moves from theology to science, from science to politics, from style to sources; and each of these moves perpetuates the story both of Dante and of his readers, proving what we have come to expect — that a text is also the history of its reception' (10). See also Peter Dronke on the 'otherness' of medieval poetry for which, he suggests, contemporary scholarship has had no critical terminology (1986: 1–8).

20. The division of the phenomenon of presence into three types is usually credited to Kwan Min Lee (2004). I set out each of these types of presence in Chapters 2, 3, and 4, and additionally discuss the avatar in relation to narrative mediation and the experience of reader identification with the protagonist in Chapter 4.

21. Arguably most noteworthy at the time of writing are: Claudia Rossignoli's 2019 essay, 'Playing the Afterlife: Dante's Otherworlds in the Gaming Age'; Katherine Powlesland, 'Dante and Video Games: The Unrealised Potential of the Virtual *Commedia*' (2022); Boccaccio scholar Brandon K. Essary's 2019 article, 'Dante's *Inferno*, Video Games, and Pop Pedagogy'; and digital theorist Timothy J. Welsh and medievalist John Sebastian's essay, 'Shades of Dante: Virtual Bodies in *Dante's Inferno*' (2014).

22. For example, Webb's *Dante's Persons: An Ethics of the Transhuman* (2016); Shaw's essay, 'Embodiment and the Human from Dante through Tomorrow' (2010); and Kline's introduction to his edited volume, *Digital Gaming Re-imagines the Middle Ages* (2014).

23. For example, Brown's essay, 'The Dark Wood of Postmodernity (Space, Faith, Allegory)' (2005); Kanekar's 'Detours through Autonomy: Mismapping the *Divine Comedy*' (2013); Kleiner's 'Mismapping the Underworld' (1989); Sinding's *Body of Vision: Northrop Frye and the Poetics of Mind* (2014).

24. Steven Botterill (1994) offers a compelling reading of Bernard's appearance in the text. His reading points out not only the surprise of Bernard's involvement (65), and the withholding of Bernard's identity for nearly forty lines (67), but also reminds the scholar not to 'underestimate its immediate impact on an unprepared reader — which is to astonish. Such "professionals" have, in a sense, forgotten that they ever did *not* know that this event was going to take place, and have lost the ability to react to it as ordinary readers — the kind to whom the *Comedy* is addressed — surely must' (66). But Botterill's focus is not on narrative mechanics, so he does not appear to spot — at least, he does not comment on — the decoupling of the reader's gaze from the protagonist's, which will be my primary focus here (and which itself supports Botterill's own commitment to reading as directed by the mechanisms of the text).

25. The early commentaries generally agree 'tal qual ei volea' to indicate a mode of acting or doing; for example, L'Ottimo Commento (ll. 49–51): 'that which [Bernard] desired, that is to say, that divine virtue drew him to itself just as to its perfection'. Anonimo Fiorentino's gloss (ll. 49–51) proposes instead a mode of being, 'content and quieted', but this is not a common interpretation.

26. In his gloss (ll. 52–54), Hollander comments: 'The poet could not be more precise. Up to now his powers of sight have improved so that he can finally see God's reflection in the universe perfectly, an ability that was far from his grasp when the poem began. Now he will see Him as Himself [...]. In the next tercet we realise that he has recorded his breakthrough. No Christian except for St Paul has seen so much — or such is the unspoken claim the poet makes us share.'

27. For an account of how a reader 'experiences' a narrative world by constructing a mental model, see Johnson-Laird (1983). I explore this further in Chapter 1, particularly in relation to affective devotion.

28. In the same gloss, Singleton defines the other such 'slip' to be at *Purg.*, XXI. 10–14: that is, the arrival of Statius.

29. The framework of reader participation offers a clear opportunity, I suggest, to explore further the highly productive relationship between narrative construction and truth claims, but this lies beyond the scope of this book. For now, it is perhaps sufficient to have in mind Moevs's presentation of the tension: 'We can imagine that Dante would smile appreciatively at Singleton's famous phrase, "the fiction of the *Divine Comedy* is that it is not fiction", but he would answer: "you have not seen the point, the *punto*". The poem's poetics, its typological and anagogical thrust, the basis of its claim to prophetic truth and its claim on the reader is grounded in its metaphysical ontology: in the self-experience of the subject of all experience, the awakening to what is not in the world, but lies outside it. The thrust of the *Comedy* is that its letter is ontologically continuous with Scripture, physical reality and history, while at the same time it also points to itself as artifice, representation, *fictio,* myth, a body or veiling of soul or spirit' (Moevs 2005: 183). The well-known Singleton reference is discussed in the latter's essay, 'The Irreducible Dove' (1957: 129).

30. I discuss focal view further in Chapter 4.

31. On autocorrection in cognitive theory, see, for example, Pervin (1978: 71).

32. See Ryan and Deci's definition of 'intrinsic motivation' as 'doing something because it is inherently interesting or enjoyable', as compared with 'extrinsic motivation', which 'refers to doing something because it leads to a separable outcome' (2000: 55). This phenomenon is elegantly expressed in William Carlos Williams's poem *Paterson*: 'Dissonance | (if you're interested) | leads to discovery' (IV. 2).

33. In 'Un'interpretazione di Dante', Contini (1976) talks of feeling the 'teeth' of the imagination bite: 'In the *allegro* movement of the tercets, with the frictionless turning of the wheels of the eschatological adventure, the great sequences give a little and soften, the lapidary words, for centuries inscribed in the national memory, stretch and slightly loosen their hold. But the reader who slows down, who delays a little, who re-engages with the techniques of traction, suddenly feels the teeth of the imagination bite, yields to the greater power of the intensity of the words. Amongst the most passionate [gli appassionati], the discrete prevails over the continuous' (1976: 69). Here, Contini appears to be describing a shift from reading in a mode of epistemic immersion and into the more participatory model of cognitive engagement I set out in this book.

34. I outline a model of 'narrative training' in Chapter 4 to propose how such refinement of the cognitions is invited throughout the poem.

35. The definition of *focal view* is in flux as narrative theory continues to extend across media. The *living handbook of narratology* routes its definition in Genette (1980: 189–94), and I follow the *lhn*'s definition in my analysis in this section: 'A selection or restriction of narrative information in relation to the experience and knowledge of the narrator, the characters or other, more hypothetical entities in the storyworld' (http://lhn.sub.uni-hamburg.de/index.php/Focalization.html).

36. See Genette (1980: 161–211, 212–62). *Mood* ('Who sees?', in Genette's shorthand) and *voice* ('Who speaks?') need not be identical, especially in a retrospective first-person narrative like the *Comedy*, in which only the narrator can 'speak' directly to the reader whilst events can be shown to her both through the narrator's eyes (looking back retrospectively) and through the eyes of the journeying protagonist (as events unfold). I discuss this further in Chapter 4.

37. Whilst here I distinguish just these two focal characters for clarity in developing my argument in relation to Bernard's interaction, I set out in Chapter 4 a more nuanced and complete proposal that the narrating Dante focal character is in fact a composite of three 'narrating instances' (building on Genette 1980: 212–15) that I label and outline as follows: (1) an *Embodied Narrator* narrating instance, located in the outer story world with subjective glossed knowledge (having undertaken the journey) and an authenticating focus on his own embodied cognition; (2) an *Implied Author* narrating instance, of no fixed location and with total knowledge/omniscience, including prophecy, conferring *auctoritas*; and (3) a *Zero-Focalised Narration* narrating instance, whose purpose is neutral propulsion of narrative action, and that has omniscient sight within the inner story world but no knowledge privileges (that is, that visually frames, but does not

interpret). I propose, then, a total of three Dantes whose framing of the action can influence or direct the reader's participation in the narrative, or four if we also include the focal character of the journeying Dante protagonist, located in the inner storyworld with restricted sight and knowledge.

38. In relation to the narrative structure of the *Vita nuova,* Singleton writes: 'With the death of Beatrice, a circle is closed. We know again what we began by knowing. And we stand at a point where we can see the movement along this line of action is not movement in a single direction. The current is alternating, which is something one had already seen in the figure of a poet–protagonist become two persons according to a situation in time: the one being he who, though ignorant of the end, moves always towards the end; and the other he who, knowing the end, is constantly retracing the whole line of events with the new awareness and transcendent understanding which such superior knowledge can give' (1977: 25). Note that the narrating Dante is omniscient only in his *Implied Author* narrating instance incarnation, not in either the *Embodied Narrator* or *Zero-Focalised Narration* narrating instances.

39. 'Buio d'inferno e di notte privata | d'ogne pianeto, sotto pover cielo, | quant' esser può di nuvol tenebrata, | non fece al viso mio sì grosso velo | come quel fummo ch'ivi ci coperse, | né a sentir di così aspro pelo, | che l'occhio stare aperto non sofferse' [Darkness in Hell, or any night stripped bare | of planets under impoverished skies | (a pall of clouds as dense as these could be), | has never formed, for me, as thick a veil | as did the smoke that now surrounded us, | or stretched a weave so rasping in its feel | that eyes could not stay open to its touch] (*Purg.,* XVI. 1–7). More generally, on seeing in the dark in Hell, see Chapter 2, n. 21.

40. Specifically, the *Zero-Focalised Narration* instance.

41. Specifically, the *Implied Author* narrating instance.

42. The word 'ma', often preceding a narrative shock and therefore inviting an experience of surprise in the reader, is likely, I propose, to be an indicator of a rupturing of Ryan's third form of immersion, *temporal* immersion. This lies outside the scope of this book, but along with 'già' [already], which I suggest to carry a similar function, merits investigation for an extended understanding of invitations to participate.

43. Such alternative interpretations may include, for example, whether it is possible that the journeying Dante can somehow see Bernard in his peripheral vision (although tracking the precise eye movements and locatives for each character from the moment Bernard took Beatrice's place in *Paradiso* XXX suggests that Bernard would need to be located some considerable distance forwards and up from Dante — themselves problematic concepts in *Paradiso* — so almost certainly not). Or again, whether Dante could infer Bernard's gesture through the phenomenon of *joint attention*, defined by Andrew Pinsent as 'a triadic person–person–object scenario in which the object is the focus of attention of both persons' (2012: 44), and of which I suggest there is an example involving Bernard, Dante and Mary at *Par.,* XXXI. 118–42. To a certain extent, this depends on how the reader mentally models Bernard's *cenno* or sign in *Paradiso* XXXIII: is it a gesture of the hand (as Singleton seems to infer)? A smile? This would be more typical of the lexicon of signs in Paradise, although it would be tautologous in this case. Or could this, too, be a 'visual' gesture, a turning of the eyes? If the latter, then the phenomenon of joint attention might be mooted, but neither of the former two could be 'read' without being seen under normal modes of human perception. What is certain though is that by *not* specifying the nature of the sign, Dante creates another gap in the narrative, since each interpretation is possible.

44. On the principle of narrative frame violations, see, for example, Debra Malina's *Breaking the Frame* in which she writes: 'Even at its mildest, metalepsis disrupts the boundary of a fictional narrative — the one between inside and outside, between story and world. When a text repeatedly indulges in such subversion, the result is inevitably jarring, and its effects run the gamut from startling diversion through destabilisation and disorientation to outright violation' (2002: 2–3).

45. Separating 'fabula' (story) and 'syuzhet' (plot), Vladimir Propp defined in 1928 the essential condition of a narrative text as being that it is 'closed': events are already over at the time of their narrating. See also Eco (1979).

46. Heather Webb (2019: 208) identifies a further instance of what I have termed an 'interaction *manqué*' in Botticelli's illustration of *Paradiso* XXVI, whereby 'Botticelli's canto 26 shows Beatrice gesturing to a Dante who does not see her; he is covering his eyes. Who, then, is the gesture for?'. She terms this a phenomenon of 'plural facing' (199).

47. Cognitive theorist Margaret Wilson proposed that the 'most powerful' of embodied cognition's new claims is that '*Off-line cognition is body based*. Even when decoupled from the environment, the activity of the mind is grounded in mechanisms that evolved for interaction with the environment — that is, mechanisms of sensory processing and motor control' (2002: 625–26; emphasis in original). To clarify: '[o]ff-line aspects of embodied cognition [...] include any cognitive activities in which sensory and motor resources are brought to bear on mental tasks whose referents are distant in time and space or are altogether imaginary' (635).

48. There have been numerous reports in the media of this phenomenon: see, for example, 'HAL 90210' (2016).

49. Bailenson, author of *Experience on Demand: What Virtual Reality Is, How It Works, and What It Can Do* (2018), is quoted in LaMotte (2017).

50. I have piloted a model of primary research on *Mirror's Edge* in Chapter 2 that has been productive and suggests opportunities to refine further such a comparative approach. For the most part, though, my thesis in this book rests on adapting and building from existing theory in video game criticism. In addition, my focus is on so-called 'interestingly hard' video games. This term was coined by Margaret Robertson (2010) to describe games that foreground 'the rich cognitive, emotional and social drivers which gamifiers are intending to connect [players] with'. Robertson is also pioneer of the concept of 'serious games', in which the primary purpose of the game is not entertainment but to train or teach. Both such types of games are typically released by independent game designers, by contrast with mainstream blockbuster games or those that focus on gamification and pointsification. This notwithstanding, the core principles discussed here, of presence and the avatar, are common to both.

51. Gee, a founder of the field of New Literacy Studies, writes that the first function of the avatar is to provide 'a *surrogate body* for the player in the game world [...], determining what and how the player can see and sense'. Two further functions are to provide: 'an *identity* that a player inhabits [...]. When we play a game, we play as the avatar ...] [or] in the spirit of the avatar'; and 'a *tool-kit*. The avatar, in terms of his or her skills, powers, and devices, offers the player a set of tools with which to accomplish goals and solve problems in the game' (2015: 17–18; emphasis in original).

52. This is the root of the illusion of interactivity in a virtual space, feeling *as if* you are there and *as if* your body has agency in the game world (you act; the world and the objects within it act reciprocally on your body). See Ryan (2001: 160–85) on 'the many forms of interactivity'.

53. There is a conflict in current video game critical theory as to whether these separate identities 'meld' (Gee 2015: 94), or whether a gap is maintained between them, as digital anthropologist Tom Boellstorff maintains (2011: 513). I follow Boellstorff, as I discuss in Chapter 4.

54. Gee writes: 'Good video games create a "projective identity". They create a double-sided stance to the world (virtual or real) in terms of which we humans see the world simultaneously as a project imposed on us and as a site onto which we can actively project our desires, values and goals' (2015: 94).

55. A specialist in digital affective participation, Calleja writes that: 'Alterbiography is the ongoing narrative generated during interaction with a game environment [...]. [T]he generation of alterbiography can feature the character as a separate entity controlled by the player or can be considered as being about the player in the world [...]. The *alterbiography of self* is most commonly evoked in first-person games [...], where players interpret the events in the game as happening to *them* specifically, rather than to an external character' (2011: 124–25; emphasis in original).

.

❖

Embodiment in Context

1.1. A fresh return to embodiment

My proposal for the reading mode I term 'first-person participation' is rooted in a model of embodied cognition that began to emerge with the so-called affective turn of the mid-1990s in the humanities and social sciences, and that is increasingly recognised in medieval scholarship as representing a return, at least in part, to medieval models of theory of mind, as I shall set out in this chapter.[1] In second-generation cognitive science, a new theory of *embodied cognition* challenges the Cartesian separation of mind from body that has come to dominate models of thought over the last four hundred or so years.[2]

Descartes's *cogito* has been, in the terms of Lakoff and Johnson, 'of special catastrophic significance' in influencing subsequent theory of mind (1999: 400).[3] They argue that Descartes presents as a 'philosophical truth' (394) an assumption about cognition rooted in an unconscious metaphor — namely, that 'knowing is seeing' (393).[4] This metaphor forces him, they write, to a 'model of deduction as a single act of vision that encompasses what is really a *series* of cognitive acts' (399; emphasis in original),[5] ultimately leading him to the conception of a disembodied mind in which all thought is conscious and where there is an objective external world to be cognised.[6] Cognitive science now offers us, in Lakoff and Johnson's terms, 'overwhelming evidence that the mind does not work like this' (1999: 414).[7] But so appealing and common-sensical is this metaphor, with its illusion of a human-centric universe to be mastered, that it has endured, shaping the way we encounter the world and separating us, I shall propose, from certain medieval habits of cognition that affect the way we engage with texts like the *Comedy*. In a Cartesian world we have come to privilege the visual and the deductive over the sensual and the intuitive, narratives of resolution over revelation, and meaning over presence.[8]

Prominent medievalist and historian of perception Brian Stock has observed that the modern humanities encounter texts as objects to master, commenting that '[c]ontemporary criticism has considerably obscured the relationship between reading and contemplation practice that was deliberately incorporated into many late ancient and medieval readings on the self' (2001: 23). More recently, medieval historian Sara Ritchey has commented that '[the medieval] affective means of interpretation and understanding has [...] lost its place of importance in contemporary humanistic programs of study which have instead [...] promoted a distanced, measured hermeneutics' (2012: 342). My suggestion in this book is that second-generation cognitive science's model of embodied cognition helps us defamiliarise essential differences between medieval modes of cognising that are instrumental in the practice of reading, and the Cartesian model through which modern scholarship has long been reading the *Comedy*, opening a path to a more historically sensitive way of interacting with the poem. Presence is the tool through which I propose the modern reader may re-encounter the *Comedy* in this way.

In Margaret Wilson's synthesis, and in opposition to a Cartesian disembodied mind, embodied cognition is born of an understanding that 'human cognition, rather than being centralised, abstract, and sharply distinct from peripheral input and output modules, may instead have deep roots in sensorimotor processing' (2002: 625). This belief is rooted in new neurobiological evidence of a phenomenon of *exaptation* — that is, the discovery that the mind adaptively co-opts or 'piggyback[s]' on neural circuits originally designed for bodily action, out of evolutionary efficiency (Lakoff and Johnson 1980: 20).[9] Human perceptual and motor systems share the same neural circuits. When we *act*, the muscles are excited and movement is observable; when we *perceive*, this motor execution is inhibited; or, in the terms of prominent neuroscientist Vittorio Gallese, in perception, 'action is not produced, it is only *simulated*' (2011: 457; my emphasis).[10]

It has become widely accepted in cognitive science that this phenomenon of embodiment extends beyond sensory perception into the other cognitive functions, such as memory, attention, language, learning, reasoning, and judgment.[11] In Lakoff and Johnson's terms, '[t]he same neural and cognitive mechanisms that allow us to perceive and to move around also create our conceptual systems and modes of reason' (1999: 4).[12] In some cases, this re-use of bodily systems becomes perceptible: in the motoric expression of language through gesture, for example, or in the offloading of a short-term memory function like enumeration by counting on the fingers. Sometimes, it is the viscera that are implicated: 'gut feel', perspiration, raised heart rate. Lakoff and Johnson further define an additional type of embodiment in relation to the cognitions, one that functions at an almost entirely unconscious level. They categorise this as 'neural embodiment' (1999: 102–03), describing it as 'all those mental operations that structure and make possible all conscious experience' (103). These are *unconscious* mental operations: neurons that fire without our conscious involvement, for example, in the way we unconsciously receive feedback from places and people that makes us feel 'present' — as if we are physically there — and that makes these interactions feel 'realistic'; in automatic imitation of others (known as neural mirroring); or in the unconscious leaps we make to bridge gaps in perception data (such as inferring a person has a lower body when we see them sitting behind a desk). Such unconscious mental operations frame the way we cognise our world. This is the type of embodiment that is of particular interest to me in this book.

Descartes's logic framed reality as, in the words of Francisco Varela et al., 'the representation of a pre-given world by a pre-given mind' (1993: 9); it naturalised a worldview of external observation that the communication technologies of print and screen reflected and endorsed.[13] Embodied cognition frames the processes of cognition instead as both *enactive* — that is, dynamic and rooted in sensorimotor processing — and *extended* — that is, constantly emerging as a result of interactions with people and with the environment.[14] In their foundational text on embodied cognition, *The Embodied Mind*, Varela, Thompson, and Rosch describe it as 'the enactment of a world and a mind on the basis of a history of the variety of actions that a being in the world performs' (1993: 9). 'To understand the mind's place in the world', suggests Susan Hurley in *Consciousness in Action*, 'we should study these complex dynamic processes as a system, not just the truncated internal portion of them' (1998: 2).

My suggestion in relation to the *Comedy* is that Dante's text recruits not only the reader's conscious cognitive processes (the 'think', 'remember', 'imagine', of the direct addresses), but also strategically targets the reader's unconscious mental processes, inviting participation at a level of neural embodiment. Specifically, I mean that there are mechanisms in the text that invite the reader's brain to accept the narrated space, the interactions within it, and the reader's own presence there, as 'realistic'; in a way, and to an extent, that we might consider unusual, and indeed innovative, in a textual artefact. Lakoff and Johnson characterise these unconscious mental operations as 'the massive portion of the iceberg that lies below the surface, below the visible tip that is consciousness' (1999: 103). Their iceberg metaphor may be useful as a means to hold in mind the notion of a continuum of invitations to the reader's cognitions in the *Comedy*. If the direct addresses represent the visible tip of the iceberg, inviting the participation of the conscious mental processes of thinking, remembering, imagining, my suggestion is that the vast bulk of the poem's invitations to cognitive participation in fact constitute the hidden portion of the iceberg: the unconscious mental processes that shape our individual perception of reality and drive our unique behaviours.

1.2. Medieval theory of mind

An analysis of late medieval understanding of cognition is not straightforward. The rediscovery of Aristotle in the late twelfth century fuelled the development of varying theories of mind by thinkers including Avicenna, Thomas Aquinas, Albertus Magnus, Roger Bacon, Peter Olivi, and William of Ockham.[15] However, what is evident is that cognition was widely held to be embodied: 'the mind–brain complex an integrated, dynamic system', in the terms of medieval historian Corinne Saunders and developmental psychologist Charles Fernyhough; the resultant *phantasmata* 'dripp[ing] with sensory qualities and emotional charge' (2016: 880).

Stephen Milner has identified, in late medieval Italy, three significant points of discussion relating to the cognitions that, we can infer, would have been in the air when Dante was writing the *Comedy*. The first is a shift towards an Aristotelian understanding of cognition as *dynamic*, away from the Platonic species theory of cognition.[16] The second was a re-focusing on cognition as *social*, through an appreciation of the self as contingent upon and shaped by interactions with others.[17] The third point of discussion was an understanding of cognition as rooted in *interaction with the environment*: the self 'a porous and sensate body that impinges [on], and is impinged upon by, the world in the accumulation of experience' (2015: 239). Milner concludes that '[a]s it moves through time and space, such a self is radically contingent as it is called into being through its bodily motility and sensitivity to different environments and encounters as a self in community' (239).

In each of these three points, I suggest, we might explore resonances with a modern understanding of embodied cognition: in the first, Varela et al.'s *enactive* model of a body in action; in the second and third, the notion of cognition as *extended*, and contingent upon social relations and spatial interactions. The medieval conception of cognition, as outlined by Milner, and our own contemporary model of embodied cognition seem to have in common a notion of a contingent, dynamic, interactive 'self in society': in both models, the body, as Suzannah Biernoff has expressed it, 'a hinge between self and world' (2002: 48).

Rediscovering such parallels offers an opportunity, I suggest, to rethink the way we have approached the *Comedy* through an inherited lens of Cartesian disembodiment, and to map together a contemporary and a medieval model of cognition in a way that scholarship on the medieval cognitions has arguably not had the tools to attempt in the past. Much of the canonical scholarship in medieval theory of mind (Kemp, Tweedale, Yates, for example, who were all writing in the second half of the twentieth century) was a product of first-generation cognitive science. Such scholars were therefore constrained by accident of context to try to read medieval theories of mind through the Cartesian legacy of computational mentalism, rather than through embodied cognition, arguably coming up against certain theoretical dead-ends as a consequence.[18] In 2012, scholar of medieval English literature Jane Chance observed that, to date, there had been 'few advances in understanding what might be termed the "medieval brain"' (2012: 251) and that 'few [...] medievalists have grasped the potential importance of a cognitive theoretical and neuroscientific approach to the late Middle Ages, particularly given the significance of the rise in affective spirituality beginning in the thirteenth century' (252).

But there is growing evidence of change. An emerging body of analysis in the humanities now seeks to read medieval theory of mind through the fresh lens of embodied cognition. Milner is a leading exponent, explicitly finding a relationship between medieval theory of mind and the mid-1990s affective turn, and writing that this turn 'can be read as little more than the re-establishment of the premodern link between cognition and sensation, a return to the long-held assertion of the interdependence of psychology and physiology in the reading of human behaviour' (2015: 238).[19] Commenting on the manifold developments in theory of mind by medieval writers, Saunders and Fernyhough suggest that '[such] writings offer sophisticated and complex ways of understanding the [medieval] relation between brain and mind in the era of neuroscience' (2016: 883). Performance theorist Jill Stevenson, writing on the English Passion plays, concludes that contemporary neuroscience invites us to '[revisit] medieval notions of perception's material interactivity' (2010: 26). And in the field of medieval affective piety, in her 2011 monograph *Imagination, Meditation, and Cognition in the Middle Ages*, Michelle Karnes has newly highlighted in relation to some of the most popular Italian gospel meditations a phenomenon of neuroplasticity that could radically extend an understanding of the purpose and ambition of such texts in terms of individual behaviour change.[20]

In the next section, I set out briefly some observations relating to medieval scholarship on the cognitions in which embodiment is already indicated in different ways: specifically, in the areas of *rhetoric*, *gesture*, and *memory*. Afterwards, I turn to the field of *affective piety*, to offer some context on medieval practices of reading, and suggest that with affective piety's focus on recruiting the cognitions in service of changing individual behaviour, and its dependence on virtual (that is, textual, as opposed to real life) sensory input data, new thinking about embodied cognition offers highly productive perspectives for an exploration of invitations to participation in the *Comedy*.

1.3. Approaches to medieval cognitive theory: rhetoric, gesture, memory

Rhetoric

Stephen Milner has foregrounded a foundational role for affect in the rhetoric of the Middle Ages, writing that '[r]hetoric called on the irrational forces of emotion to move the will, requiring the orator to possess a level of emotional intelligence if he was to carry the hearts, as well as the minds, of his audience' (2015: 244).[21] Its purpose, he writes, was to move (*per-suadere*, to strongly urge or induce) individuals and communities:

> As the handmaiden to ethical discourse, [rhetoric] delivered right reason concerning the obligations and duties of the good citizen in persuasive form, stressing the virtue of action over the attainment of knowledge, the primacy of the good over the identification of the true. Unlike logical and dialectical argumentation, rhetorical argumentation and invention were far more suited to the contingent world of communal political and social life. (243)

It did so by 'engag[ing] the senses' (243); by an 'appeal to the sensitive soul and the channelling of its desires and appetites' (244). The methods of rhetoric as he describes them are highly evocative of the *enactive* and *extended* models of embodied cognition, Milner arguing that 'rhetorical argumentation was applied and situated' (244) and that '[r]hetoric put the specificity of situation [*extended* cognition], [and] the contingency of action [*enactive* cognition], back into the frame as it uses emotions to affect judgment' (243).

I suggest that Milner's reading of medieval rhetoric through a frame of affective reason reinforces the importance, in considering the *Comedy*, of fully allowing that the rhetorical figures of the poem seek to engage the reader's emotions as well as her intellect. To be persuaded, the reader must first *feel*, and indeed yield to 'the irrational forces of emotion'. I return to what this might mean in practice in the section on affective piety.

Gesture

In *Gestures and Looks in Medieval Narrative* (2002), John Burrow sets out the distinction in Augustine's theory of signs in *De Doctrina Christiana* between gestures and postures consciously adopted to encode and express a specific meaning or intention (which would come under the classification of *signa data*), and non-verbal messages unconsciously communicated (*signa naturalia*).[22] Barański has demonstrated that Dante had a sophisticated appreciation of learned thinking about *signa*,[23] and of course there is much evidence in the text of embodied utterance in the *Comedy*, both in terms of the often explicit encoding of postures of penitence in *Purgatorio* recently discussed by Heather Webb in *Dante's Persons* (2016), and in her 2013 essay, 'Postures of Penitence in Dante's *Purgatory*'; and the arguably less conscious notional 'leakage' of body language (Farinata's raised eyebrows in *Inferno* X, or Malacoda's expression of contempt in *Inferno* XXI, for example), as I explore in Chapter 3.[24]

My proposal is that embodied cognition offers a fresh lens for exploring embodied utterance in one particular way that might alter engagement with the poem; namely, that gesture, posture, and facial expression are fundamental mechanisms of intersubjectivity at an unconscious level.[25] The notion of neural embodiment offers a new model for thinking about this in relation to a mechanism of 'neural mirroring', which proposes that we unconsciously, or 'directly', read another's actions or intentions through their so-called 'body language' by automatically simulating the same neural activity that underpins such body language ourselves.[26] Neuroscientist Vittorio Gallese names this phenomenon *embodied simulation*, writing with literary theorist Hannah Wojciehowski in 2011 that:

> Embodied simulation creates internal non-linguistic 'representations' of the body-states associated with actions, emotions, and sensations within the observer, as if he or she were performing a similar action or experiencing a similar emotion or sensation [...]. [It] is a mandatory, pre-rational, non-introspective process — that is, a physical, and not simply 'mental' experience of the mind, emotions, lived experiences and motor intentions of other people. (Wojciehowski and Gallese 2011: 15)[27]

It is pre-rational and unconscious because 'mirror neurons allow a *direct* form of action understanding' (13), and it occurs constantly in real life when we observe and come into interaction with other people. It is 'direct' because 'it does not require any inference by analogy or other more cognitively sophisticated and explicit forms of mentalisation. When we see someone acting or expressing a given emotional or somatosensory state, we can directly grasp its content without the need to reason explicitly about it' (13). Embodied simulation is increasingly widely accepted to be the root of empathy and catharsis; and the mirroring upon which it is based, a plastic skill: that is, one that can be refined.

Crucially, for a new understanding of user participation in a virtual artefact like a text, Wojciehowski and Gallese further suggest that embodied simulation is triggered *not only* when we observe such body states in real life, but can also be triggered when we *imagine* observing them; that is, in response to appropriate virtual data: imagined, remembered, or mentally modelled in response to narrated information in a text. They write that:

> Embodied simulation [...] can also occur when we *imagine* doing or perceiving something [...]. [B]rain imaging studies show that when we imagine a visual scene, we activate the same visual regions of our brain normally active when we actually perceive the same visual scene. (16)

As a result, they hypothesise, in neural processing terms 'the border between real and fictional worlds is much more blurred than one would expect' (17). There are manifold examples in the *Comedy* of narrated gesture, posture, and facial expression, including some instances of explicit mirroring between interacting characters, as I discuss in Chapter 3. My suggestion is that a new sensitivity to the mechanism of neural mirroring — as made manifest in narration of behaviours in the text — may invite us to consider the possibility that gesture, appropriately and realistically rendered through narrative data of observed bodily behaviour, may have the neurobiological potential to work metaleptically in a text. By this I mean that it may be possible to build a case in relation to the *Comedy* (as others already have in relation to other texts, as I discuss later) to argue that the reader's own mirror mechanism may be triggered in response to what she reads, setting up the possibility of an additional level of 'direct' understanding by the reader of the intentions and body states of the characters in the poem. I return to this in Chapter 3.

Memory

In the Middle Ages, memory was accorded a different status than it is given today, as scholarship has extensively shown. In 1966, Frances Yates alluded famously to '[w]e moderns who have no memories at all' (1984: 4); 'we moderns' having made a virtue of developing technologies designed to offload or externalise most memorial work, from pen and paper note-taking to photography, paper archives, and now satellite navigation, Google searching, and cloud data storage. In 1993, cognitive neuroscientist Merlin Donald commented that: 'Cognitive evolution is not yet complete: the externalisation of memory has altered the actual memory architecture within which humans think' (737).[28] It is well established that we must interrogate our modern assumptions about this cognitive function when we try to engage with a medieval conception of memory.

Scholarship on medieval conceptions of the memorial faculty suggests that memory was seen as a trainable tool; a notion we also embrace today in the principle of neuroplasticity and so-called 'brain training'. Significantly, for medieval thinkers, training of this faculty was seen as a virtue. Mary Carruthers writes that memory was identified with 'creative thinking, learning (invention and recollection), and the ability to make judgments (prudence or wisdom)' (2008: 195).[29] Memory training served, then, not only to support the convenience and wellbeing of better recall, but also underpinned a crucial *ethical* purpose: providing and continually strengthening the mental architecture that supports good judgment and the capacity for virtuous and independent thought.

Medieval people also sought to offload cognitive memorial work to a certain degree. However, rather than the prosthetic technological externalisation we embrace today, medieval offloading focused primarily on mnemonics to trigger retrieval of units of remembered data. These included such embodied practices as the spatial model of the 'memory palace', rooted in the classical method of *loci*; or in certain of the so-called spiritual exercises often outlined in devotional literature that sought to create associations between tapping a certain body part and bringing to mind a particular affective state.[30] But, importantly, there is the suggestion in medieval scholarship that books, too, could also be seen as mnemonics; and I propose that this notion may offer another contextualising model for thinking about cognitive participation in the *Comedy*.

Carruthers writes:

> A book is not necessarily the same thing as a text. 'Texts' are the material out of which human beings make 'literature'. For us, texts only come in books, and so the distinction between the two is blurred and even lost. But, in a memorial culture, a 'book' is only one way among several to remember a 'text', to provision and cue one's memory with 'dicta et facta memorabilia'. So a book is itself a mnemonic, among many other functions it can also have. (2008: 9–10)

Considering a book as a cue to individual memorial work opens up the possibility of doing all sorts of cognitive work in interaction with it, in the same way that a memory palace furnishes a system for then placing and retrieving all the objects that are the ultimate focus of the cognitive memorial work. Under this model, a book is not simply a narrative in itself as we might habitually perceive it today, but rather a system of stimuli to independent, personal, cognitive work; a device for cueing retrieval of other 'objects' from personal memory, that may include personal sensory experiences (emerging from hill-fog into watery sun, for example) or other foundational texts, particularly Scripture, as I discuss in Chapter 4. Under such a model, we might perceive that the *Comedy* invites and requires a very different form of highly individuated cognitive engagement than today's readers may habitually expect to deploy in reading a narrative text — much more active engagement of the memory and importing of remembered experiences, resulting in a much more personal, participatory mode of reading.[31]

The *Comedy* has already been proposed as mnemonic. Harald Weinrich suggested in 1994 that Dante's three realms 'compose [...] a vast mnemonic system', supported by 'the most appealing, welcoming or repugnant images' (1994: 16). Frances Yates famously wrote in 1966: 'That Dante's *Inferno* could be regarded as a kind of memory system for memorising Hell and its punishments with striking images on orders of places, will come as a great shock, and I must leave it as a shock' (repr. 1984: 95).[32] She offers little elaboration, but it is apparent that she envisages the mnemonic function as inviting the participation of the imagination:

> In this interpretation [of the *Comedy* as mnemonic] the principles of artificial memory, as understood in the Middle Ages, would stimulate the intense visualisation of many similitudes in the intense effort to hold in memory the scheme of salvation, and the complex network of virtues and vices and their rewards and punishments. (1984: 95)

Yates appears to suggest that the principal memorial work is spatial in nature: first, holding in mind 'the scheme of salvation' — the structure of the three worlds of the afterlife as they appear to the journeying Dante, and the equivalent, I suggest, of building the 'rooms' of the memory palace; then, second, appending to this architectural schema the taxonomy of 'virtues and vices and their rewards and punishments' — that is, visualising the objects and interactions contained in Hell, Purgatory, and Paradise. I wonder if, through the lens of embodied cognition, we can push this model further. Rather than focusing on using the text to build the rooms of the memory palace and then furnish them with observable paraphernalia such that the schema becomes memorable at a visual level — a working spatial model and the events that play out in it observed from a position of exteriority — perhaps instead the *Comedy* can be understood to function as a mnemonic for retrieval of personal *feeling*, cueing remembered *experience* of interactions, even if those interactions were or are virtual rather than taking place in the real world.[33] As I explore further in Chapter 5, a hypothetical reader engaging with the text in the mode I describe in this book as first-person participation would import her own remembered experiences into the fabric of the text in service, I propose, of simulating her own journey through the virtual space of Dante's afterlife. In subsequent revisiting of each virtual room in memory, what will be recalled are not simply events observed (watching the journeying Dante's interactions) but, rather, feelings experienced. The point of remembering then becomes not only to *see* again but also to *feel* again.

Affective piety may offer a model for better expressing the individually transformative purpose of remembering a virtual experience, so I turn to this next.

1.4. Medieval affective piety

New medieval models of reading

The practice of reading underwent a period of substantial change in Europe in the twelfth and thirteenth centuries. There was a major shift in communication technologies as a textual tradition gained traction alongside oral, visual and performance traditions, yielding a fertile period of multi-modality in reception that continued well after Dante's lifetime.[34] Consequently, practices of reading a written text were very often informed by both visual and oral or performative cognitive behaviours and habits. Jessica Brantley, for example, has discussed 'the diagramming of the Lord's Prayer as a visual object' (2007: 202) in the fourteenth-century English Vernon Paternoster, concluding that the modality of reading invited in its tabular form 'is far from a static looking — it is as various, as contingent, as active, as any oral performance could be' (212). Brantley suggests that this tabular form disrupts 'the left-to-right protocols [in left-to-right writing systems] of modern silent reading' (212), operating instead as 'a matrix, or a network, or even a hypertext, for it provides multiple reading paths that link dispersed nodes or chunks of meaning to others in a variety of ways' (208). Similarly, in *Textual Situations: Three Medieval Manuscripts and their Readers*, Andrew Taylor warns against an habitual depriviliging of the body in contemporary reading practices compared with medieval habits, writing that '[t]he influence of print and its dominant mode, silent reading, may encourage us to think that questions of performance can be ignored' (2002: 21). He goes on to add that 'we have read medieval texts as if they belonged to the world of print, divorcing the works from their codicological context and thus from the music and conversation that once surrounded them, from their institutional situation, and from the lives they helped shape' (24–25).

Alongside this technology change was an explosion in new reading communities. Sabrina Corbellini has listed a number of factors driving this new turn to reading.[35] Coinciding with what she terms the 'media revolution' that 'changed the way books were copied and made accessible as well as the networks of diffusion of texts and manuscripts' (2013: 5), Corbellini includes in this list the twelfth-century development of the advanced schools and universities, a widespread increase in literacy in the laity, a vast translation movement bringing established texts within the reach of new readers, and the emergence of new writers, including women, and new genres of writing, including quest narratives, so-called vernacular theology, and the spiritual exercises of affective devotion.[36]

From these new reading communities emerged new models of reading, as more people had greater direct access to books as material objects with which to interact, and more opportunities to read alone or in private; a mode of 'silent reading' that, in practical terms, privileged reading at your own pace, re-reading, and cross-referencing one section or text with another.[37] And reading alone also gave the time and space for a deep affective response to a text that sometimes manifested in bodily responses, both observable through sensorimotor gesture, and the invisible but felt sensations of somatic and visceral responses.[38] Heather Blatt has drawn attention to what she proposes to be models of invited 'bodily experience' in medieval reading practices, in focusing on practices of emendation, non-linear reading, and the negotiation of physical architectural spaces (2018: 12).[39] Simultaneously, there was an increase in public reading or oral performances which, as Stock writes, invited commentary and interpretation: the group members 'must make the hermeneutic leap from what the text says to what they think it means; the common understanding provides the foundation of changing thought and behaviour' (Stock 1983: 522). In total, it is evident that reading was not the primarily mental and solitary process of cognitive assimilation of information that we might assume today. Barański has written that '[d]uring the course of his life, Dante displayed a coherent yet continually evolving and increasingly original understanding of the nature of writing, which culminated in the composition (and exegesis) of the *Comedy*' (2005: 563).[40] I suggest we might add to Barański's synthesis that Dante also demonstrates an evolving and original understanding of the flowering of different modes of reading and, as I shall argue in this book, invites active participation in those different modes. Perhaps the most interesting and instructive of these for my purposes is the medieval model of affective piety.

Affective piety

In his survey of the Passion narratives and devotional meditations of the late Middle Ages, Thomas Bestul locates the 'full flowering' of the affective piety movement 'in the Franciscan spirituality of the thirteenth and fourteenth centuries', observing that its subsequent diffusion through the aristocratic laity and amongst women led to 'a great demand for devotional texts' (1996: 35).[41] Such texts functioned as devotional icons for the pious laity, modelling meditations for the reader's use, in service of providing an interactable framework to support a powerfully vivid and visceral imaginative reconstruction of Christ's Passion — the final events of his life from his entry into Jerusalem to the crucifixion. Bestul refers to this process of vivid imaginative reconstruction through the multiple senses as 'affective meditation' (1996: 38). Sara Ritchey retrieves from Ludolph of Saxony's *Vita Christi* [1374] the terms *recordatio* ('dramatic visualisation in the imagination') and *compassio* ('an emotional response to the imagined past') (2012: 350).

Arguably the best known of these meditations is the pseudo-Bonaventuran *Meditationes Vitae Christi* [*MVC*], allegedly written by an Italian Franciscan in Tuscany to a Poor Clare sometime between 1336 and 1364.[42] Immensely popular, it was translated into all the major European vernaculars. But if the most popular texts for affective devotion came after Dante, it seems certain the model was already established in texts familiar to Dante.

Bestul traces the model for the Passion narrative back to Bernard of Clairvaux (the same Bernard of *Paradiso* XXXIII) who, whilst writing 'no independent treatise on the Passion', demonstrated 'unremitting zeal for affective meditation on the Passion of Christ as a way toward spiritual perfection' (1996: 38).[43] The meditation model itself, suggests Bestul, derives directly from Bonaventure:

> To stimulate the emotions, Bonaventure relies on the techniques of 'vivid representation' he commended to his readers as a meditative strategy. The work has many concrete, visual evocations of the events of the Passion, employing an intimate, affective, apostrophic style [...] [and is] notable for its attention to the physical details of Christ's suffering, bleeding body, deformed by pain and injury. (1996: 44)

What is crucial about this imaginative work of 'vivid representation' is that its goal is not solely to *see*, as external observer, the events of the Passion (arguably a 'Cartesian theatre' model of mental representation), but also to *feel* the associated emotions: to imaginatively participate in Christ's suffering, representing so vividly the associated body states in the meditant's own body that it is 'as if [...] she were performing a similar action or experiencing a similar emotion or sensation' (Wojciehowski and Gallese 2011: 15). Emotions, particularly those directed towards Christ, writes Bestul, 'are not regarded as deleterious but are esteemed as a means of opening the way toward spiritual perfection' (35). Writing on Ludolph's *Vita Christi*, Ritchey describes this as a process of 'enscript[ing] Christic emotions' (2012: 350).[44] The point of this process of imaginatively representing in your own person the pain of Christ's suffering is to '*incorporate* the subjectivity of another' (Ritchey 2012: 341; my emphasis) — that is, to simulate in your own body the physical and emotional pain experienced by Christ in the Passion.[45] Such embodied affective acts, Ritchey proposes, are 'designed ultimately to lead to new ethical, emotional, and physical dispositions' (341). My suggestion is that second-generation cognitive science would classify this precisely as an act of embodied projective identification — that is, a representation of the body states of the other (Christ, in this case) in the reader's own body in an enactive model of imaginative representation. In exploring this potential parallel we might, with an alertness to contextual authenticity, find a way to begin to make use of contemporary theories of embodied cognition to newly defamiliarise those mechanisms in the text that I propose constitute invitations to reader embodied participation in the *Comedy*. This is what I address in the main, technical, section of this book.

Crucially, the text of the *MVC* provides a step-by-step script for representing these emotions in the meditant's body. Such guidance is helpful, and even necessary, suggests Bestul, because the Gospels themselves provide little detail for the reader requiring assistance to identify with Christ's suffering, being 'meagre in the specifics of Christ's sufferings and death' (Bestul 1996: 27). Devotional texts help to plug this gap for the reader struggling to project herself into the virtual space of the gospel narrative by providing cues to help the reader elaborate physical and affective details for herself. These manifest both in the form of explicit prompts to imagine ('Hora torniamo a miser Iesù Cristo, il qualle va solo. Or vàtene cum lui. Ma di che viveva miser Iesù per camino?' [Now let us return to our Lord Jesus, who goes alone. Now go with him. But how did Lord Jesus make his way on the path?]);[46] and particular details to model, with Bestul offering the example 'that Christ's hands were bound so tightly that blood burst from his fingernails' (27).

The goal is presence — in Latin, *praesentia*: the perceptual illusion of direct participation in the events of the Passion themselves via an experience of an embodied (somatic, visceral) projection into a virtual (imagined) space. Bestul notes the *MVC*'s 'frequent exhortations to visualise the scene in the mind's eye as if one were actually present at the events' (48);[47] Ritchey again cites Ludolph: '"Lege ergo quae facta sunt tanquam fiant; pone ante oculos gesta praeterita tanquam praesentia"' [Read therefore about what was being done as if it were being done. Place before your eyes these past things as if they were present] (349).

The expressed purpose of such meditations was affective, in the sense of feeling greater love, or compassion, for Christ. In Karnes's words, 'creating vivid mental images of Christ's sacrifice of himself for mankind heightens affection for him' (2011: 10). This affective purpose is well established in medieval scholarship. But Karnes further proposes something new.

Karnes's thesis in *Imagination, Meditation, and Cognition in the Middle Ages* is that the gospel meditations may have had a *cognitive* purpose in addition to their affective purpose. By this, she means specifically the engagement of the imagination as 'a trainable tool' (2011: 20). Neuroscience tells us that cognitive capacities are plastic. Karnes asks whether the act of repeatedly participating in the cognitive work of the meditations was in fact designed to train the faculty of imagination to ever greater heights of sustainable and immersive realism.

The writer of the *MVC*, she notes, 'could not be clearer that meditation occurs in the mind, specifically, the actively thinking mind. The meditant who maximises the activity of the mind thus *augments the imaginative power of meditation*' (Karnes 2011: 174; my emphasis).[48] 'Training' the imagination will furnish an extraordinary level of 'imaginative vivacity', an unleashing of its 'greatest potential', which is to render the imagined 'real'; that is, to make the absent Christ present to the meditant (177):

> The components that make for successful meditation according to the *MVC* [are]: invention, detail, mental labour, emotion, and rational deliberation. Their ultimate effect is to create imaginative vivacity [...]. Only a fully activated imagination can realise its greatest potential, which is to turn the merely imagined presence of Christ into real, spiritual presence, in turn enabling the meditant to conform to him. Imagination thus acts creatively, cognitively, and affectively. (177)

The goal of this imagination 'training' through the guided steps offered by the meditations is to 'become capable of sharing, eventually, [Christ's] journey to heaven, finding in such meditation a path toward salvation' (20). The meditation functions, then, in Karnes's formulation, as a 'means to fulfil [the] Pauline prescription, and to fulfil it particularly well' (20).[49] For Karnes, the *MVC*:

> promises nothing less than *direct access to Christ*, who will appear to the dutiful meditant in the same way that he appeared to his disciples after his resurrection. Referring to Christ's post-resurrection appearances, the author [of the *MVC*] writes, 'I think that if you knew how to share in his sufferings ... you would realise an Easter in each and every one of these appearances'.[50] (154; my emphasis)

I stop short here of a suggestion that the programme of invitations to participate in the *Comedy* may be designed to directly facilitate an encounter between the reader and the divine. As Barański sets out in 'Dottrina degli affetti e teologia' (2018), the question of whether it is possible or impossible for a mortal human being still *in via* to 'see' God face-to-face has a long and complex history.[51] Dante's framing of his vision begins from the premise that only God can elect the very few to this possibility (Moses, Saint Paul, the Apostle John). The narration of the *visio Dei* represents *not* the event of the encounter itself but, rather, the profoundly flawed memory of the protagonist's experience. It is a memory trace of a signal experienced: narrative cannot call into being the divine, but only a representation of the journey towards the divine.[52] The purpose of the programme of invitations in the *Comedy*, I suggest, is to burnish in life, in the living human individual, the desire for this encounter.

The key point in Karnes's proposal in relation to my thesis for the *Comedy* is that she finds in the meditations a qualitative, plastic element to the fulfilling of the Pauline prescription. Some meditants will 'fulfil it *particularly well*' (2011: 20; my emphasis). Some, by extension, will do a bare minimum and achieve the sketchiest of imaginative experiences of participation in the journey to salvation. But those who have finessed their capacity to imagine vividly, immersively, and to sustainably enter into a realistic illusion of presence, will — according to Karnes — experience Christ resurrected: 'direct access to Christ' (154). 'Training' — repeated finessing of the plastic capacity of the imagination — is the key.

Karnes roots this element of plasticity in Bernard of Clairvaux's conceit of an exceptional level of imaginative capability resulting in a capacity for 'imageless devotion', available only to the precious few possessed of 'angelic purity'.[53]

> Bernard admits the near-impossibility of attaining this ideal [of 'imageless devotion'] — he reserves it for those precious few with 'angelic purity' (*angelicae puritatis*) and endorses image-based devotion as profitable for the masses — but imageless devotion nevertheless remains his ideal. (Karnes 2011: 17)

Perhaps some Dante scholars may find a resonance in the *Comedy*, with the invitation in *Paradiso* II to make a personal judgment about readiness to read the third canticle, an act counselled only to '[v]oialtri pochi che drizzaste il collo | per tempo al pan de li angeli' [You other few who have already stretched, | straight-necked, through time to reach for angel-bread] (*Par.*, II. 10–11). Whilst the *Comedy* pre-dates the *MVC*, it is subsequent to the works of Bernard and Bonaventure in which Karnes finds the basis for her claim to a cognitive purpose. It is not unreasonable, I would therefore suggest, to ask whether the *Comedy* also indexes a similar model of strategic invitations to a finessing of the imaginative capacity that for some will yield a realistic, fully credible, persuasive mental experience of present participation in their own journey of desire for the encounter with the divine.

Finally, I propose a further innovation in Dante's model for inviting such participation. The gospel meditations are made up to a large degree of their framework of instructions to the meditant's conscious cognitions, written in the second person: 'imagine this', 'think about that'. Dante instead constructs a narrative of an event, a *story* (even if the reader accepts it as a truthful account of a lived personal experience): the *Comedy* is a first-person immersive narrative. Within this story, there are some twenty metalepses explicitly inviting the conscious cognitive participation of the reader (the direct addresses, as I discuss in Chapter 4). The narration of this story is exceptionally open: full of similes inviting imaginative comparison of narrated phenomena in Dante's virtual world with phenomena the reader is likely to have personally experienced in the material world (also set out in Chapter 4).

Karnes is of the belief that narrative is more powerful in inviting the participation of the imagination than factual information. Referencing Hume's *An Enquiry Concerning Human Understanding*, she concludes: 'The key variable is narrative: because imagination associates like ideas, it transfers to one literary scene the passions elicited in another. As a result, literature can derive more vividness from imagination than, to use Hume's own example, history' (2011: 169).[54] Albertus Magnus and Aquinas were of the same belief, as Frances Yates also writes in relation to memory. Albertus Magnus suggested in regard to poetic similes, in Yates's synopsis, that 'the wonderful moves the memory more than the ordinary' (1984: 66); Aquinas's first precept for memory proposes 'choosing striking and unusual images as being the most likely to stick in memory' (Yates 1984: 75).

This framework of a first-person narrative permits Dante, I shall argue in this book, to invite the participation not only of the conscious cognitions, through the device of the direct address that models the step-by-step instruction format of the gospel meditations; but also to invite the participation of the unconscious cognitions, of those mental operations that function beneath the surface of consciousness and construct our sense of presence, of reality, and of personal agency, and that shape our beliefs and our behaviours.

The embodied reader

The narrating Dante, we might note, makes explicit mention of the reader's body. This body permits her to sit on a bench, for example: 'Or ti riman, lettor, sovra 'l tuo banco, | dietro pensando a ciò che si preliba, | s'esser vuoi lieto assai prima che stanco' [Now, reader, sit there at your lecture bench. | And if you want not tedium but joy, | continue thinking of the sip you've had] (*Par.*, X. 22–24);[55] her act of reading is a material event in the physical world: 'ma leggi Ezechïele [...] | e quali *i troverai ne le sue carte* | tali era quivi [...]' [But read Ezekiel [...] | And as you'll find them [the animals drawing the chariot] *written on his page*, | so were they there] (*Purg.* XXIX. 100, 103–04; my emphasis). She is in possession of specific sensory and somatic modalities. She has a voice capable of speech (even if she is asked to withhold that speech): 'Com' io divenni allor gelato e fioco, | nol dimandar, lettor, ch'i' non lo scrivo' [How weak I now became, how faded, dry — | reader, don't ask, I shall not write it down] (*Inf.*, XXXIV. 22–23). She has ears, permitting her to hear the narrator's oral performance: 'O tu che leggi, udirai nuovo ludo' [O you there as you read! Hear this new game] (*Inf.*, XXII. 118); 'Se tu se' or, lettore, a creder lento | ciò ch'io dirò' [If you are slow, my reader, to receive, | in faith, what I'll say now] (*Inf.*, XXV. 46–47). And she has eyes that are invoked not only in metaphorical expressions of attention (for example, 'Aguzza qui, lettor, ben li occhi al vero' [Reader, now fix a needle eye on truth] (*Purg.*, VIII. 19)), but can also be materially directed, in an act of situated co-presence ('meco' [with me]) alongside the narrating Dante, jointly attending to the same night sky: 'Leva dunque, lettore, a l'alte rote | meco la vista, dritto a quella parte | dove l'un moto e l'altro si percuote' [Lift up your eyes, then, reader, and, along with | me, look to those wheels directed to that part | where motions — yearly and diurnal — clash] (*Par.*, X. 7–9).

Whilst such references are few in number, they correlate with the direct addresses with a consistency that might alert us to the possibility of a strategy at work. We can, of course, ask whether the reader is to conceive of these bodily actions as literally intended, rather than simply metaphorical constructs (a question arguably along the same lines as whether we are really to break off reading the poem in order to re-engage with the Scriptural intertexts, or really to do the cognitively demanding imaginative and memorial work invited in the direct addresses, to both of which I return in Chapter 4). The reader has a choice about the extent to which she wishes to vividly model these embodied images: will she really imagine herself on a bench with the narrator, investing cognitive energy in *recordatio*? (Ritchey 2012: 350). Or will she mentally skip over this image as a figure of speech superfluous to an understanding of what the poem *means* at this point? This notwithstanding, under the terms of embodied simulation, the narration of such an action or body state (sitting on a bench, turning a page, hearing speech, looking upwards alongside someone), even when not acted upon, is nonetheless registered as data that can trigger the same neural pathways in the attending reader. Regardless of whether the reader engages, Dante has embedded this narrative datapoint in the text: it is an observable mechanism, an invitation to cognitive participation.

Importantly, the narrating Dante also gives us an indication of the purpose of vivid imagination of these body states. Such a reader, he explicitly suggests on at least two occasions, will attain some quality of simulation of the journeying Dante's own felt experience at key points. Arguably the best example of this is in *Paradiso* XIII. Here, in the direct address that opens the canto (1–21), the narrating Dante sets out a sequence of astral phenomena for the reader to imagine for herself, reconfigure, then animate; a set of components that, together, could help to evoke the protagonist's experience of being encircled by the twenty-four theologians in the Heaven of the Sun. 'Imagini [...] | imagini [...] | imagini' [imagine] (1, 7, 10), the reader is invited; then, following successful modelling of this data,

> [...] avrà quasi l'ombra de la vera
> costellazione e de la doppia danza
> che circulava il punto dov' io era. (19–21)

> you'll have a shade, then, almost, of that true
> constellation — of the dance that, doubled,
> circled round the point where I was now.

The reader who has vividly imagined each astral component and then set them into dynamic interaction will finally have an 'ombra' [shade] of the journeying Dante's own experience; an analogue or approximation of the journeying Dante's body state; personal experience of how it feels to be at the still centre ('il punto') of this 'vera | costellazione', the dynamic 'doppia danza' that encircles him.[56]

Similarly, in *Purgatorio* XVII, the reader that vividly brings to mind an embodied experience of being caught in the hills in a fog (seeing through your skin, like a mole) will 'see', says the narrating Dante, 'in giugnere a veder' (8), just how the journeying Dante re-saw the sun, 'com' io rividi | lo sole' (8–9), on emerging from the blackness of the terrace of Wrath.[57] In fact, this deployment of the reader's own body to model, step by step, the journeying Dante's reported experience, is directly invited in most of the direct addresses: modelling his discomfitedness in *Inferno* VIII (94–96), for example; his distress and struggle not to cry in *Inferno* XX (20–21); his liminal state of feeling neither dead nor alive in *Inferno* XXXIV (25–27); his wonder at the gryphon in *Purgatorio* XXXI (124–26); his desire to see the conditions of the blessed in *Paradiso* V (109–14); his sense of the speed of his ascent in *Paradiso* XXII (106–11). Essentially, it seems, in these instances the reader's body is invoked as a mechanism by which the reader may reconstruct or simulate the journeying Dante's embodied experience, or body state, in her own body; that is, precisely as Gallese sets out in his model of *embodied simulation* that allows us to project ourselves into another's experience, to feel what they feel.

1.6. Personal response and subjectivity

The history of the practice of affective devotion in the Middle Ages establishes a precedent for invitations to a personal response to a text; one that might lead to the possibility of individual behaviour change. Such responses are normally understood to be subjective: a unique individual interaction between one person's accumulated experiences or apperceptual frame and particular units of content in the text, experienced as a particular feeling or feelings. Often such feelings will be emotions or visceral signs, rendered perceptible to others by self-report — although the medieval model of affective piety also invites us consider a set of observable behaviours as external evidence of affective response, including weeping, swooning, or kissing, which arguably has offered some basis for discussion of replicated responses. Essentially, though, subjective response is problematic as a basis for analysis because the strongly bipartite nature of the interaction means the data is not replicable: just because one person, with their own particular triggers, has one particular response, it does not follow that another person will have the same.

However, whilst it is difficult to find reliable objective terms through which to discuss the personal response, I suggest it is extremely important that we try in relation to the *Comedy*. An experience of presence is rooted in knowledge that is mediated through the body, rendering it inherently personal: each reader feels present on their own account; each reader experiences the journey as realistic to a greater or lesser degree only through their own response. This question of experientiality was central to medieval meditative practices. Ritchey writes that 'the practice of meditation as it was taught in later medieval schools and religious houses [...] was a means of interpreting and comprehending a text through *experiencing it*' (2012: 1; my emphasis). Bernard of Clairvaux wrote: 'I believe what I have experienced: certain things you find better in the forest than in books. Woods and stones will teach you what you cannot hear from the teachers.'[58] The late-medieval theologian and philosopher John Wyclif describes 'the truth of Holy Scripture', in Mary Carruthers's synthesis, as follows: 'A work is not truly read until one has made it part of oneself [...]; the writing must be transferred into memory, from graphemes on parchment or papyrus or paper to images written in one's brain by emotion and sense' (Carruthers 2008: 11). An experience of self-presence in particular, as I shall explore in Chapter 4, cannot be rendered through an experience of external observation or spectatorship, but is contingent upon individual participation.

Milner points towards an idea that a return to an understanding of a medieval 'embodied self', through the current 'turn to the senses', allows us to conceive of the reader as 'freestanding instrumental philosopher', suggesting that:

> Particular, contingent, and socialised, such a self sought to understand the nature of its being less through abstract philosophical speculation than as a freestanding instrumental philosopher who was repeatedly called upon to make his/her own judgments within a demanding and unstable social world. (2015: 240)

Each reader of the *Comedy*, I suggest, is invited to act as precisely such a 'freestanding instrumental philosopher', repeatedly offered cues to simulate in her own body the experience of the virtual world of the afterlife and the interactions within it, and thereby finessing her ability to make her own judgments based on the certainty of embodied knowledge.

My proposed solution to the problem of the instability of subjective response as a basis for discussion, then, is to focus *not* on reported feelings but instead to look for the specific mechanisms in the text that cue or invite the possibility of some form of response, regardless of whether one reader registers a response and another does not.[59] Being *observable*, such mechanisms are objectively perceptible and therefore operate as stable units for discussion and analysis, as in the example set out in the Introduction of Singleton's subjective response of discomfort in relation to the narration of Bernard's sign, at the root of which we can identify the observable mechanism of a dissonant focal view switch. I focus only on mechanisms that appear repeatedly — hence the repeated exercises of quantification in this book — and in relation to which a strategy can therefore reasonably be proposed. My thesis for this book has no interest in constructing a defence of subjective readings but, rather, it aims to identify a series of observable narratological mechanisms that invite the participation of the cognitive functions, as a proposed basis for discussion of individual response in reading the *Comedy*.

Notes to Chapter 1

1. For an introduction to the affective turn, see *The Affective Turn: Theorising the Social*, ed. by Patricia Clough and Jean Halley (2008).
2. For a specifically humanities-oriented introduction to second-generation cognitive science, see Kukkonen and Caracciolo's essay, 'What is the "Second Generation?"' (2014). For a general introduction to second-generation approaches to embodied cognition, see, for example: Margaret Wilson, 'Six Views of Embodied Cognition' (2002); Raymond Gibbs, *Embodiment and Cognitive Science* (2006); and *The Routledge Handbook of Embodied Cognition*, ed. by Lawrence A. Shapiro (2011). Descartes's *cogito* formulation was first published in 1637.
3. On the Cartesian legacy, see especially Chapter 19, 'Descartes and the Enlightenment Mind'.
4. 'We cannot doubt "what we can clearly and perspicuously behold and with certainty deduce"' (395, citing Descartes's *Rules for the Direction of the Mind*, V).
5. Their full exploration of the consequences of this metaphor unfolds over pp. 393–400.
6. On disembodiment in the *cogito*, see *Meditations*, 78: 'Thus, simply by knowing that I exist and seeing at the same time that absolutely nothing else belongs to my nature or essence except that I am a thinking thing, I can infer correctly that my essence consists solely in the fact that I am a thinking thing. It is true that I may have (or, to anticipate, that I certainly have) a body that is very closely joined to me. But nevertheless, on the one hand I have a clear and distinct idea of myself in so far as I am simply a thinking, non-extended thing; and on the other hand, I have a distinct idea of body, in so far as this is simply an extended, non-thinking thing. And accordingly, it is certain that I am really distinct from my body and can exist without it' (Descartes 2013: 109).
7. Antonio Damasio's widely accepted 'somatic marker hypothesis', set out in his monograph, *Descartes' Error: Emotion, Reason, and the Human Brain* (1994), offers neurobiological evidence of reason's indivorcibility from affect. Quantum mechanics, via phenomenology, has radically challenged the common-sense notion of an objective external reality. For a lay introduction to the constructed nature of human cognitive experience in the context of quantum theory (so-called 'first-person reality'), see David Hoffmann's *Visual Intelligence: How the Mind Creates Visual Worlds* (1998).
8. On these tensions, see Hans Ulrich Gumbrecht, *The Production of Presence: What Meaning Cannot Convey* (2004). See also Stephen Milner's 2015 essay, ' "Bene comune e benessere": Rhetoric

and the Affective Economy of Communal Life'. Following Gumbrecht, Milner proposes that 'the aesthetics of presence' 'has seen an attempt to foreground "being" rather than "meaning" in the description of affects rather than the reading of texts, privileging phenomenology over hermeneutics' (237).

9. *Exaptation* is defined by Oxford Reference as follows: '[Biology:] The process by which features acquire functions for which they were not originally adapted or selected' (<https://www.lexico.com/definition/exaptation> [accessed 15 September 2021]). Originally a Darwinian notion ('preadaptation'), the term *exaptation* was coined by Stephen Jay Gould and Elisabeth Vrba in 1982. In his essay 'Mirror Neurons and Art', Gallese explains exaptation as follows: 'Key aspects of human social cognition are produced by neural exploitation, that is, by the exaptation of neural mechanisms originally evolved for sensory–motor integration, later on also employed to contribute to the neurofunctional architecture of thought and language, while retaining their original functions as well' (2011: 457). Further, in AI pioneer Andy Clark's formulation: 'Biological brains are first and foremost the control systems for biological bodies' (1999: 506). Clark's revolutionary research into robotics in the 1990s (and continuing into the 2020s) foregrounded a notion of emergent interaction that opened the path to the models of presence in virtual worlds that I discuss in this book.

10. '[T]he [neural] circuit structures action execution and action perception, imitation, and imagination, with neural connections to motor effectors and/or other sensory cortical areas. When the action is executed or imitated, the corticospinal pathway is activated, leading to the excitation of muscles and the ensuing movements. When the action is observed or imagined, its actual execution is inhibited. The cortical motor network is activated (though, not in all of its components and, likely, not with the same intensity), but action is not produced, it is only simulated' (Gallese 2011: 457).

11. Based in Damasio's work on affective reason and Lakoff and Johnson's notion of 'concepts', amongst others.

12. That is, 'the same neural system engaged in *perception* (or in bodily movement) plays a central role in *conception*' (1999: 38; emphasis in original), modelling relationships between things and performing abstract inferences.

13. In *Consciousness Explained*, Daniel Dennett describes as the 'Cartesian theatre' this notion of an inner mental stage upon which metaphorical objects (our ideas) are observed by a metaphorical spectator (our faculty of understanding) (1991: 107).

14. A so-called '4E' model distinguishes between 'embodied', 'enactive', 'embedded', and 'extended' cognition. For an introduction, see Richard Menary's 'Introduction to the Special Edition on 4E Cognition', in *Phenomenology and the Cognitive Sciences*, 9.4 (2010). I share cognitive literary theorist Emily Troscianko's position that *embodied* cognition usually contains the other three: 'a body being inherently situated [embedded/extended], and always in action [enactive]' (2014: 24). My exploration of spatial presence (Chapter 2) primarily foregrounds principles of extended cognition; social presence (Chapter 3), both extended and enactive; self-presence (Chapter 4), primarily enactive.

15. For an introduction to individual thinkers and theories, see, for example: Robert Pasnau's *Theories of Cognition in the Later Middle Ages* (1997), which focuses particularly on Thomas Aquinas and subsequent challenges to his models by Peter John Olivi and William Ockham; Leen Spruit's *Species Intelligibilis: From Perception to Knowledge* (1994); or Simon Kemp's *Medieval Psychology* (1990), which includes an account of the inner senses and of memory (53–76). For a short introduction to the mechanics of medieval cognition for non-specialists, see Corinne Saunders and Charles Fernyhough's essay, 'The Medieval Mind' (2016).

16. In his essay '"Bene comune e benessere"', Milner writes: '[A]s Dante put it in *Convivio* citing Aristotle: "vivere è l'essere de li viventi" [life is the mode of being of living things] [*Conv.*, IV, 7, 11]. The faculties of the soul were what furnished the "motus" or engine of movement' (2015: 239). On this shift from what Simon Kemp describes as the 'generally held' medieval Platonic metaphor — the so-called 'tablet metaphor' — of stored mental representations as 'preserv[ing] the form or species of objects or events', to William of Ockham's claim that 'mental representations are not stored but instead constructed on the basis of past learned experiences',

see Simon Kemp's 1998 essay, 'Medieval Theories of Representation' (especially p. 275), and also Mary J. Carruthers's *The Book of Memory: A Study of Memory in Medieval Culture*, especially pp. 18–19. Dante explicitly deploys the wax tablet metaphor in the *Comedy* several times (including at *Purg.*, XVIII. 39; *Purg.*, XXXIII. 79; *Par.*, I. 41; and *Par.*, XIII. 67, 73). My suggestion is that the enactive model is, additionally, powerfully encoded into the mechanisms of Dante's text.

17. Milner proposes that 'medieval Aristotelianism [...] furnished a sophisticated but coherent psychological, physiological, and ethical interpretative framework that sought to make sense of the "self in society" while acknowledging the susceptibility of the self to external stimulus [...]. This framework conditioned how contemporaries read the world and sought to make sense of human interaction, from Dante to Machiavelli' (2015: 238).

18. For example, Patrick Hutton comments that Frances Yates's rendering of the role of the art of memory suggests 'an arcane method in an errant search for divine wisdom. Such an interpretation, however, marginalised the topic by characterising it as a line of intellectual inquiry' (1993: 11–12). Such scholarship, I would suggest, could now very productively be re-examined in the light of second-generation cognitive science.

19. Indeed, Milner suggests, the turn from Cartesianism can be read as a mirror of the medieval turn away from Scholasticism towards affective spirituality and a new vernacularity: 'In many ways Cartesian method shared much in common with the scholastic method as carried out in the medieval classroom which privileged logical and dialectical argumentation in the analysis of set questions' (2015: 238).

20. I discuss this further in the section on Affective Piety in this chapter.

21. Earlier approaches to an understanding of rhetoric in the late medieval period may be found in, for example: Rita Copeland, *Rhetoric, Hermeneutics, and Translation in the Middle Ages* (1991); Suzanne Reynolds, *Medieval Reading: Grammar, Rhetoric, and the Classical Text* (1996); and *Medieval Grammar and Rhetoric: Language, Arts, and Literary Theory, AD 300–1475*, ed. by Rita Copeland and Ineke Sluiter (2009). For other recent and varied perspectives in relation to Dante and rhetoric, see, amongst others: *Dante e la Retorica*, ed. by Luca Marcozzi (2017); Joseph P. Zompetti, 'A Theory of Vernacular Rhetoric: Reading Dante's *De Vulgari Eloquentia*' (2017); Ronald Martínez's essay, 'Rhetoric, Literary Theory, and Practical Criticism' (2015); and Claire Honess's essay, 'The Language(s) of Civic Invective in Dante: Rhetoric, Satire, and Politics' (2013).

22. Citing Augustine (*De Doctrina*, II, 5), Burrow describes the distinction as follows: *naturalia*: '"those which without a wish or any urge to signify cause something else beside themselves to be known from them", including in his examples facial expressions where they are involuntary signs of emotion'; *data*: '"those which living things give to each other, in order to show, to the best of their ability, the emotions of their minds, or anything they have felt or learnt"' (2002: 1–2).

23. See: Barański, 'Dante's Signs' (1995: 139–80). More generally on signs in Dante's works, see Barański's monograph, *Dante e i segni* (2000). On gesture in Dante, see Burrow's *Gestures and Looks* for a broad survey (2002: 156–79); for more detailed analysis, see Webb (2016), *Dante's Persons*, Chapter 2.

24. Although I would suggest that the two categories and their respective degree of apparent intentionality or consciousness overlap substantially in the *Comedy*.

25. Further, and beyond the scope of this particular study, new scientific evidence suggesting that gesture helps us *think* and *remember* might also invite new perspectives on gesture in the *Comedy*. See, respectively: David McNeill, *Hand and Mind: What Gestures Reveal about Thought* (1996), and John Sutton and Kellie Williamson, 'Embodied Remembering', in *The Routledge Handbook of Embodied Cognition* (2014). See also Dijkstra, Kaschak, and Zwaan's 2007 essay, 'Body Posture Facilitates Retrieval of Autobiographical Memories' (2007), which proposes that retrieval of a memory of a past experience is facilitated if the body posture assumed during the past experience is re-enacted.

26. There is a large body of replicated empirical research data and associated literature on the phenomenon of neural mirroring and the mirror mechanism that supports it, of which a useful synthetic introduction can be found in Rizzolatti and Craighero's essay, 'The Mirror-

Neuron System', in the *Annual Review of Neuroscience* (2004). For a list of publications that shows the wide range of recent applications of mirror neuron theory (for example, on yawning, smiling, empathy, Theory of Mind), see Jan Plamper, *The History of Emotions*, trans. by Keith Tribe (2017: particularly 219 nn. 234 & 235). The presence of so-called 'mirror neurons' was originally observed in macaques in 1996 by neuroscientist Vittorio Gallese and others, and reported in *Cognitive Brain Research* (1996); Gallese has since become a key international figure in understanding the relationship between action–perception and cognition in humans. The same mirror mechanism was discovered in humans in 2010 (see Keysers and Gazzola (2010), 'Social Neuroscience: Mirror Neurons Recorded in Humans'). There has been debate about the extension of mirror neuron theory into certain of the higher cognitive functions, but my work rests only on widely accepted evidence relating to the sensorimotor circuit (see Plamper 2017: 220–22).

27. Further: 'Mirror neurons [...] typically discharge both when a motor act is executed and when it is observed being performed by someone else [...]. | Observing an action causes in the observer the automatic activation of the same neural mechanism that is triggered by executing that action oneself [...]. [For example], [w]atching someone grasp a cup of coffee, biting an apple, or kicking a football activates the same cortical regions of our brain that would be activated if we were doing the same thing' (12–13). Importantly, they go on to propose that this is true not only for motor action, but also for emotion and sensation: 'When we perceive others expressing a given basic emotion such as disgust, some of the same brain areas are activated as when we subjectively experience the same emotion' (13–14).

28. In 1991, Donald proposed in *Origins of the Modern Mind* that we have adaptively used parts of our bodies, our surroundings, and technology to offload and externalise memory storage. He later commented that 'the externalisation of memory has altered the actual memory architecture within which humans think. This is changing the role of biological memory and the way in which the human brain deploys its resources'; for example, 'increasing the degree to which our minds share representations' (1993: 748).

29. She writes that this association of memory and ethics was a cultural one, and not simply a technological one: '[T]he valuing of *memoria* persisted long after book technology itself had changed. That is why the facts of [newly-available] books in themselves [...] did not profoundly disturb the essential value of memory training until many centuries had passed' (9). For further discussion on the question of the ethics of memory, see Spencer Pearce who, in 'Dante and the Art of Memory', comments on medieval memory training as 'the fundamental educational requirement [...]; needful for salvation' (1996: 20).

30. On the medieval memory palace, see Carruthers (2008), including the influence of Thomas Aquinas; and Yates (1984) on medieval 'artificial memory', and the classical method of *loci*. On the practice in medieval affective devotion of creating associations between specific body parts and affective states, see Ritchey (2012).

31. Interestingly, Spencer Pearce proposed of memory in 1996 — in the early stages in the revival of thinking of cognition as enactive — that the art of local memory is most effective when images interact *dynamically* (1996: 40), concluding that: '[w]e may begin to appreciate the activity of memory — or at least of the memory-image — if we discard the notion that mental images are somehow akin to photographic reproductions of past perception' (41). Thus, Dante's poem 'is not simply a design, it is an enactment' (48).

32. William Franke issued a corrective to Yates's claim to novelty in 2012, observing in *Dante and the Sense of Transgression* that 'taking Dante as the culmination of the ancient rhetorical tradition of the *ars memorativa* is actually an idea that has a considerable history in critical theory and comparative literature' (2012: 6).

33. Justin Steinberg makes the point in *Accounting for Dante* that in the *Comedy*, Dante may be seeking 'to influence the books of memory of his urban readers'. He continues: 'For Dante, the book of memory is a psychic container as real as the material spaces of contemporary books. Indeed, the complicated formal structures, rationalised topography, and heightened visuality Dante employs in his work can be seen as a means of maintaining spatial–textual integrity within the "place" of the memory of individual readers, a sort of memorial transmission that

rivals and might even replace the unstable material circulation that he would have witnessed in the early dissemination of his lyrics. If the vernacular poet cannot control the new methods of book production, perhaps he can influence the books of memory of his urban readers' (2007: 10).

34. On this technology change see, for example, Armando Petrucci, *Writers and Readers in Medieval Italy* (1995); and Brian Stock, *The Implications of Literacy: Written Language and Models of Interpretation in the Eleventh and Twelfth Centuries* (1983). Stock prefers to speak of 'the occasioned use of texts' rather than 'literacy', because 'one can be literate without the overt use of texts, and one can use texts extensively without evidencing genuine literacy' (7). It is also interesting to consider the medieval 'read and hear' model of concurrent modes of reception: *legere* and *audire* were 'used as synonyms', according to Giles Constable (1996: 48). The narration of the poem switches between the two modalities on several occasions, most obviously in *Inferno* XXII: 'O tu che *leggi, udirai* nuovo ludo' [O you there, as you *read*! *Hear* this new game] (line 118, my emphasis; Kirkpatrick's translation adapted); and *Inf.*, XXV. 47; and *Inf.*, XXII. 118.

35. See her introductory essay in *Cultures of Religious Reading in the Late Middle Ages* (Corbellini 2013).

36. For more on the emergence of new reading communities, see also Petrucci (1995, particularly pp. 133–37). Specifically, on the earlier shift from monastic models of reading to scholastic, see Malcolm Parkes's essay, 'Influence of the Concepts of *Ordinatio* and *Compilatio* in the Development of the Book' (1976). Peter Hawkins points out in his essay 'Religious Culture' (2015) that the Franciscans influenced a turn 'to narrative, emotion, and the language of the marketplace' (327). In his 2015 essay, Andrea A. Robiglio points out that 'the trope of the "quest"' — 'the pursuit to understand oneself and one's relationship to God' — 'take[s] us away from the world of the universities' (153). In *Augustine the Reader*, Brian Stock writes that Augustine conceived of the act of reading as 'a critical step in a mental ascent: it is both an awakening from sensory illusion and a rite of initiation, in which the reader crosses the threshold from the outside to the inside world. This upward and inward movement takes place when the appropriate text is transformed into an object of contemplation. *Lectio* becomes *meditatio*' (1996: 1–2). For an outline of medieval reading practices, see also Joyce Coleman's entry in *The Encyclopaedia of Medieval Literature in Britain*. She describes the multi-stage monastic reading practice of *lectio divina* as follows: 'First came private (though usually vocalised) reading of scripture and related Latin works, in order to grasp their literal meaning and to commit them to memory. The reader then proceeded to meditative reading, pondering the text and its spiritual messages. From there, he or she moved on to prayer and, ideally, to contemplation of the divine' (Coleman 2017: 1573). Scholarly practices, and then public reading, she observes, invited commentary and glossing (1573). But there was also a practice of lay silent reading: 'nothing prevented any literate person from also taking up the book in some quiet moment to read it privately' (1574). Finally, '[d]evotional reading among the laity [...] descended from earlier monastic practices but [was] augmented by the late medieval emphasis on projecting oneself into the Passion story (a practice known as "affective piety")' (1574).

37. On silent reading, see Paul Saenger, *Space Between Words* (1997).

38. In *The Wings of the Doves*, Elena Lombardi writes that '[t]he act of reading involved the body and the person's emotions much more than today. Not only were books touched, kissed and caressed, but reading was also held to stimulate intense responses such as happiness, anger, shame, and even sexual arousal' (2012: 214). Further, elaborating a notion of 'affective literacy', Mark Amsler has conceived medieval writing and reading practices as 'a semiotic matrix of acts and bodies', denoting 'a range of emotional, spiritual, physiological, somatic responses readers have when reading or perceiving a text, such as crying, laughing, imagining, or becoming aroused' (2012: 101, 103).

39. Blatt and I share a conviction that digital media studies and its model of participation is a powerful tool for exploration of medieval practices of reading (Blatt 2018: 3). However, our respective focus is different, Blatt exploring motor practices alone (emendation, sitting, walking), whereas my primary focus is on neural embodiment; and through a thematic lens, rather than my technical narratological one.

40. Further, 'he expected his readers to follow his metaliterary suggestions and be actively involved in interpreting his "new" poem [...]. Exegesis was central to the medieval literary experience, and in the *Commedia* Dante called his readers to this in ways which would have been immediately recognisable' (Barański 2005: 576).

41. See also Sarah McNamer, *Affective Meditation and the Invention of Medieval Compassion* (2010).

42. On dating and authorship of the *MVC*, see Karnes (2011: 8, 145), and Bestul (1996: 48). More widely, see Sarah McNamer's essay, 'The Origins of the *Meditationes Vitae Christi*' (2009).

43. Bestul references specifically Bernard's Sermons 20 and 43.

44. 'Meditation for Ludolph is thus a self-perpetuating loop of autoconstitution in which the practitioner enscripts Christic emotions by journeying through the past then redelivering the meditant to the present' (Ritchey 2012: 350).

45. Further on this question of embodied participation in the Passion, see Kerstin Pfeiffer's discussion of 'tactile empathy' in her essay, 'Feeling the Passion: Neuropsychological Perspectives on Audience Response' (2012). Writing of the later (fifteenth-century) N-Town Second Passion Play and the York Crucifixion, she proposes that: 'Unlike purely static depictions of Christological suffering such as crucifixes, which foreground the wounds left by the buffeting and scourging, the captivating [enacted] images of violence against the body of the actor standing in for Christ in the N-Town trial pageants re-create for the audience the sensation of painful touch. By allowing the spectator to see blow after blow land on the body of an actor standing in for Christ, these pageants allow him or her to feel the pain they cause not only vicariously but also personally because the feeling is reproduced in them' (Pfeiffer 2012: 335).

46. Quoted from *Meditations on the Life of Christ* (McNamer 2018: 70).

47. Further, from the *MVC*, Chapter 12: 'Et tuto il fondamento del spirito me pare che stia in çiò: che sempre in ogni luocho riguardi lui cum li ochi della mente tua [...]. Adonca considera tuti li soi acti et costumi, et specialmente contemplando la sua faça, se la pòi contemplare — la qualle cosa mi pare malagievole sopra tute le altre cose, ma credo che questo te saria la maçore consolatione che tu potesti bonamente havere' [And it seems to me that the foundation of the spirit is this: that always in every place regard him with the eyes of your mind [...]. Consider all his acts and behaviours, and contemplate especially his face, if you can — which seems to me the hardest thing, but I believe that this is the best consolation that truly you could have] (82).

48. Note that Karnes's analysis explicitly invites a revision of conventional (Cartesian) scholarship in relation to the medieval concept of the imagination. Twentieth-century medieval scholarship largely cleft to the view that imagination was less esteemed than memory in the theocentric culture of the Middle Ages. Perceived as 'prone to fanciful inventions', the imagination 'was a mental faculty run amok' (Karnes 2011: 2), only released from its divine shackles to the full human power of its inventiveness and creativity with the Enlightenment, in the common view. Karnes proposes a significant corrective in favour of a medieval rich inner life. She argues that in fact the late Middle Ages saw the imagination 'invested [...] with a new authority' (3). She roots this development in the twelfth century's return to Aristotle and specifically his notion that the imagination is 'involved centrally in every act of knowledge acquisition. As Aristotle famously said, "The soul never thinks without an image", an image provided by imagination (*De Anima* III. 7, 431a 16–17)' (3). In relation to her field of interest in the gospel meditations of the period, she concludes that 'imaginative meditations on Christ were more ambitious and purposeful than the scholarship on them has recognised' (5). The notion of a medieval distrust of the imagination has arguably been foregrounded in Dante studies: see, for example, Pearce on the imagination's 'distorted representations of reality' (1996: 29). My suggestion is that in her reformulation, Karnes offers a new and considerably more nuanced picture of the medieval notion of imagination that may much more sympathetically reflect the *Comedy*'s complex relationship with the human imagination in its interactions with the divine. This potentially opens a new and productive path for Dante studies in relation to the faculty of the imagination, but one that extends much further than my preliminary analysis here.

49. Karnes notes that Paul's Epistles encourage communities to suffer with Christ in order to rejoice with him: 'God forbid that I should glory, save in the cross of our Lord Jesus Christ' (Gal. 6:4), and cross-references the *MVC*: 'A person who wishes *to glory in* the passion and *cross of the Lord* (Gal. 6:4) should persevere in earnest meditation on it' (2011: 154; emphasis in original).

50. Further: 'Meditation enables the meditant to share Christ's suffering, and Christ appears to her as a result' (Karnes 2011: 154). She sees the same purpose in the meditations of James of Milan (155–61), whose meditation, she suggests, makes the human mind capable of 'travel[ling] a mental pathway from Christ's humanity to his divinity' (155); and in those of Ludolph (166–67).

51. As I mention in the Introduction (n. 26), Hollander comments in his gloss on *Par.*, XXXIII. 52–54 that 'the poet [...] can finally see God's *reflection* in the universe perfectly, an ability that was far from his grasp when the poem began' (my emphasis).

52. 'In the examination of beatitude in the *Commedia*, as with the entire metaphysical system of the poem, it is essential to recognise that we are dealing not with the divine but with *the representation of* the divine' (Barański 2018: 275; my emphasis).

53. Yates proposes a similar plasticity in relation to memory, writing of the classical sources in which she bases her medieval 'art of memory' that they 'seem to be describing inner techniques which depend on visual impressions of *almost incredible intensity*' (1984: 4; my emphasis).

54. In 1748, Hume had suggested that the imagination works better with literary images: 'The imagination [...] is more enlivened, and the passions more enflamed than in history, biography, or any species of narration which confine themselves to strict truth and reality' (2013: 81).

55. In *Representative Essays*, Spitzer notes of this tercet: 'We see for the first time the *figure* of the reader: he has a body (whereas before he had only a mind or eye or ear) and he sits [...]. Here Dante truly has "created the reader"' (1988: 190). In relation to the reader's mental model of the situation of this body, Steinberg discusses 'the university-standard *libro da banco* (desk book) implicit in *Paradiso* 10' (2007: 9). It is worth pointing out that the reader has immediately previously been invited to lift her eyes to the night sky along with the narrating Dante (*Par.*, X. 7–9), so either this *banco* needs to be assimilated as being positioned outside, or the reader needs to rapidly switch locations in her mind, from outside looking at the night sky, to being inside a library. Preliminary analysis suggests that in the *Comedy*, the reader's body is typically characterised as very mobile across worlds, suggesting a strategy is at play and meriting further research.

56. In her essay 'I miti biblici. La sapienza di Salomone e le arti magiche', Alison Cornish writes that the value in this 'extremely laborious' 'cogitative exercise' lies in its doing, rather than in the 'scarce fruit' (1999: 394) that it yields to the mind's eye: 'The value of this exercise, then, must be in its execution; imaginative effort for its own sake is at the heart of the passage, an effort that becomes an attempt to reproduce through the imagination the fundamental composition of the created universe' (395).

57. 'Ricorditi, lettor, se mai ne l'alpe | ti colse nebbia per la qual vedessi | non altrimenti che per pelle talpe, | come, quando i vapori umidi e spessi | a diradar cominciansi, la spera del sol debilemente entra per essi; | e fia la tua imagine leggera | in giugner a veder com' io rividi lo sole in pria, che già nel corcar era. | Sì, pareggiando i miei co' passi fidi | del mio maestro, usci' fuor di tal nube | ai raggi morti già ne' bassi lidi' [Reader, recall, if ever in the hills | a fog has caught you so you couldn't see | (or only as a mole does through its skin), | then how, as vapours, clinging, damp and dense, | began to dissipate, the sun's round disc | enters, and feebly makes its way through these. | From this, you'll easily be brought to see, | in your imagination, how I saw | the sun again, already setting now. | So, levelling with my teacher's trusted steps, | I came out from that cloud, along with him, | to rays, down on the shore, already dead] (*Purg.*, XVII. 1–12).

58. 'Experto crede: aliquid amplius invenies in silvis, quam in libris. Ligna et lapides docebunt te, quod a magistris audire non possis' (*Epistolae* 106 in Leclerq et al. (1957–1977, VII: 266)). English translation from Heffernan and Burman (2005: 118).

59. There are growing efforts to seek to quantify replicated reader responses to texts — for example, Giulia Cartocci et al.'s 'The "NeuroDante Project"' (2016) — but this is not my interest here.

CHAPTER 2

❖

Spatial Presence

2.1. 'Tu non se' in terra': being transported

Dante's journey through Paradise begins with Beatrice telling him, in *Paradiso* I, not where he is (transiting from the Earthly Paradise to the heaven of the Moon) but rather where he *isn't*:

> 'Tu stesso ti fai grosso
> col falso imaginar, sì che non vedi
> ciò che vedresti se l'avessi scosso.
>
> Tu non se' in terra, sì come tu credi;
> ma folgore, fuggendo il proprio sito,
> non corse come tu ch'ad esso riedi.' (88–93)

> 'With false imaginings
> you make yourself so dull you fail to see
> what, shaking off this cloud, you'd see quite well.
>
> You are not still on earth as you suppose.
> No thunderbolt that flees its proper place
> ran at such speed as you return to yours.'

In *Paradiso*, the journeying Dante is entering a new space in which expectations or assumptions rooted in earthly laws of physics, such as perspective and gravity, no longer apply, and where the mistaken application of such assumptions, resulting in false imaginings, 'falso imaginar' (89), can act as an impediment to understanding.[1] The journeying Dante is gazing into the sun, 'e fissi li occhi al sole oltre nostr' uso' [and fix[ed] my eyes — beyond our norm — straight at the sun] (54), when suddenly, the narrating Dante writes, it was as if God had adorned the sky with a second sun: 'come quei che puote | avesse il ciel d'un altro sole addorno' (62–63). Beatrice has intuited his wonder at seeing what appears to be the sun and the moon occupying the same sky above him, but this wonderment is misplaced: he misinterprets what he sees — 'non vedi | ciò che vedresti [...]' [you fail to see | what, [...], you'd see quite well] (89–90) — because he has presumed an erroneous standpoint: he assumes that he is still on earth.[2]

His spatial understanding has been challenged before, perhaps most notably in his transit out of hell, when the unexpected rotation around the 'punto' of Satan's hips left him disorientated and confused, seeing Satan's legs apparently above him:[3]

> Io levai li occhi e credetti vedere
> Lucifero com' io l'avea lasciato,
> e vidili le gambe in sù tenere. (*Inf.*, XXXIV. 88–90)

> Raising my eyes, I thought that I should see
> Lucifer where I, just now, had left him,
> but saw instead his legs held upwards there.

But whilst in *Inferno* XXXIV Virgil did little to clarify what seeing differently might mean, with his extended narrativised observation of how he, Virgil, effected the physical transition for Dante ('Di là fosti cotanto quant' io scesi; | quand' io mi volsi, tu passasti 'l punto | al qual si traggon d'ogne parte i pesi' [While I was still descending, you were there. | But once I turned, you crossed, with me, the point | to which from every part all weight drags down] (109–10)), here in *Paradiso* Beatrice instead frames the notion of seeing anew as a principle to be embodied, inviting Dante to understand the distorting effects of mistaken perception through physically enacting, attentively, this new standpoint for himself. Were he on earth, it would indeed be extraordinary to see 'un altro sole' (63) alongside the first. But his physical standpoint now is different: he is no longer on earth as he imagines, 'tu non se'' in terra' (91), but rather — and travelling faster than a bolt of lightning — he is in return transit to his 'principio' (111), his origin. If he shakes off the cloud of 'falso imaginar' and looks afresh, he will see this.

Aristotle writes in the *Metaphysics* of 'the delight we take in our senses; for even apart from their usefulness they are loved for themselves; and above all others the sense of sight'.[4] But in the same way that optical illusions remind us that our eyes can deceive us, so Dante's experience here invites the reader, I propose, to consider that human visual perception is cognitively mediated, rendering it essentially subjective.[5] And if this process of mediation rests on an inappropriate inference, then we may misconstrue what we see.

So, the mediated nature of visual perception makes our grasp of place potentially fallible. However, a human understanding of place is based on more than just the physical, or what appears to be materially present through visual perception. Place is also *relational*, constituted by our relationship with it and other objects in it. Indeed, as Lakoff and Johnson proposed in *Metaphors We Live By*, this quality of spatial relationality is so essential in human understanding that it pervades our language in many of the metaphors we use. Such embedded 'spatial orientations', they write, are a function of 'the fact that we have bodies of the sort we have and that they function as they do in our physical environment' (1980: 14). Maurice Merleau-Ponty wrote of a body as not 'a thing in objective space, but as a system of possible actions, a virtual body with its phenomenal "place" defined by its task and its situation. My body is wherever there is something to be done' (2002: 291). More recently, theories of situated cognition have identified this continually emerging relationality of body and place as the basis of human understanding. Cognitive scientists Wolff-Michael Roth and Alfredo Jornet propose that:

> The central aspect of the situated cognition hypothesis is that intelligent behaviour arises from the dynamic coupling between intelligent subject and

its environment rather than only from the agent's mind (brain, control system) itself. (2013: 465; emphasis in original)

Further, place is *experiential*, encountered not only through the eyes but through the other senses and bodily systems; a phenomenon that many theorists have referred to as 'sense of place', or a figurative notion of atmosphere or *Stimmung*.[6] On the evocativeness of place, in *The Image of the City*, urban design scholar Kevin Lynch suggested that 'a sense of place in itself enhances every human activity that occurs there, and encourages the deposit of a memory trace' (1960: 119). In *The Poetics of Space*, Gaston Bachelard explored a notion of lived experience or personal interaction with space, writing, for example, that 'a house that has been experienced is not an inert box. Inhabited space transcends geometrical space' (1969: 47). But there is also the question of a literal experience of atmosphere or the 'aerial medium', to borrow Tim Ingold's term (2008: 1796), with which individuals interact when not contained within built architecture, and which includes weather conditions, atmospheric pressure, temperature, and air quality, for example.[7] Such atmospheric phenomena, writes Ingold, 'fundamentally affect [the situated individual's] moods and motivations, their movements, and their possibilities of subsistence' (1802).

Importantly for my argument in this book, such phenomena are experienced not only through visual perception, and the other senses, but also through the *visceromotor* system, which underpins affective response to a place — Bachelard's house that is no longer an 'inert box', Lynch's experience of a 'memory trace'; and through the *somatosensory* system, which processes sensations on or in the body, including those that derive from Ingold's 'aerial medium', such as temperature, pressure, and pain, and also an awareness of the body's position in space and movement, or proprioception.

Visual perception, as discussed earlier, is fallible because it relies on an unconscious process of inference in the brain. In real life, an understanding of place is constructed not only via the visual and wider sensorimotor system, but also the somatosensory and visceromotor systems; that is, the 'feel' of it, in the broadest sense. It is these systems that convert data of temperature, airflow, local threat, and proprioception into an embodied understanding of a place as hot, windy, frightening, and one through which we are falling at speed, for example.

In relation to a virtual rather than a real-life space my suggestion, rooted in Wojciehowski and Gallese's observation that 'embodied simulation [...] can also occur when we *imagine* doing or perceiving something' (2011: 16), is that the same 'realistic' sense of place can be invited in the reader of a text, *provided that* the text reproduces the same stimuli to not only the reader's sensorimotor system (most commonly visual data, but also sound, smell, touch), but also to her somatosensory and visceromotor systems. These systems, I propose, serve to authenticate (as in real life) the readily observable visual data, reassuring the reader's brain of the 'realism' of the place narrated.[8]

A feeling of genuine transportation into a narrated world — what I describe in this chapter as *spatial presence* — is rooted, I suggest, in a direct, embodied experience of place constructed through a combination of the sensory, visceral, and somatic systems of the body. Narratives that deliver a less convincing sense of place, by contrast, I suggest, tend to rely only or primarily on visual description. The provision of multi-sensory data, particularly sight, sound, and smell, to evoke a sense of place is not uncommon in well-constructed narrative texts, but Dante's innovation in relation to setting and spatial evocation, I will suggest, is to have found ways to consistently invite the perceptual illusion of spatial presence in the reader. Further, he deploys this mechanism specifically in service of assisting the earth-bound reader to arrive at a new understanding of place as relational and *emergent*, rather than fixed;[9] and of the virtual as every bit as 'real' as the material, enabling the reader to conceive of Paradise not as 'there', a specific end or destination, but rather as 'here': that is, simultaneously present with the reader's living experience of the physical world.

2.2. Literary setting versus spatial presence

In *Story and Discourse*, textual and film narrative theorist Seymour Chatman defined 'literary space' as more than simply place or 'setting', suggesting it also includes landscapes, climatic conditions, domestic spaces: everything that can be conceived of as spatially located (1980: 96–106, 138–45). More recently, Marie-Laure Ryan insisted on separating the experiential and the orientational, writing that 'a sense of place is not the same thing as a mental model of space: through the former, readers inhale an atmosphere; through the latter, they orient themselves on the map of the fictional world' (2001: 123). Video game criticism, I propose, now gives us a new tool for thinking about how these two elements combine in a fictional narrative, as they do in the real world, through the notion of *spatial presence*.

One of the three forms of presence defined by interaction theorist Kwan Min Lee (2004), and by far the most commonly discussed, spatial presence is commonly understood in video game criticism as 'the subjective experience of being in one place or environment, even when one is physically situated in another' (Witmer and Singer 1998: 225) — an early definition, but one that has endured; or, simply, the sense of 'being there'.[10] This sense of feeling oneself to be somewhere other than where one rationally knows one's body to be is recognised as a 'perceptual illusion of non-mediation' that occurs 'when a person fails to perceive or acknowledge the existence of a medium in his/her communication environment and responds as he/she would if the medium were not there' (Lombard and Ditton 1997).[11] The literary notion of immersion and the video game notion of spatial presence have often been unhelpfully conflated.[12] However, my analysis of the narrative mechanics in the *Comedy* that invite spatial presence strongly supports IJsselsteijn's definition of presence as 'the experiential counterpart of immersion', confirming that the key difference between a notion of immersion in a sense of place and spatial presence is the trigger to *embodied simulation* that sparks a sense of dynamic reciprocal interaction between body and location.[13]

Pioneer of VR theory Brenda Laurel observed that VR offers the player the potential to '[take] your body with you into worlds of the imagination' (1993: 14). In this chapter, I will seek to establish that this transformation depends on the brain being given cues in the narration that suggest a narrated virtual world is like, or behaves like, the real world. Specifically, this means that the reader encounters data that repeatedly engages her diverse bodily systems, and the world responds to her presence in it; that is, in Calleja's terms, 'having one's [...] presence [...] acknowledged by the system itself' (2011: 22).

2.3. A mortal human body in a virtual space

It is a commonplace that place is evocative; and this is a notion that applies to the virtual places of narrative as well as to the physical world. Mandler and Johnson reported from empirical research that 'setting' is the most frequently remembered component of a textual narrative (1977: 144); Marie-Laure Ryan adds that setting promotes 'emotional attachment' in a narrative experience (2009: 54).

In the *Comedy*, there is a vast amount of data related to spatial evocation: a preliminary tally suggests at least twelve hundred instances in the poem in total, or an average of twelve references to location per canto. These instances range from real and fictional named locations, landscape features, architectural structures, astronomical co-ordinates, environmental and atmospheric conditions, and spatial and orientational metaphors ('qui', 'là', 'giù', 'su': here, there, down, up) — that is, all the components of spatial evocation discussed above: physical, relational and orientational. At around four hundred references per canticle, the distribution of spatial data might be surprising in its consistency, given the apparently much more substantial nature of the pit of Hell and Purgatory's mountain than of what is set out in *Paradiso*. It becomes perhaps less surprising, though, when we consider the distribution of the different types of spatial evocation in each canticle: a dominant focus on physical features (geographical and architectural) in *Inferno* and *Purgatorio*; but on spatial metaphor instead in *Paradiso*, particularly orientational metaphor. Another major difference is in the openness and relational nature of each world with the other realms and with the *mondo mortal*, suggesting differences in the evident ability of those within each world to conceive of and enact the integration of 'here' with 'there'. Hell is rendered essentially separate and contained, not only through the sealed (dark, starless) nature of its geography, but also by its oppressive weather systems (that account for around a tenth of all spatial evocation data in *Inferno*). Purgatory is constantly connected with the mortal world through the naming of worldly cities and regions, and with the heavens through astronomical references; and Paradise with the physical world both in time and in eternity, and through the naming of specific locations and via a totalising notion of the world, 'il mondo', 'il mondo mortal', as that with which it is always and fundamentally in relation. There is a great deal of productive work to be undertaken in relation to further mapping and analysis of this spatial data and its cumulative effect in the poem, but in this chapter I shall of necessity focus only on establishing the principle of the particular textual narrative mechanics by which spatial presence may be invited.[14]

The familiar, apparently material features of Hell (including even a material city) make it a place that at first glance would seem highly relatable and interactable through the medium of the body, as is our own physical world. Purgatory, too, with its mountain, its stone fabric interwoven with the penitents' aerial bodies, its *intagli*, its steps and narrow fissures, seems, on the surface at least, rich with physically interactable features. And by writing what he has seen on his journey through these realms, as Beatrice instructs the journeying Dante in the Earthly Paradise — 'quel che vedi, | ritornato di là, fa che tu scrive' [And what you see write down when you go back] (*Purg.*, XXXII. 104–05) — and writing, too, what he hears, touches, smells, senses through his body, experiences, and feels, as he comes into relation with other objects and forces, the narrating Dante can re-mediate these places for the reader in the same perceptible terms.[15]

But in *Paradiso*, of course, there *are* no physical features or locations to see, touch, feel, smell, so the reader's transportation to Paradise will rest much more fully on successfully experiencing the perceptual illusion of spatial presence — feeling herself 'there', rather than relying on seeing what it looks like; but this requires a cognitive approach at odds with our 'falso imaginar' assumption of a perceptible external material world. One of the many challenges for the reader in *Paradiso* will be to come to experience space not as material but as relational, a medium that houses, or emerges as the site of, interactions. Place does not exist as a concept independent of interaction. The interactable objects which will underpin the reader's experience of spatial presence will be not geographical or architectural features, but the souls of the blessed. The possibility of profoundly and meaningfully grasping such an understanding, I suggest, is greatly enhanced when the reader can experiment with experiencing it for herself in *Inferno* and *Purgatorio* through invitations in the narrative to spatial presence.

In the next two sections, I explore two sequences in the poem that I suggest powerfully illustrate the mechanisms by which Dante invites reader spatial presence, catalysing a capacity to participate: first, the descent on Geryon in *Inferno* XVII and, afterwards, the ascent of the celestial ladder in *Paradiso* XXII.

2.4. 'Being there': Geryon

The action of the flight on Geryon — a descent narrative (*katabasis*) within the *katabasis* of *Inferno* as a whole — takes place at the end of *Inferno* XVII.[16] Dante and Virgil are at the top of the abyss that will take them into Malebolge; Geryon, that filthy image of deceit, 'sozza imagine di froda' (7), has been summoned from the depths of Hell by Virgil to carry them down. With echoes of mythological over-reaching and failure resonating throughout the episode, Dante imagines the terror he feels as he realises they are in mid-air, 'ne l'aere d'ogne parte' (113), on the back of this monstrous vehicle to be similar to that experienced by Phaeton and Icarus at the point at which their own vehicles of flight began to fail.[17] From the handily remembered cord around Dante's waist that facilitates the initial sounding of the abyss to the notionally terrifying city-wall-and-weapon-shattering monster who eventually comes in to land with all the grace of a sulky captive falcon, 'disdegnoso e fello' (131), the episode is a challenge to the reader's sense of realism.[18] Hollander, in his gloss (ll. 115–26), proposes it to be 'perhaps the single most melodramatic and implausible narrative passage in the *Comedy*'; yet, as Barolini writes, it is 'remarkably successful' in engendering 'willing suspension of disbelief' (1992: 61). In their gloss (ll. 115–17), Bosco and Reggio credit Dante's realism, noting 'the extraordinary power of the Dantean imagination in representing as a felt experience that which was barely even conceivable'. The episode is undoubtedly epistemically immersive: there is both suspense (will fraudulent Geryon deliver them safely?) and mystery (what horrors are causing the screams from below?). But I propose that what really makes this implausible descent so compellingly plausible, despite the preposterousness of the vehicle, are Dante's invitations to the reader to feel spatially present: as though she, herself, is physically 'there'.

The narration of the descent is as follows:

> Come la navicella esce di loco
> in dietro in dietro, sì quindi si tolse;
> e poi ch'al tutto si sentì a gioco,
>> là 'v' era 'l petto, la coda rivolse,   103
> e quella tesa, come anguilla, mosse,
> e con le branche l'aere a sé raccolse.
>> Maggior paura non credo che fosse
> quando Fetonte abbandonò li freni,
> per che 'l ciel, come pare ancor, si cosse;
>> né quando Icaro misero le reni   109
> sentì spennar per la scaldata cera,
> gridando il padre a lui 'Mala via tieni!'
>> che fu la mia, quando vidi ch'i' era
> ne l'aere d'ogne parte, e vidi spenta
> ogne veduta fuor che de la fera.
>> Ella sen va notando lenta lenta;   115
> rota e discende, ma non me n'accorgo
> se non che al viso e di sotto mi venta.
>> Io sentia già da la man destra il gorgo
> far sotto noi un orribile scroscio,
> per che con li occhi 'n giù la testa sporgo.
>> Allor fu' io più timido a lo stoscio,   121
> però ch'i' vidi fuochi e senti' pianti;
> ond' io tremando tutto mi raccoscio.
>> E vidi poi, ché nol vedea davanti,
> lo scendere e 'l girar per li gran mali
> che s'appressavan da diversi canti. (*Inf.*, XVII. 100–26)

> Slowly astern, astern, as ferries leave
> the quay where they had docked, so he moved out.
> Then, only when he felt himself ride free,
>> he turned the tail where breast had been before,   103
> and — stretching long, as eels might do — set sail,
> paddling the air towards him with his paws.
>> No greater fear (so, truly, I believe)
> was felt as Phaeton let the reins go loose,
> and scorched the sky as still it is today,

nor yet by ill-starred Icarus — his loins   109
unfeathering as the wax grew warm — to whom
his father screamed aloud: 'You're going wrong!'
    And then with fear I saw, on every side,
that I was now in air, and every sight
extinguished, save my view of that great beast.
    So swimming slowly, it goes on its way.   115
It wheels. It descends. This I don't notice —
except for the breeze on my face and from below.
    By then I heard, beneath us to the right,
the roar of some appalling cataract.
And so I leant my head out, looking down.
    More timorous of falling still, I saw   121
that there were fires down there and heard shrill screams.
Trembling, I huddled back and locked my thighs.
    And then I saw, as I had not before,
the going-down — the spirals of great harm —
on every side now coming ever nearer.

(Here I have slightly amended Kirkpatrick's translation at line 117 to clarify the narratological mechanism.) The relative absence of *visual* description is arresting. The flight, of course, as we are told at the end of canto XVI, is in the dark, through 'aere grosso e scuro' [dark and fatty air] (130), so the journeying Dante cannot actually see for most of the descent, despite the four uses of 'I saw', 'vidi' (specifically: seeing that he is in mid-air (112); that, recursively, all sight is extinguished (113–14); seeing the fires (122); and seeing the 'gran mali' (125)). And even were the thick dark air visually penetrable, Geryon's body gets in the way: 'vidi spenta | ogne veduta fuor che de la fera' (113–14), unless the journeying Dante leans his head out. It is only as they come in to land that we have some visual description of the environment: the 'gran mali', the walls of the abyss. But even this is evoked not through material description — they are anyway represented through metaphor, 'the spirals of great harm' in Kirkpatrick's rendering — but instead by the dynamic sensation of their pressing ever closer, 'li gran mali | che s'appressavan da diversi canti' (125–26). The reader, then, has very little data with which to construct a precise visual image of the place. All she knows is that Geryon backed out into the space like a ferry; that Dante and Virgil, on Geryon's back, descended in circles towards cries and fires beneath; that the abyss gets tighter the closer they come to the bottom; and that Dante is terrified. She knows nothing of the depth, fabric, shape, or colour of the abyss. This is nothing like the God's-eye perspective that will open *Inferno* XVIII, allowing the reader to construct a visual model of the place from a position of external observation.[19] Here, if the reader wants to get an idea of what this place is like, she will need not simply to try to visualise it but to simulate in her own body *how it feels* to be there.

Cognitive narrative theory suggests there is a strategic benefit to this paucity of visual description. An excess of spatial data, it is held, diverts the brain from the other mental operations, particularly imagining, that assist the reader to generate a more personal mental model of the text and that is said to be indicative of the 'skilled' reader.[20] And this paucity of visual data is not just a feature of the Geryon *katabasis*. It is characteristic of *Inferno* generally, although it has been little commented on in scholarship — testament, I would suggest, to its success as a narrative strategy. In *Inferno*, there are many geographical and architectural objects located in the space — battlements, gates, walls, valleys, woods, sands, ditches, bridges, towers, giants — but the descriptions are almost always neutral, even bland. The battlements are high ('alti', IX. 133), the wall, high ('alto', XXXII. 18), the ditches, high ('alte', VIII. 76), the sink or 'burrato' from the depths of which Geryon will emerge, high ('alto', XVI. 114). Elsewhere, the broken bridge is simply 'old' (XVIII. 79); the valley just 'dark' ('buia', XII. 86); the shores, 'hard' ('duri', XV. 1); the 'riva' [bank] is just a 'riva' (XVII. 9), the 'rena' [sand] simply 'rena' (XVII. 33 and 35), as too the 'fosso' [ditch], 'scoglio' [ridge] and 'abisso' [abyss] (XXII. 183, XXVII. 134, XXXIV. 1, amongst others). Things are generally tall, dark, hard, old, numbered, or just themselves in their least evocative form — not vividly visualisable places but rather signs denoting relatable objects.[21]

As a strategy, this has its risks: for the less imaginative or 'skilled' reader, it may feel disappointingly spare (perhaps leading such a reader to lean more heavily on illustrations). For the reader in participatory mode, though, I suggest this pictorial or visual sparseness is liberating (indeed, Botticelli reproduces it extremely effectively in his line drawings in his illustrations for the poem): it both invites active imaginative collaboration between reader and text, and also, importantly, invites the reader to dedicate cognitive resource to attending to the human interactions unfolding at that site. The journeying Dante's interactions in *Inferno* are with the sinners; the notionally material nature of Hell as place is relevant and meaningful only insofar as it situates these interactions and, indeed, collaborates in the punishment of the sinners in their eternal damnation, a continually emergent medium of punishment. In fact, unimplicated in any such punishment, the journeying Dante, we might observe, very rarely interacts with or disturbs the fabric of Hell at any material level.[22] Instead, he operates in a kind of 'safe' mode (a phenomenon even more apparent in relation to social presence, as I discuss in Chapter 3): remaining notably *on*, rather than engaging *with*, its features — standing on a bank, on an edge, crossing a river (in a boat), standing above a ditch, and even being carried by Virgil, protecting him from contact with the surface of the notional place.

But whilst the journeying Dante might not be interacting much with the material fabric of Hell, the participatory reader needs to be able to construct a series of mental models that simulate the experience of 'being there'. In the episode with Geryon, it becomes evident that Dante's focus is on narrating *not what the descent* through the abyss looks like to the external observer, but instead on *how it feels* to be there. He will achieve this by a mechanism I shall refer to as *narration through situated body states*.

What spatial data is available to the reader in the sequence? The marked-up text below identifies triggers to each of the three bodily systems discussed earlier: **sensorimotor data** (data received via the senses; marked up here in **bold type**), <u>visceromotor data</u> (viscera, like blood flow and breath; <u>underlined</u>), and *somatosensory data* (sensation, like temperature and movement; *italics*).[23]

Come la navicella *esce di loco*
in dietro in dietro, sì quindi si tolse;
e poi ch'al tutto si sentì a gioco,
    là 'v' era 'l petto, la coda rivolse,   103
e quella tesa, *come anguilla, mosse*,
e con le branche l'aere a sé raccolse.
    <u>Maggior paura</u> non credo che fosse
quando Fetonte abbandonò li freni,
per che 'l ciel, come pare ancor, si cosse;
    né quando Icaro misero **le reni**   109
senti spennar per la scaldata cera,
gridando il padre a lui 'Mala via tieni!'
    <u>che fu la mia</u>, quando **vidi** ch'i' era
ne l'aere d'ogne parte, e **vidi spenta**
ogne veduta fuor che de la fera.
    Ella sen va *notando lenta lenta*;   115
rota e discende, ma non me n'accorgo
se non che *al viso e di sotto mi venta*.
    Io **sentia** già da la man destra il gorgo
far sotto noi un orribile scroscio,
per che con li occhi 'n giù la testa sporgo.
    Allor fu' io <u>più timido a lo stoscio</u>,   121
però ch'i' **vidi** fuochi e **senti'** pianti;
ond' io <u>tremando</u> tutto mi raccoscio.
    E **vidi** poi, ché nol vedea davanti,
lo scendere e 'l girar per li gran mali
che s'appressavan da diversi canti. (*Inf.*, XVII. 100–26)

Slowly astern, astern, as ferries leave
the quay where they had docked, so *he moved out.*
Then, only when he felt himself ride free,
    he turned the tail where breast had been before,   103
and — stretching long, *as eels might do* — set sail,
paddling the air towards him with his paws.
    <u>No greater fear</u> (so, truly, I believe)
was felt as Phaeton let the reins go loose,
and scorched the sky as still it is today,
    nor yet by ill-starred Icarus — **his loins**   109
unfeathering as the wax grew warm — to whom
his father screamed aloud: 'You're going wrong!'
    And then <u>with fear</u> I **saw**, on every side,
that I was now in air, and **every sight**
extinguished, save my view of that great beast.
    So *swimming slowly*, it goes on its way.   115
It wheels. It descends. This I don't notice —
except for the breeze on my face and from below.
    By then **I heard**, beneath us to the right,
the roar of some appalling cataract.
And so I leant my head out, looking down.
    <u>More timorous of falling still</u>, **I saw**   121
that there were fires down there and **heard** shrill screams.
<u>Trembling</u>, I huddled back and locked my thighs.

> And **then I saw**, as I had not before,
> the going-down — the spirals of great harm —
> on every side *now coming ever nearer.*

I discussed the visual earlier, but there is other *sensory* data too that describes the interaction of the journeying Dante's body with the physical conditions of the space: the sound of the 'orribile scroscio' (119) and the 'pianti' (122); the haptic sensation of the double wind, both coming up vertically from the bottom of the sink, and the wind in the journeying Dante's face as Geryon pierces the thick air, and which indeed is what alerts him to the fact of their rotational descent (115–17) (I shall come back to this). There is *visceromotor* data that conveys his response of terror to being in that space: the explicit analogy with Phaeton and Icarus' fear (beginning at line 106 and resolved at 112) that is particularly powerfully embodied in Icarus' experience of the progressive melting of the wax that held together his feathers of flight ('sentì spennar', 110); there is his fear of falling ('Allor fu' io più timido a lo stoscio', 121), that triggers the visceral trembling that triggers in turn the motor response of the gripping of his thighs ('ond' io tremando tutto mi raccoscio', 123). And there is *somatosensory* data that narrates, particularly, the experience of movement through the space, or *vection*: the feeling of being on a reversing ferry ('in dietro in dietro', 101), an embodied sensation many readers may be able to retrieve from memory; feeling Geryon stretch out beneath him like an eel ('quella tesa, come anguilla, mosse', 104); and Geryon's slow, slow swimming round and down through the thick air ('Ella sen va notando lenta lenta; | rota e discende', 115–16) — data the narration *does* provide to the reader, so she *may* mentally model it for herself (exactly as we saw in Bernard's redundant invitation, in the Introduction), even if the narration does instantly offer a corrective in relation to the protagonist's experience of the event (the equivalent of the 'già' in relation to Bernard's sign): 'ma non me n'accorgo | se non che al viso e di sotto mi venta' (116–17).

In summary, then, it is an extremely rich, well-observed, *realistic* description of the dynamic effect of a terrifying descent on the body. It is dynamic because it invokes the continuous loop of human perception–action: sensory, visceral, and somatic data is explicitly linked with the resulting motor responses through repeated conjunctions: 'per che' [and so] (120), 'allor' [then] (121), 'però ch'i'' [for I] (122), 'ond' io' [at which I] (123). By bringing to consciousness the body's processing of the event in the form of a sequence of discrete steps, Dante effectively slows down, separates and invites the reader to attend to these individual components of a normal embodied process usually experienced as automatic. I propose that the reader who attentively seeks to reproduce each step, through imaginative enactment (and re-reading — and it takes some considerable work), and becomes 'skilled' in so doing, will find herself rewarded by experiencing for herself a sense of how it feels to be there, spiralling down through that abyss on the terrifying monster's back.

This is the first component of spatial presence, I propose. But there is a second, mentioned earlier: the question of reciprocal feedback or 'having one's [...] presence [...] acknowledged by the system itself' (Calleja 2011: 22). For the reader's brain to accept the virtual world as 'real', that world needs to behave in a 'realistic' way, responding to her body's presence in it by providing feedback data — that is, acting reciprocally on her body as her body acts on it.

There is a single detail in the episode with Geryon, I suggest, that triggers this second component of the illusion. It is a detail that has drawn the attention of many commentators but as yet without a clear explanation of what this detail does that is so powerful, and by what mechanism. This is an instance in which an understanding of the mechanisms of spatial presence in video games is particularly able to help us, I suggest; so perhaps the best way to try and explain it is by examining one particular video game, *Mirror's Edge*, that was an innovator in constructing the illusion of spatial presence.

Originally released in 2008 and considered a classic, *Mirror's Edge* is a first-person action–adventure game set on the rooftops of a futuristic dystopian city.[24] The player controls a female avatar called Faith and uses free-running or *parkour*-style movements to navigate the rooftop game space. The game is famous for inducing motion sickness and is critically rated for its immersive properties.[25] A short clip of a play-through on an Oculus Rift by game blogger TCTNGaming ('Tony') is available on YouTube.[26]

The main point of interest for the purposes of this chapter occurs when the player has to get his avatar Faith across a narrow pipe that stretches between two high rooftops (at 68 seconds into the clip noted above).

FIG. 2.1. *Mirror's Edge* gameplay screenshot: Faith falling.

The player fails, so Faith falls, and the player can be heard crying, 'Don't fall, don't fall, don't fall, no, oh, crap, no!', as his avatar crashes to the ground. In the webcam view of the player, inset into the top left corner of the screen, we can see him hold his hands to his chest, breathing quickly (see Fig. 2.2).

He whispers, 'OK, right, never again', kicks a box over the edge experimentally,

FIG. 2.2. *Mirror's Edge* gameplay screenshot: player's embodied response.

and exhales an 'ohhhh', as he watches it fly down. This visual and aural evidence of a strong visceral reaction suggests an apparent transfer of bodily sensations from avatar to player — that is, that Gallese's mode of *embodied simulation* has been triggered. And indeed, just watching the clip may be enough for you to find your own stomach seems to lurch upwards as Faith plummets. This being the case, we might conclude that the player has attained Lombard and Ditton's 'perceptual illusion of non-mediation' — that is, his brain is engaging with the space as though it were 'real', with the result that the player feels spatially present in the game world.

There are several mechanisms in the game design that could be implicated in this illusion.[27] First, and most obviously, there is so much *visual data,* rendered realistically (comprehensive, and consistent with material laws such as perspective) that even though the world is clearly not 'real', the player's brain has no trouble in constructing a credible mental model of how it looks: all the imaginative work has been done, freeing the player's cognitive processes to attend fully to experiencing the space. This is not an option available to the author of a textual narrative artefact, of course: it would take pages and pages of visual description to render a similarly detailed mental model, taxing the reader with visuospatial complexity and making the episode unreadable. As discussed earlier, Dante does not even try.

The second tactic the game employs in terms of mechanics of spatial presence is to make it very easy for the player to enter the mode of embodied simulation. This is because the game makes it extremely easy to identify with the body of the avatar. The primary illusion is a visual one: through the first-person camera view, the player sees exactly what the avatar sees, including the visual data of the player's (surrogate) body — bits of 'your' legs, hands, torso in line with your movement. Controlling Faith's movements, you *are* Faith's body; you and your avatar are already operating, in Gallese and Guerra's terms, a 'shared motor code' (2014: 106). The other senses are evoked too, such as the sound of your breath as you run, and your gasp as you fall, but also, and particularly innovatively in *Mirror's Edge*, the sense of *proprioception* — the perception of the position of the body in space. This is invoked particularly by the game's unusually sensitive freedom of camera movement that is reportedly designed to 'transmit motion' from the avatar's body to yours (and this is what contributes to motion-sickness in some players).[28] In the *Comedy*, as we have seen, this same mechanism of embodied simulation is triggered through narration of situated body states, although the restrictions of the textual medium mean that the reader is required to actively collaborate through engaging her imagination to catalyse the narrated data.

This brings us to the third mechanism in the game: the illusion of reciprocal feedback — the main reason that your brain is prepared to accept the game space as 'real'. *You* act on the environment, by falling; the environment acts reciprocally on you, responding to your weight, your acceleration, your changing location. This is how a human body (an object with mass) experiences the material world: twigs that break underfoot in a wood, the resistance against your arms and legs as you paddle through water; or the triple phenomena of acceleration, rotation, and upward force responsible for that uncanny feeling of your stomach lurching upwards when you fall through the air.

In the material world, this latter happens because your organs experience a reduction in the gravitational force normally exerted on them by the ground, via your feet, when you are the right way up, and this gives the illusion that they are lifting upwards. When you are playing (or watching a play-through of) a game like *Mirror's Edge*, of course there *is* no reduction in the force acting on your stomach; you are not physically plummeting through gravitational space. But your brain is sending neural messages *as if* you really were present there, despite being 'physically situated in another [place]' (Witmer and Singer 1998: 225): as if, in Beatrice's words, 'tu non se' in terra' (*Par.*, I. 91).

In the game, reciprocal feedback data is primarily rendered through graphics — that is, visual means. Velocity is evoked through the illusion of the ground rushing up to meet you, graphically represented by distant objects getting progressively larger. In the episode with Geryon, Dante's narration of the effect of the 'gran mali' coming closer, 's'appressavan' (126), is equivalent visual environmental feedback data doing essentially the same job, notwithstanding the characteristic 'gappy' presentation mode of textual narrative.[29] My own research into the graphical rendering of effects in *Mirror's Edge* suggests that rotation is rendered by successive representations of parts of your shadow, evoking its twisting as you fall.[30] This is an effect so subtle it only becomes perceptible to the naked eye when the play-through footage is advanced frame-by-frame, as can be seen in Figure 2.3.

The poem also evokes rotation, gappily: Geryon 'rota e discende' [It wheels. It descends] (116) — although, as discussed, the journeying Dante only registers it as a result of the wind on his face.[31] In the game, these two devices — the ground rushing up, your shadow twisting — are sufficient to persuade the brain that you really are falling, and hence the response of your stomach leaping upwards, together

FIG. 2.3. *Mirror's Edge* gameplay screenshot: body shadow effect.

with other observable visceromotor reflexes in the player, such as his touching his chest and his breath coming short.

However, the game differs from the text in its ability to update this reciprocal feedback data constantly (the standard frame rate for a game engine of *Mirror's Edge*'s era is 60 frames per second). The poem simply cannot offer this quantity of repeated update information in a text. There is the mention of rotation and descent ('Ella sen va [...] | rota e discende', 116). But there is an additional device that invites the imaginatively responsive reader to experience the descent as dynamic and happening in time.

This is the device of the *wind* — 'se non che al viso e di sotto mi venta' [except for the breeze on my face and from below] (117; my translation): the double wind that hits your face and signals Geryon's speed as he circles down through the filthy air, and the wind that blasts up from the sink below, catching you as you lean out. *You* act on *it*, by being in its path; *it* acts on *you*, by striking your face. It is a tiny detail of the body's reciprocal relationship with the environment in which it is situated and one that has drawn much attention in the commentaries but without necessarily, I would suggest, any conclusion previously being offered as to why it is so powerful an observation for the reader's experience of the sequence. In his gloss (ll. 124–25), Sapegno notes that the dearth of the visual means that it is only the wind that communicates the sense of spiralling descent: 'Descent and rotation is registered only because of the breath of wind, with the visual sense having no kind of reference point.' Bosco and Reggio (ll. 115–17) note the doubling of sensation of the wind, from both in front and below: 'Geryon rotates and descends and thereby causes a double ventilation: to the face, from the rotational movement; from underneath, from the downward movement.'

My suggestion is that the power of this detail of the wind lies, first, in its conferral of the illusion of reciprocal feedback from the environment to the subject, and second, in the suggestion of dynamism: that the wind is a continuously emerging factor, constantly in Dante's face as they cut through the air, constantly experienced from below ('al viso e di sotto mi venta', 117), and, we might feel invited to infer, a blast even more powerfully experienced when he leans his head out, face down, to hear the racket beneath.

This detail, I suggest, completes the invitation to spatial presence in this sequence. The narration of the descent offers an unusual level of data evoking *how it feels* to move through that space. This invites not simply immersion in the narrated event of the journeying Dante's progress, but instead provides cues for the responsive reader to neurally simulate the journeying Dante's embodied experience as he descends through the black space: a transfer of effect that, 'done well' (Bailenson's term), temporarily invites the reader's brain to experience the narrated space as 'real'.

The 'responsiveness' of the reader is key. As discussed in the Introduction, the model of embodied simulation described here is rooted in a pre-rational, automatic, 'direct' neural response in the reader's brain to virtual cues to spatial presence; that is, it is an unconscious process of neural embodiment (Wojciehowski and Gallese 2011: 13). Some readers, we may suppose, are simply more sensitive to this than others, and so somehow 'naturally' more adept in feeling transported. However, as discussed in relation to affective devotion and spiritual exercises in Chapter 1, the ability to imaginatively elaborate on given narrative data is a *plastic* skill that can be refined with practice. In this instance of the descent on Geryon, the reader is representing in her own body not Christic emotions in modelling the Passion, but the journeying Dante's visceral experience of the terrifying circling descent. The reader of the *Comedy* who seeks to more vividly and more realistically model this visceral experience of 'being there' can finesse her skills in the same way as the reader of the spiritual exercise: by consciously responding, in step-by-step narrative sequences like the descent on Geryon (and also, as I discuss later, in certain of the ascents in Paradise), to cues in the text to imaginative elaboration of body states rendered modellable through very specific narrative detail. With practice the reader may become increasingly skilled in entering the perceptual illusion of spatial presence; the first cognitive building-block, I suggest, to developing the skill of reading in the mode of first-person participation.

To summarise, the illusion of spatial presence is invited through a compound narratological mechanism I have described as *narration through situated body states,* whose twin components I set out below.

First, the narration triggers embodied simulation in the reader by evoking situated body states, that is, the responses of the protagonist's sensorimotor, visceromotor, and somatosensory systems in relation with the environment. This includes not only what can be seen (flames), heard (cries), and felt (wind), but also his 'looped' embodied response: fear causes trembling, trembling results in his thighs gripping more tightly.[32]

Second, the experience is then *animated*, inviting the reader to construct not a static pictorial mental model but a *dynamic* one. This comes in part from the initial information of Geryon's spiralling motion through the space, 'Ella sen va notando lenta lenta; | rota e discende' (115–16), in which the gerund ('notando'), the present tense ('sen va'), and the repetition ('lenta lenta') all invite the reader to mentally model this sequence as extending in time, such that she may imagine not a static picture of one moment in Geryon's rotating descent but the animated sequence of rotations as he spirals down. But this is still rooted more in propositional understanding than in embodied understanding. The second key element in animating the sequence in an enactable way is the detail of the wind that invites the reader to infer dynamic, constant feedback from the environment onto the protagonist's body. If the reader has successfully animated her mental model, a sense of the wind may be imaginatively elaborated continuously both on the face and from below; even if she is not yet fully proficient in this mode of imagining, the narration of the head movement to look down constitutes another reminder of its effect. Like the piecemeal, constantly altering shadow in the game, the wind, I suggest, offers the dynamic environmental feedback necessary for the brain to accept the space as interactable, and therefore realistic, inviting the experience of spatial presence.

For all the apparent materiality of Hell, in the narration of the descent on Geryon a sense of place is evoked *not* through interaction with the features and objects of a landscape, but instead through narration of how it feels to move through that space: this is a narration of *vection*. The poem has invited a sense of being 'there' without the requirement that 'there' should have any material anchors. As such, and as I will explore next, it offers the reader an excellent rehearsal space for the real challenge of modelling spatial presence in Paradise.

Creating 'here': the celestial ladder

The journeying Dante will only gain Paradise proper when he attains the Empyrean — the gathering of all the blessed — in *Paradiso* XXX. Prior to that, in *Paradiso*, he will experience instead a temporary reconfiguration of the Empyrean, linearised and quasi-materialised, and rendered by the paradisiacal phenomenon of *condescension*, as Beatrice will explain in *Paradiso* IV.[33] Condescension makes Paradise interactable for the still-mortal journeying Dante in terms of his encounters with the blessed: he will meet the souls within the linear structure of Aristotle's eight concentric crystalline planetary heavens, to which the *Primum Mobile* has been added, each sphere acting as a medium for his interactions with the blessed.

The spheres themselves are perceptible in so far as they have shape, movement (rotation), and some form of substance, being crystalline ('cristallo', *Par.*, XXI. 25),[34] but they are not materially interactable in the sense of offering sense data to the eyes, the hands, or the feet, as the landscapes of Hell and Purgatory were, to be climbed over or squeezed through. There are spatial 'features' in condescended Paradise — the cross, skywriting, the eagle — but these are contingent, ephemeral structures, constructed of the lights of the blessed themselves; dynamic, constantly and visibly in motion, and reconfiguring through mutual correspondence.[35] Such spatial features, then, progressively depict place in Paradise as the nexus of dynamic force, the intersection of divine and human energies, coming into being through reciprocal action; and always returning to the engagement of individual with individual through the necessity of human perception, as Dante observes in the Heaven of Jupiter: 'parea ciascuna rubinetto in cui | raggio di sole ardesse sì acceso, | che ne' miei occhi rifrangesse lui' [Each soul showed forth as minute rubies might. | In each a sun ray burned with such new fire | its light, reflected, broke back from my eyes] (*Par.*, XIX. 4–6). Indeed, this epitomises *situated cognition* as set out by Jornet and Roth — namely, that 'information exists not prior to, but emerges from, and is a function of, the organism–environment relation (coupling)' (2013: 466).

For most of *Paradiso*, then, the journeying Dante will experience Paradise not in its 'real' form, but in its 'realistic' form, to borrow Barolini's terms (2013: 199) — that is, as a temporary spatial illusion. But the Empyrean, too, represents a challenge to a mortal human understanding of place: whilst it *appears*, as narrated in *Paradiso* XXXI, to have form — a rose 'in shape' — 'In forma dunque di candida rosa | mi si mostrava la milizia santa | che nel suo sangue Cristo fece sposa' [In form, then, as a rose, pure, brilliant, white, | there stood before me now the sacred ranks | that Christ, by His own blood, has made His bride] (1–3) — it is constructed of pure light, 'Fassi di raggio tutta sua parvenza' [All that appears is made there by a ray] (XXX. 106); and the shape of the rose emerges constantly as a result of the ceaseless interrelations of light energies, the eternal transfer of love.[36]

Different to an earthly manifestation of place then (material, observable, fixed), in *Paradiso* place will ultimately need to be understood as a quality of *emergence*: contingent, relational, coming into being at the point of intersection of reciprocal forces or energies. In this largely abstract space, the features or 'objects' with which the journeying Dante will interact will be not geographical or architectural objects; rather, the relational 'objects' in this space that will underpin the experience of realism and presence will be the souls of the blessed. However, in this otherwise spatially abstract place, there is a series of specific opportunities by which the reader may experience a sense of place; and that, as with Geryon, is through the narration of *vection* — as much a subjective experience as a visually observable phenomenon of movement. In *Paradiso*, the journeying Dante will make ten ascents through the spheres. This time, though, the reader will be entirely dependent on visceral and somatic data, without even the scant supporting visual and environmental data of *Inferno*.

But this may not be such an improbable leap for the earth-bound reader as it sounds. In fact, the reader could be argued to share the same combination of orders of reality as the journeying Dante himself: both still-mortal embodied subjects in a virtual space. The journeying Dante, like the reader, will continue to use his senses, viscera, and somatic responses in his journey through the heavens, but he will largely suspend his motor functions.[37] He enters the temporary virtual spatial illusion of condescended Paradise as the reader enters the virtual (imagined) space of Dante's narrative. This combination of a motorically suspended sensate body operating in a virtual space is one we experience when dreaming and is also a waking experience now made manifest through VR technology. I explore this next, but would first briefly suggest here that permitting these two orders of reality to intersect in this way (real body, virtual world) may perhaps offer new terms by which we could begin to consider afresh the so-called 'truth claims' of the poem. 'A culturally fractious issue that raises the question of the reader's beliefs', in earlier words of Barolini (2006: 2), such truth claims historically depend on an argument that has focused on whether Dante invites the reader to believe in a 'real' experience (a real body in a real place), or a fiction or vision (a virtual body in a virtual place).

The journeying Dante will make ten ascents in *Paradiso*. A mutuality of forces — a yielding, rather than autonomous agency — will characterise each: rising imperceptibly, being lifted up, collected, finding himself within, impelled, and arriving.[38] I propose that, as in the narrative of the descent on Geryon, one of these ascents — coincident with the final direct address to the reader — offers the reader a step-by-step rehearsal to construct, through the mode of embodied simulation, an experience of spatial presence, even in the largely abstract, virtual space of Paradise. This opportunity occurs in the eighth ascent: the ascent of the celestial ladder in *Paradiso* XXII.

The eighth ascent takes the journeying Dante from the heaven of Saturn into the constellation of Gemini in the heaven of the fixed stars by means of the celestial ladder.[39] The ascent is described as follows:

> La dolce donna dietro a lor mi pinse
> con un sol cenno su per quella scala,
> sì sua virtù la mia natura vinse;
>   né mai qua giù dove si monta e cala   103
> naturalmente, fu sì ratto moto
> ch'agguagliar si potesse a la mia ala.
>   S'io torni mai, lettore, a quel divoto   106
> trïunfo per lo quale io piango spesso
> le mie peccata e 'l petto mi percuoto,
>   tu non avresti in tanto tratto e messo   109
> nel foco il dito, in quant' io vidi 'l segno
> che segue il Tauro e fui dentro da esso. (100–11)

> My sweetest lady with a single sign –
> the powers she had so vanquished what I was –
> drove me to mount the ladder after them.
>   Nor where, in natural terms, we climb or sink   103
> is any motion ever swift enough
> to match the speed of what my wings could do.
>   So may I, reader, sometime join once more   106
> that prayerful march of victory (for which
> I often weep my sins and beat my breast),
>   you'd not so swiftly have withdrawn and thrust   109
> your finger in the fire as I first saw
> the sign that follows Taurus ... and was in!

A vast distance, as Dante reminds the reader in the *catascopia* at the end of the canto, is covered at unimaginable speed.[40] With a single sign, 'un sol cenno' (101), Beatrice triggers an impulse in the journeying Dante ('mi pinse', 100) to mount the ladder, a trigger to the yielding he is still learning.[41] He then experiences a sense of vection comparable to no force of gravity or upward ascent on earth, 'qua giù' (103), but that is approximated in a metaphor of flight, 'la mia ala' (105). The narration of the action pauses for a moment for the returned poet, back in his own physical location on earth, to avow his desire to return (107–08). Finally, in the poem's last direct address to the reader, the narrating Dante proposes that you, reader, could not have stuck your finger in and out of a fire (109–10) in the time it took him to arrive in his natal constellation.

Unusually amongst the other paradisiacal ascents, the eighth occurs in time, even if that time is almost imperceptible: a near-simultaneous departure and arrival, but it does have a duration, however infinitesimal, as Bosco writes in his gloss (ll. 100–11).[42] This, I suggest, allows Dante to invite the triggering of embodied simulation in the reader, by presenting as discrete steps the dynamic processes of sensory perception and embodied response, as we saw in the descent on Geryon but with greater subtlety: the journeying Dante sees Beatrice's sign and reflexively begins to ascend the ladder; he sees the constellation of Gemini then feels himself present within it. In the real world, these steps happen so quickly as to appear virtually simultaneous — precisely as the simile of pulling your finger from a fire illustrates.

In total, Dante offers the reader eight instances of modellable body state data in the sequence, heavily privileging the somatosensory (sensations in or on the body, including proprioception and vection), as marked up below. I use the same coding system as with the Geryon sequence: **sensorimotor** data in **bold type**, <u>visceromotor</u> data <u>underlined</u>, and *somatosensory* data in *italics*.

> La dolce donna dietro a lor *mi pinse*
> **con un sol cenno** su per quella scala,
> sì sua virtù la mia natura <u>vinse</u>;
>   né mai qua giù dove *si monta e cala*   103
> *naturalmente*, fu sì ratto moto
> ch'agguagliar si potesse *a la mia ala*.
>   S'io torni mai, lettore, a quel divoto   106
> trïunfo per lo quale io piango spesso
> le mie peccata e 'l petto mi percuoto,
>   tu non avresti in tanto *tratto e messo*   109
> *nel foco il dito*, in quant' io **vidi** 'l segno
> che segue il Tauro e *fui dentro* da esso. (100–11)

> My sweetest lady **with a single sign** –
> the powers she had so <u>vanquished</u> what I was –
> *drove me* to mount the ladder after them.
>   Nor where, *in natural terms, we climb or sink*   103
> is any motion ever swift enough
> to match the speed of *what my wings could do*.
>   So may I, reader, sometime join once more   106
> that prayerful march of victory (for which
> I often weep my sins and beat my breast),
>   you'd not so swiftly have *withdrawn and thrust*   109
> *your finger in the fire* as **I first saw**
> the sign that follows Taurus ... and *was in!*

There are two instances of visual data: the implied sighting of Beatrice's 'cenno' (101), and when he sees, 'vidi' (110) that he has attained Gemini. There is one notable visceromotor body state: his sensation of being overcome, 'vinse' (102), by Beatrice's 'virtù' (102). And there are five instances of somatosensory body states, all associated with vection or proprioception: the sense of being impelled, 'mi pinse' (100); the retrieved experience of gravity on earth, 'dove si monta e cala | naturalmente' (103); the sense of flight, 'la mia ala' (105); the imagined experience of pulling your finger straight out of a fire, 'tratto e messo | nel foco il dito' (109–10); and, finally, the experience of being 'in', 'dentro' (111), the eighth sphere. Unrelated to vection, there is one further instance of motor data that I propose has a different strategic purpose in relation to the Embodied Narrator narrating instance of the narrating Dante character,[43] to which I will briefly return later: the narrator's reported self-flagellation, weeping and beating his chest (107–08) in his longing to return to the 'devoto | triunfo' [prayerful march of victory] (106–07).

What is particularly important and interesting here is that almost all the body state data is deployed figuratively or comparatively, as metaphor or simile. Yielding, Dante feels himself 'pushed' up the ladder by Beatrice's sign, but there is no motor force from Beatrice; he feels vanquished, 'vinse' (102), but not by her physical strength but rather her 'virtù' (102). Vection is described initially through a null comparison with earthly motion ('né mai qua giù dove si monta e cala | naturalmente, fu sì ratto moto | ch'[...]' [Nowhere in natural terms we climb or sink | is any motion ever swift enough | to [...]] (103–05)), that might help the reader propositionally understand what Dante *means* — it was an astonishingly rapid movement — but arguably, as a null comparison, it will not help her experience it for herself. His second effort invokes the metaphor of flight ('la mia ala' [my wings] (105)): whether avian or angelic, this requires imaginative projection since the reader is neither. Finally, he offers the comparison of the earthly experience of pulling your finger from a fire, a simile that functions by inviting an embodied, enactive, dynamic memory (not a static visual picture): if the reader can retrieve a similar dynamic felt experience from memory, she will understand not only what he *means* but can also simulate the same dynamic internal body state, experiencing it for herself in an embodied way. In this ascent, the physical, the corporeal, is almost entirely invoked in support of enactive imagination, not as a reality in itself. Motoric progression from A to B is not the point: what *is* important is to participate in the same body states as the journeying Dante, co-present with him in this space, not observing him from a position outside.

The ladder itself, like Geryon, is a vehicle of travel, but rather than evoking physical interaction (the locking of the thighs on Geryon), it functions here instead as a site of spatial metaphor and relationality: Dante travels up, 'su per quella scala' (101), behind the 'collegio', 'dietro a lor' (100). But interestingly, in this paradisiacal space of ephemerality and emergence, when the ladder was first encountered in canto XXI, it was evoked in terms that leave open what seems to be a clear possibility of materiality, certainly by contrast with the other spatial features of *Paradiso*: the cross, the skywriting, the eagle. Dante describes it in the following terms:

> Dentro al cristallo che 'l vocabol porta,
> cerchiando il mondo, del suo caro duce
> sotto cui giacque ogne malizia morta,
> di color d'oro in che raggio traluce
> vid' io uno scaleo eretto in suso
> tanto, che nol seguiva la mia luce.
> Vidi anche per li gradi scender giuso
> tanti splendor, ch'io pensai ch'ogne lume
> che par nel ciel, quindi fosse diffuso. (25–33)

> Within the crystal, circling round the world,
> which bears the etymon of that dear lord —
> under whose sway all evil thoughts lie dead,
> I saw, as gold in which a ray shines through,
> a ladder stretching upwards — and so far —
> my eye-lights could not follow where it led.
> I also saw descending, rung by rung,
> so many brilliancies that every flare
> the sky displays I thought was flowing down.

Gold in colour, 'di color d'oro' (28) and stretching up as far as his eyes can see ('eretto in suso | tanto, che nol seguiva la mia luce', 29–30), the ladder is composed of rungs, 'gradi' (31) that seem very clearly to offer reciprocal feedback to the lights of the contemplatives as they dance down it, their percussive interactions with each step, 'si percosse' (42) seeming to send up a shower of sparks:

> tal modo parve me che quivi fosse
> in quello sfavillar che 'nsieme venne,
> sì come in certo grado si percosse. (40–42)

> In just that way, these sparks appeared to me,
> combining in their scintillating showers
> as each one struck upon a certain step.

Such interactions suggest materiality, inviting a special capacity for this particular ladder to be both material (as here) and immaterial (as in canto XXII). This capacity for simultaneous reality and virtuality perhaps mirrors the much more widely discussed duality of the ladder in Christian thought; Bosco, for example, commenting on 'l'immagine fisico–allegorica della scala' [the physical-allegorical image of the ladder], being both physical apparatus and signifier of the path of the Christian ascent to God.[44] My suggestion in relation to the reader's spatial experience of the journey is that this dual nature of the ladder allows and invites the reader to conceive of it as both material and virtual, both 'there' (with its percussive contemplatives) and 'here': a place she need not enter physically but can always access virtually, that is, through the imagination.

For, we might recall, Dante himself is not only in one place in the poem. The *journeying* Dante, of course, is located in this inner story world. But the *narrating* Dante is also *situated*: located not 'there', in the inner story world, but instead in his own 'here'; an outer story world, somewhere in Italy, some short time after his journey of Easter 1300. (The reader herself, of course, is physically situated in yet another 'here', her own physical reality.) And in the ascent of the celestial ladder, the narrating Dante reminds the reader very powerfully of his own 'here', with his disruptive and powerful observation of his weeping and flagellation back on earth:

> S'io torni mai, lettore, a quel divoto
> trïunfo per lo quale io piango spesso
> le mie peccata e 'l petto mi percuoto. (*Par.*, XXII. 106–08)

> So may I, reader, sometime join once more
> that prayerful march of victory (for which
> I often weep my sins and beat my breast) | [...]

Like Bernard's perspectively disruptive sign, this intrusion from another world — at a point of such powerful spatial presence in the first — seems paradoxical: a wilful threat to the reader's immersion. But again, as with Bernard's sign, I suggest this dissonant disruption has a strategic function.

This interjection from another world, I propose, opens up a space for the reader to experiment with holding different orders of reality concurrent in her mind — the real world and the virtual space of her imagination or belief — or, more accurately, in the terms of cognitive processing, switching very rapidly between them. The more the reader practices such a skill, the more adept she will become at investing equivalent mental resources to each, not privileging one as more 'real' than the other simply because it is more easily perceptible (the physical world), or disfavouring the other (any virtual world, including the afterlife) because it places a higher load on the cognitive functions, particularly the imagination.

Peter Hawkins writes of the narrating poet's interjection in this episode that it 'places Benedict's ladder and all it represents outside the sphere of fiction and into that world in which the poet writes and reader reads — the world in which we live' (1999: 243). Indeed, Hawkins talks not of the reader feeling present 'there', in Dante's narrated world; but rather of an outcome in which Dante's world is transposed to 'here', the present world of each one of us.[45] In holding the two 'reals', the material and the virtual, in balance, the reader may find that an idea of Paradise becomes accessible on earth. In Dante's deployment of the mechanics of spatial presence, then — triggering embodied simulation through narration of situated body states, and then animating that experience — I propose that the poem supports the reader in passing through a realistic experience of embodied transportation (the 'being there' of video game criticism, entering one world by leaving another behind) to a fluid, dynamic 'here' that emerges in dynamic relationship with others; feeling herself located, in Merleau-Ponty's terms, 'wherever there is something to be done' (2002: 291).

Notes to Chapter 2

1. As Beatrice will clarify in relation to Dante's mode of travel at the end of the canto: 'Non dei più ammirar, se bene stimo, | lo tuo salir, se non come d'un rivo | se d'alto monte scende giuso ad imo' [You ought not, if I'm right, be more amazed | at rising up than when you see a stream | descending from a hill's crest to its base] (*Par.*, I. 136–38). In his gloss (ll. 88–90), Hollander comments: 'He thinks of what his senses are experiencing as though it were sensed on earth.'

2. From a physical standpoint on the surface of the earth, this would infer a transgression of the diurnal cycle, the earthly natural law by which the moon appears luminously visible only once the sun has set. See Hollander (gloss on *Par.*, I. 61–63) on discussion in the commentaries regarding whether the 'altro sole' is understood as the moon (my reading here) or the sphere of fire.

3. The 'punto' is referred to at *Inf.*, XXXIV. 77 and 109.

4. Aristotle, *Metaphysics*, Book I, Chapter I.

5. This is a basic tenet of Maurice Merleau-Ponty's 1945 *Phenomenology of Perception* (Merleau-Ponty 2002). Visual perception consists of two key processes: light hits the retina and is converted into neuronal signals; the visual association cortex combines these signals and performs *inferences* derived from prior experience (such as the perspectival assumption above) in order to derive meaning.

6. See, for example, Gumbrecht's *Atmosphere, Mood, Stimmung: On a Hidden Potential of Literature* (2012).

7. Ingold proposes that: 'To progress beyond the idea that life is played out upon the surface of a furnished world, we need to attend to those fluxes of the medium we call weather. To inhabit the open is to be immersed in these fluxes. Life is lived in a zone in which earthly substances and aerial media are brought together in the constitution of beings which, in their activity, participate in weaving the textures of the land. Here, organisms figure not as externally bounded entities but as bundles of interwoven lines of growth and movement, together constituting a meshwork in fluid space' (2008: 1796).

8. Or indeed to contradict it, creating dissonance, and a trigger to stop and excavate the text.

9. Emergence is an important phenomenon in video game criticism, as well as in theories of consciousness. See, for example, the definition offered by video game and performance theorist Ragnhild Tronstad in *The Johns Hopkins Guide to Digital Media*: 'Associated with complexity and unpredictability, a general notion of emergence depicts a situation or phenomenon that evolves in a direction that could not have been predicted beforehand by studying the agents and rules involved [...]. Digital games stand out in showing a particular disposition towards emergence in its many configurations [...]. [G]ames of emergence are characterised by the combination of few and simple rules leading to varied and unexpected outcomes' (2014: 180–81).

10. International Society for Presence Research (2000), 'The Concept of Presence: Explication Statement'.

11. Cited from the section 'Presence Explicated' in their article 'At the Heart of it All: The Concept of Presence', in the *Journal of Computer-Mediated Communication*.

12. Debate is ongoing in video game criticism about the differences between immersion and spatial presence. Summarising the debate in their essay, 'Gaming and the Limits of Digital Embodiment', Farrow and Iacovides concluded: 'There is persistent ambiguity within the literature on virtual realities and games over "immersion, engagement and presence" [...], since the terms are often used interchangeably' (2013: 233).

13. IJsselsteijn writes: 'The experience of presence appears to be a complex perception, formed through an interplay of raw multisensory data, spatial perception, attention, cognition, and motor action, all coupled through a constant dynamic loop of sensorimotor correspondence [...]. The perception of ourselves as part of an environment, virtual or real, critically depends on the ability to actively explore the environment, allowing the perceptual systems to construct a spatial map based on sensorimotor dependencies. Provided the real-time, reliable correlations between motor actions and multisensory inputs remain intact, the integration of telepresence technologies into our ongoing perceptual–motor loop can be usefully understood as a change in body image perception — a phenomenal extension of the self' (2005: 25).

14. I have also focused here only on spatial evocation in the inner story world — that is, the three realms of Hell, Purgatory, and Paradise, but there is further work to be done on spatial presence in relation to the narrating Dante's outer story world.

15. In fact, Dante surpasses Beatrice's instruction, I shall suggest, privileging narration of bodily sensation (the multiple senses, or *how it feels* to be there), over external observation or what can be *seen* ('quel che vedi'), as I will discuss throughout this chapter.

16. John Freccero aligns *katabasis* with the pursuit of knowledge: 'In the ancient world, [the] descent in search of understanding was known as *katabasis*' (1986: 107).

17. See Nick Havely: 'Geryon is thus a powerful example of how, when imagining evil, Dante outdoes his traditional sources. The precariousness of his venture, balancing between due audacity and over-reaching pride, is evident in the fearful way he imagines the novelty of the experience of flight on the monster's back at the end of the Geryon canto [...]. Yet even here the poet is busy invoking and outdoing Ovid and classical myth' (Havely 2007: 163).

18. 'Io avea una corda intorno cinta, | e con essa pensai alcuna volta | prender la lonza a la pelle dipinta. | Poscia ch'io l'ebbi tutta da me sciolta, | sì come 'l duca m'avea comandato, | porsila a lui aggroppata e ravvolta. | Ond' ei si volse inver' lo destro lato, | e alquanto di lunge da la sponda | la gittò giuso in quell' alto burrato' [Around my waist I wore a braided cord, | and had on past occasion thought, by this, | to snare the leopard with its painted hide. | My leader told me I should slip this off. | And when I'd got it wound from round my waist, | I handed it across in twisted knots] (*Inf.*, XVI. 106–14). According to Virgil, at least: '"Ecco la fiera con la coda aguzza, | che passa i monti e rompe i muri e l'armi! | Ecco colei che tutto 'l mondo appuzza!"' [Behold! The beast who soars with needle tail | through mountains, shattering shields and city walls! | Behold! The beast that stinks out all the world!] (*Inf.*, XVII. 1–3). 'Come 'l falcon ch'è stato assai sul'ali, | che sanza veder logoro o uccello | fa dire al falconiere "Omè, tu cali!" | discende lasso onde si move isnello, | per cento rote, e da lunge sipone | dal suo maestro, disdegnoso e fello; | così ne puose al fondo Gerïone | al piè al piè de la stagliata rocca' [A falcon, having long been on the wing, | and seeing neither lure nor bird to prey on, | compels the falconer to sigh: "You're coming in," | then sinks down wearily to where it left so fast. | A hundred turns — and then, far from its lord, | it lands, disdainful, spiteful in its scorn. | So, too, did Geryon, to place us on the floor, | the very foot of that sheer, towering cliff] (*Inf.*, XVII. 127–34).

19. The unusual use of an extended diegetic visual description to open *Inferno* XVIII functions, I suggest, to restate narratorial authority after what I will propose to be a highly participatory ending to canto XVII.

20. 'The text representation is likely to include inferences that specify (a) spatial relations among objects, (b) goals and motivations of characters [...], and (c) causal relations among events, actions and episodes. Thus, the ability to make knowledge-based inferences is viewed as an important component of skilled reading.' (Golding, et al. 2014: 191).

21. Jonathan Usher has raised the interesting question of the poet's apparent ability in Hell to 'see perfectly well in the dark' (1982: 24), asking whether this denotes 'a strange loss of logical coherence, or whether it marked the poet's imaginative triumph over the laws of optics' (24) — with which, he points out, Dante had demonstrated his familiarity in both *Convivio* (see III 9, 5) and *Rime* (see XC). Observing how, in *Inferno* IV, the hemisphere of darkness is described as conquering the fire ('un foco | ch'emisperio di tenebre vincia', 68–69), rather than the more normative conceit of light conquering the dark, Usher concludes that a strategy is at work: 'This apparent contradiction is immensely valuable, for it allows us to grasp that Dante has made a fundamental artistic discovery: there is nothing like light for emphasising darkness. The poet is deploying the literary equivalent of *chiaroscuro*, and its effect is as dramatic as in the paintings of Georges de La Tour, where the light-source is a single candle' (27). As a result, 'perspective is foreshortened: everything happens very close to the pilgrims. They practically trip up over the inhabitants before they are able to see them' (27). I suggest that the apparent banality of the poet's adjectives in evoking spatial features in Hell, described above, is consistent with what Usher describes as a strategy of structural 'short-sightedness' in Hell: encounters are foregrounded; geographical features, the perception of which is incompatible with the 'short focal length' (27) of Hell, are visible but indistinct.

22. Notable exceptions include when his body weight troubles the still-loose stones from the landslide triggered during the Harrowing of Hell (XII. 29–30), and the craggy rock-face of lower hell with its surface tissue that requires careful manhandling, as Virgil advises: 'Sovra quella poi t'aggrappa; | ma tenta pria s'è tal ch'ella ti reggia' [Next, take your hold on that niche there. | But test it first to see how well it bears] (XXIV. 29–30).

23. In one instance, more than one system is indicated ('al viso e di sotto mi venta'), as I explore later.

24. I discuss here the original *Mirror's Edge* (DICE/Electronic Arts: 2008), Playstation 3, Xbox 360, MS Windows. A sequel, *Mirror's Edge Catalyst*, was released in May 2016.

25. See Alison McMahan's 2003 essay, 'Immersion, Engagement and Presence: A Method for Analysing 3-D Video Games'.

26. TCTNGaming ('Tony') is Serbian game blogger Nenad Krstić, who at the time of writing had over a million subscribers to his YouTube channel. Link to play-through: <https://www.youtube.com/watch?v=3v9snDQ_dV8> [accessed 16 June 2021].

27. Lombard and Ditton (1997: in the section 'Causes and Effects of Presence') suggested a range of potential mechanisms for assisting in the rendering of spatial presence in video games, all of which, I propose, merit investigation in relation to literary texts, and most of which by coincidence I already cover in this book. Their list included: image size and viewing distance, motion and colour, dimensionality variables, camera techniques, direct address to camera, rapid PoV movement, over the shoulder shots, conversation off, body movement (vection), tactile stimuli (haptic), and force feedback.

28. '*Mirror's Edge* is intended to convey realism and physical contact with the environment [...]. This is achieved not only by freely moving around the stage, but also by linking the movement of the camera with character movement, such as the speed at which the camera moves up and down to increase as Faith builds up momentum while running or turn the camera rolling when Faith does a barrel roll after landing. Moreover, the arms, legs, and torso are prominent and visibility is used to transmit motion and momentum, such as when Faith's arms go up and down and her increased stride length when walking.' *Mirror's Edge Wiki*, 'Gameplay' section (<https://mirrorsedge.fandom.com/wiki/Mirror%27s_Edge#Gameplay>, last accessed 21 September 2021). See also Chapter 4, on the mechanism of *Steadicam*.

29. I explore a notion of textual 'gappiness' in Chapter 4.

30. See, for example, on the clip at 00:01:37–00:01:41.

31. Even though the journeying Dante is not free-falling here, the narrative choice to render Geryon's style of winged descent as wheeling is highly evocative of the natural rotation of a body in free-fall.

32. See IJsselsteijn on the integration of 'telepresence technologies' into the 'perceptual–motor loop' (2005: 25; and this chapter, n. 13).

33. In relation to the souls manifesting in the sphere of the Moon, Beatrice explains: 'D'i Serafin colui che più s'india, | Moïsè, Samuel, e quel Giovanni | che prender vuoli, io dico, non Maria, | non hanno in altro cielo i loro scanni | che questi spirti che mo t'appariro, | né hanno a l'esser lor più o meno anni; | ma tutti fanno bello il primo giro, | e differentemente han dolce vita | per sentir più e men l'etterno spiro. | Qui si mostraro, non perché sortita | sia questa spera lor, ma per far segno | de la celestïal c'ha men salita' [The most in-god-ed of the Seraphim, | Moses and Samuel — and either John | you care to mention — even Maria, | none is enthroned in any other sphere | than those souls who've just appeared to you. | Nor are their years, existing, more or less. | All add in beauty to the highest gyre. | Some sense the eternal breathing more, some less. | So life is sweet to all in differing ways. | They did, here, show themselves, but not because | this sphere has been allotted them as theirs. | They signify celestial power last raised] (*Par.*, IV. 28–39). On the notion of condescension as a performative act, see Lombardi (2016: 154).

34. They are therefore 'real' in so far as the Aristotelian model of the universe was accepted to be so in medieval Italy, being material (made of ether), observable and located in time.

35. The cross, made of light, shows itself to the journeying Dante as he and Beatrice rise imperceptibly from the Heaven of the Sun to the Heaven of Mars (canto XIV), 'm'apparvero splendor dentro a due raggi' [splendour appeared to me in two crossed rays] (95), blazing out

Christ, 'quella croce lampeggiava Cristo' [that cross, in sudden flaring, blazed out Christ] (104), before lights begin to trace the shape: 'Di corno in corno e tra la cima e 'l basso | si movien lumi, scintillando forte | nel congiugnersi insieme e nel trapasso' [From horn to horn, from summit down to base, | there moved here scintillating points of light, | bright as their paths met, bright in passing on] (109–11). In the travelling of the lights, Dante highlights the mutuality and the self-reflexivity of the fleeting interconnections: '*con*-giugner-*si*' (XIV. 111; my emphasis); it is an event both of individual and mutual force.

36. In *The Syntax of Desire*, Lombardi discusses the arrangement of the blessed in the rose in terms of 'a sentence', its components arranged in order 'according to the rules of contiguity (binding) and hierarchy (government)' (2016: 172). Joseph Anthony Mazzeo has pointed out that '[t]he rose [...] undergoes transformations. It becomes successively a garden, a kingdom, an empire. As a flower it has two roots; but it also has a stairway and keys' (1958: 48).

37. The journeying Dante will not need to use his body for independent movement through the space: his motor system will not function as it does on earth. Instead, as Beatrice tells him in *Paradiso* I, the independent motile agency necessary for transportational movement on earth here gives way to the instinctual impulse of all things to return to their source, to which Dante must simply yield: 'Non dei più ammirar, se bene stimo, | lo tuo salir, se non come d'un rivo | se d'alto monte scende giuso ad imo' [You ought not, if I'm right, be more amazed | at rising up than when you see a stream | descending from a hill's crest to its base] (136–38). This represents a radical shift in thinking for the embodied human being: on earth, motor agency bears an association with effort and will, enacted in the notion of the pilgrimage, but here, such autonomous action is redundant.

38. This reciprocal action of forces is characteristic of most of the ascents, as the verb deployed usually illustrates: thus, in the sphere of the Moon, the verb 'ricevette' (II. 35) — the Moon receives them; Mercury: 'corremmo' (V. 93) — corporeal but rendered metaphorical by its inclusion within the simile of an arrow fired; Venus: an upward impulsion, 'salire' (VIII. 13) — but registered only retrospectively; the Sun: similarly, 'salire' (X. 34); Mars: of having been lifted up, 'levato' (XIV. 85); Jupiter: of having been 'collected', 'ricolto' (XVIII. 69); Saturn: of having been lifted, 'levati' (XXI. 13); Fixed Stars: of being within, 'fui dentro' (XX. 111); Primum Mobile: impelled by Beatrice's glance, 'm'impulse' (XXVII. 99); the Empyrean: having left and arrived, 'siamo usciti fore | del maggior corpo al ciel ch'è pura luce' (XXX. 38–39).

39. That is, the Biblical Jacob's ladder, as confirmed by St Benedict in the canto, echoing *Genesis* 28, 12: 'e nostra scala infino ad essa ['l'ultima spera', 62] varca, | onde così dal viso ti s'invola. | Infin là sù la vide il patriarca | Iacobbe porger la superna parte, | quando li apparve d'angeli sì carca' [Our ladder, rising, spans across to that ['the final sphere', 62], | and therefore steals in flight away from view. | Up there, to where its highest part extends, | the Patriarch beheld it all — Jacob | who saw the angels loading all its length] (*Par.*, XXII. 68–72); the ladder 'symbol [...] of the contemplation that gradually leads to contact with divinity' (Mocan 2012: 216).

40. Specifically, 'e tutti e sette mi si dimostraro | quanto son grandi e quanto son veloci | e come sono in distante riparo' [And all these seven spheres displayed to me | their magnitude, their speed, the distance, too | that lay between the dwelling place of each] (*Par.*, XXII. 148–50), within the wider narration of the episode, lines 133–53).

41. Peter Hawkins points out that in every ascent, Dante 'makes these transitions by looking into the face of Beatrice' (1999: 230). It is interesting to note that here her *cenno*, like Bernard's in *Paradiso* XXXII, as discussed in the Introduction, is an open sign of a nature that can be mentally modelled as the reader desires.

42. 'The ascent is very quick but not instantaneous; it is not like any natural motion, not even that of immediately retracting a finger from a fire, but it can be compared to this; it therefore has a duration, albeit infinitesimal.'

43. My model of Narrating Instances, outlined in the Introduction, is set out fully in Chapter 4.

44. More widely on this point, see Hawkins (1999). Note too that the poem itself alludes to the figurative or virtual manifestation in Benedict's own references to his *Rule* (*Par.*, XXII. 73–75). My narratological analysis that seeks here to foreground the mechanisms of the enactment imagination sits within a large bibliography on an historicised understanding of the visual

imagination in relation to the ladder including, particularly, Mocan (2012): specifically, on contemplation as action (197–98); contemplation as 'continual compenetration between vision, intellect, and affectivity' (199); on the influence of Richard of St Victor in relation to the *vis imaginativa* (especially 216–21); and 'a climb that turns into a flight' (223): on the twin metaphors of the ladder and flight (222–26). See also Barański (2002).

45. This finds an echo in Luke, 17: 20–21: 'And being asked by the Pharisees, when the kingdom of God should come? he answered them and said: The kingdom of God cometh not with observation. Neither shall they say: Behold here, or behold there. For lo, the kingdom of God is within you.'

CHAPTER 3

❖

Social Presence

In the previous chapter, I explored how the poem invites the reader to experience the illusion of *spatial* presence in the virtual worlds of Dante's afterlife through a mechanism of neural embodiment triggered by multi-sensory environmental feedback data in the narrative. In this chapter, my focus moves to whether and how the narration of the poem also invites the reader to feel present at the many *social* encounters of the poem through a further process of neural embodiment, in this instance linked to the mirror mechanism in the brain.

To establish some parameters in terms of how a subject may experience a virtual social encounter, I borrow from discourse analysts Clark and Carlson's model of 'hearer roles' in relation to a speech act in real life, which identified three key roles: *addressee*, *overhearer* and *participant*. I shall bracket for now the first two: *addressees*, defined by Clark and Carlson as 'the ostensible targets of what is being said' (1982: 344), to which I return in Chapter 4 in relation to the direct addresses to the reader; and *overhearers*, defined as being neither directly nor indirectly addressed but 'nevertheless listening in' (343), a position I would align with that of the epistemically immersed reader of the *Comedy*, spectating on the protagonist's encounters but not expecting to participate in the ways I set out in this book.

Clark and Carlson's third category, *participants*, is particularly relevant to a discussion of reader social presence. In their model, a participant need not be directly addressed but is nonetheless an intended recipient of the propositional content of the speech act, distinguished from overhearers in two key ways: one, if he or she feels electively addressed; and two, 'by physical arrangement' — or, in my terms, if they feel spatially co-present ('the people must be near each other relative to the space available', 346).[1] My hypothesis is that if the reader can experience the illusion of spatial presence, then she may also be able to experience the illusion of being a *participant* in social discourse in a very particular way in the medium of a narrative text.

In the 1970s, when social presence was first theorised as a communications phenomenon, Short, Williams, and Christie defined it as the degree of salience, usually understood in terms of richness of awareness, between two communicators using a communication medium (1976: 48). Face-to-face interaction was generally considered to invite the richest experience and text the least rich (65). Since then — and rapidly accelerated by the Covid-19 global pandemic that emerged in 2020 — computer-mediated interaction has revolutionised the possibilities for rich and realistic social interaction in a virtual medium, regardless of where the participants are physically located (we can see and hear one another in real time, interact in virtual groups, share documents and images, 'break out' into separate 'rooms', explore alternative realities together in games, and choose to experience these interactions as an alternative self by adopting different avatars). Consequently, definitions of social presence are in flux but have evolved to include the possibility of social presence between a human and a *virtual* other (Lee's definition of social presence as 'a psychological state in which virtual [...] social actors are experienced as actual social actors in either sensory or non-sensory ways' (2004: 45)); and between a human and a *non-human* other (Lee's 'virtual social actors' can include any 'virtual social objects' or 'other intelligences' co-located at the designated site of interaction (2004: 45)). In video game criticism terms, this allows for the illusion of realistic interaction with bots and cyborgs and other artificial intelligences. In terms of the *Comedy*, it gives us a model of social presence that can tolerate the particular and varying phenomena of the souls of the dead in Dante's afterlife.

I root my analysis of social presence in interaction theorist John Waterworth and neuropsychologist Giuseppe Riva's definition designed expressly to take account of, and apply equally to, social interactions both in the real world and in the virtual space of a mediated artefact like a video game. Crucially, their definition characterises social presence not simply as an awareness of another human being ('salience'), but specifically a recognition of the other's *intention*. They propose social presence to be:

> the sensation of 'being with other Selves' in a real or virtual environment, resulting from the ability to intuitively recognise the intentions of others in our surroundings. (Waterworth and Riva 2014: 81)

This understanding of intention is key. In real life, our interactions with others give us the opportunity to gather information by which we may come to understand, and potentially even share, their intentions — a foundational component of community. In real life, we will often achieve this through conversation: but authentic reproduction of the turn-taking mechanism of real-time conversation in a narrative artefact, from early efforts using algorithms in Interactive Fiction to procedurally generated video games, remains a challenge.[2] Indeed, in video games, believable player–character dialogic interaction has been referred to as 'the hard AI problem' (Alderman 2016). 'To properly engage in a conversation', emergence theorist Penny Sweetser has written, 'the character [in a video game] must have an awareness of the state of the game world, an attitude towards the player, a memory of previous interactions, their own motivations and goals, and appropriate reactions to the player's conversation choices' (2008: 101). Even the slightest dissonance in generated content or delivery — saying something that is not quite what you might expect a human to say in a given context — can trigger a sense of the uncanny, risking rupture of player immersion.

But as Waterworth and Riva indicate, there is another key source of data by which we may grasp one another's intention — that is, through the medium of the *body*. In the experience of social presence, they propose, this recognition of intention is 'intuitive' — that is, pre-rational, automatic, and immediate. As such, like the experience of spatial presence, it qualifies as another example of Gallese's 'direct' form of action understanding, one where 'when we see someone acting or expressing a given emotional or somatosensory state, we can directly grasp its content without the need to reason explicitly about it' (Wojciehowski and Gallese 2011: 12).

Video games focus on the *body* as the principal site of interactive social understanding between player and characters, with direct discourse currently largely restricted to character monologue or expositional dialogue in cutscenes. Emergent embodied utterance is much easier to script than believable speech, requiring, as leading video game designer Rob O'Neill has observed, only a 'small amount of performance randomness' to give the illusion of autonomous, responsive characters that are 'alive'; so there is simply less data from which internal conflict (a disruptive sense of the uncanny) might arise (2016: 239).[3] Further, it increases the player's possibility of participation in the production of meaning: she can *infer* character intention based on her reading of embodied utterance.

Commonly, in real life, this phenomenon of embodied utterance is referred to as 'body language'. In literary theory, Adam Kendon has termed it 'visible action as utterance' (2004: 2).[4] It is a phenomenon Dante explicitly recognises in *Paradiso* XXVI when he compares the way in which Adam's joy is transmitted through his dazzling 'coverta' [covering] (101), to the way an animal in a sack, for example, transmits its inner 'affetto' [feeling] (98) through the movement of the material:

> Talvolta un animal coverto broglia,
> sì che l'affetto convien che si paia
> per lo seguir che face a lui la 'nvoglia;
> e similmente l'anima primaia
> mi facea trasparer per la coverta
> quant' ella a compiacermi venìa gaia. (97–102)[5]

> A beast will sometimes wriggle in a sack,
> and so display the feelings that it has
> from how the wrapping follows what it does.
> In that same way, the first of human souls
> made me see clearly, through his covering,
> how light of heart he was to meet my will.

For Dante, the process is subjective: 'mi facea trasparer'. Literary theorist Guillemette Bolens offers a new understanding of a narrative mechanism that triggers this phenomenon of embodied simulation when we encounter narration of an embodied utterance, a mechanism she terms 'kinaesthetic empathy'. She writes:

> I cannot feel the kinaesthetic sensations in another person's arm. Yet I may infer his kinaesthetic sensations on the basis of the kinesic signals I perceive in his movements. In an act of kinaesthetic empathy, I may internally simulate what these inferred sensations possibly feel like via my own kinaesthetic memory and knowledge. (Bolens 2012: 3)

The key for Bolens is that when a gesture, posture, or facial expression is narrated, the 'kinesically intelligent reader' (2) — that is, one with the practice or habit of assimilating and responding to the narration of kinesic signals in the text — unconsciously reactivates earlier personal instances of the experiences she reads such signals as expressing. The reader reflexively finds a match between what she perceives in the character's narrated body state and a stored prior experience of her own — a process Bolens terms 'semantic retrieval' (2) — and from this she is able, 'directly', to read or infer intention in the other. Because this depends on finding a match with personal experiential data, it is subjective (we may misread, or over-read); but it also, I suggest, invites the possibility of a powerful participatory experience of social presence. We can get better at it — misread less, intuit more accurately — if we attend well, read carefully, and refine and exercise our judgment, to modify immediate reflex inferences. Imaginative simulation through the medium of a text provides one route to doing this.

In this chapter, I will suggest that in a large number of episodes in the *Comedy*, the narration invites the reader to experience an illusion of social presence at the encounters in the poem. Such an invitation is constituted through strategic narration of embodied utterance that allows the reader to empathically infer the intention of the speaker and, where strategically invited, to share in it. Not all embodied actions constitute 'utterances': walking, reaching for an object, stopping, looking can all be semantically neutral. Some are more clearly encoded, socially or culturally: raising the eyebrows, making the sign of the cross, bowing the head.[6] Some can be rendered utterance by elaboration through simile (such as, in *Inferno* XIII, 'stetti come l'uom che teme' [I stood like someone terror-struck] (45)), or a qualifier that suggests an emotional association — reaching out a hand *a little*, 'un poco', as I shall explore in this chapter in relation to the narration of a gesture in the Wood of the Suicides. I propose that the text frequently narrates not semantically neutral *actions* but instead transforms such actions into gestures, postures, gait, carriage, or facial expression, a mode of narration to which I shall refer (acknowledging my debt to Bolens) as *narration through kinaesthetic empathy*. I have mapped and quantified the instances of such narration in the poem but my primary focus here, as throughout this book, is to establish a principle — that of a strategic programme of invitations to social presence in the poem — and to set out its mechanisms in the narration.

3.1. Readable bodies in the *Comedy*

In 1929, Erich Auerbach wrote that the gestures of the figures encountered in the *Comedy* are never 'an idle display of naturalistic observation' (2001: 152). But Dante's dead — the damned, the penitential, the blessed — are not, of course, equipped with bodies in the same way that the mortal human reader understands and experiences her own body. Their souls are presently separated from their mortal body in the afterlife, and will remain so until the Day of Judgment, after which body and soul will be reunited to greater 'perfection'.[7] The souls have, nonetheless, a visible, embodied form: a shade or aerial body (although embodied utterance is largely invisible in *Paradiso* where the aerial body is sheathed in progressively more dazzling light); and, in *Purgatorio* XXV, Statius sets out how this aerial body is formed when, once 'spatially' arrived in the afterlife ('Tosto che loco lì circunscrive' [As soon as it is circumscribed by place] (88)), the soul radiates out a kind of substitute body from itself, a 'forma' (99). This 'forma' is sensible ('e quindi organa poi | ciascun sentire infino a la veduta' [And from this there will form | the organs of all sense, including sight] (101–02)), so in theory the shade or soul can still communicate via the body in such a way that intention may be intuitively recognised or inferred.[8]

But can it? In *Purgatorio* and *Paradiso*, as Webb writes, 'the aerial body permits the shades to act as persons, as if they had their animate bodies, and as individuals that can love and be loved in return' (2016: 14).[9] The journeying Dante, and the reader, can reliably read the embodied utterances of the penitents (in *Purgatorio*) and the blessed (in *Paradiso*) as authentic. But reading the bodies of the shades in *Inferno*, I suggest, is more problematic. As Webb writes, infernal bodies are 'parodic' (2016: 5): sensate but not, I suggest, communicating authentically and consonantly in the way that a mortal human being's body does. Authentic intention is communicated when word, gesture and sign generatively endorse one another — as Virgil demonstrates, for example, on the shores of Mount Purgatory when, 'con parole e con mani e con cenni' [with gestures, hands and words] (*Purg.*, I. 50), he urges the journeying Dante to demonstrate his reverence to Cato. The verbal testaments of the souls are only one element in fully grasping an intuitive understanding of the souls' condition; they must be *authenticated* through empathic reading of gesture and signs.

The poem is dense with instances of narration of embodied action, with a preliminary count suggesting some eleven hundred in total. Some are simply unqualified actions which invite no inference of emotional association, and these are often verbs of linear progression (setting off, walking, stopping). For example, compare, on one hand, the semantically neutral narration of Virgil and Dante's starting out in *Inferno* I, 'Allor si mosse, e io li tenni dietro' [He made to move; and I came close behind] (136), that narrates a physical action with, on the other hand, narration of their progress along the shore of Mount Purgatory:

> Noi eravam lunghesso mare ancora,
> come gente che pensa a suo cammino,
> che va col cuore e col corpo dimora. (*Purg.*, II. 10–12)

> We went on walking, still beside the sea,
> as people do when pondering the road.
> (Their hearts go forward, though their limbs delay.)

This second is both more elaborate but also explicitly — through the simile — invites a reading or recognition of the inner body state (glossed by Singleton as 'the proper spiritual condition of the Christian pilgrim'); and indeed, so powerful is the semantic retrieval expected to be that the reader may infer the inner body state from the outer even though, in fact, the two describe a paradox, the heart pushing ahead as the body delays.[10] But the vast majority are narrated as embodied utterances, such as when the journeying Dante lowers his eyes following Francesca's eloquent first speech, 'china' il viso' (*Inf.*, V. 110), and keeps them downturned for so long that Virgil cannot help but notice and explicitly asks for clarification: 'e tanto li tenni basso | fin che 'l poeta mi disse: "Che pense?" ' [I bowed my eyes and held them low, until, | at length, the poet said: 'What thoughts are these?'] (110–11).[11] Under Bolens's model of kinaesthetic empathy, Dante's lowered eyes are not simply propositional information about *him* and how he might have looked to the external observer at that moment in time; via semantic retrieval, the reader can access through embodied simulation his inner body state for herself — she can imagine how he *feels*.

The embodied actions of the souls are often visually evocative and memorable, and especially so in *Inferno*: the yielding passivity embodied in the lustful, wafted like birds on the wing, 'di qua, di là, di giù, di sù li mena' [This way and that and up and down they're borne] (*Inf.*, V. 43); Farinata's thrusting chest and brow in which the narrating Dante explicitly infers ('*com*' avesse') disdain in its 'as if' construction, 'ed el s'ergea col petto e con la fronte | com' avesse l'inferno a gran dispitto' [he, brow raised, was thrusting out his chest, | as though he held all Hell in high disdain] (*Inf.*, X. 35–36); Ulysses' wrenching and thrashing flame, 'come fosse la lingua che parlasse' [as though this truly were a tongue that spoke] (*Inf.*, XXVI. 89). Auerbach writes: 'they wish to speak and must speak [...]: it is their torment and effort that gives their words and gestures such compelling power' (2001: 140). But it is important not to be seduced into reflex inference by the visual alone. The bodies of the penitents in *Purgatorio* speak of greater integration between outer and inner, communicating their practices of penitence: the weeping, prostrate bodies of the avaricious amplify their barely audible verbal utterance — 'I cleave to the ground', '*Adhaesit pavimento anima mea*' (*Purg.*, XIX. 73); the sustained penitence of the gluttons in canto XXIII reveals the 'M' of the 'OMO' enscribed in their faces (the gothic 'm' in question formed, as Martinez and Durling note, 'by the arching brows and the cheekbones, along with the line of the nose' (2004: 393)).[12] And in *Paradiso,* the focus is on dynamic, relational embodied utterance; the temporary emergence of compound bodies in constant, ecstatic configuration and re-configuration. There is the cross that suddenly blazes out Christ, 'quella croce lampeggiava Cristo' (*Par.*, XIV. 104); the so-called sky-writing of canto XVIII where the souls of the Just spell out, with the dazzling intensities that constitute their visible presence, the words '*DILIGITE IUSTITIAM* [...] | [...] | *QUI IUDICATIS TERRAM*' (91–93); and the breadth and intensity of intention intuitable within the narratively economical, polysemous gesture of the smile.[13]

However, the souls account for fewer than half of all the instances of narrated embodied action in the poem. The other half, in fact, is accounted for by the journeying Dante protagonist.[14] Some of his embodied utterances may be easily recalled: his swoon at the end of *Inferno* V ('e caddi come corpo morto cade' [And now I fell as bodies fall, for dead] (142)); reaching down to touch Brunetto Latini's face, 'chinando la mano a la sua faccia' [And, reaching down a hand towards his face] (*Inf.*, XV. 29); and perhaps, too, his grief at his loss of Virgil in the Earthly Paradise, expressed through allusive narration of inner physical sensation become outer manifestation, an embodied utterance in slow-motion visible in its constituent parts — bursting into tears described as a process of ice melting in his heart and issuing through mouth and eye, 'lo gel che m'era intorno al cor ristretto, | spirito e acqua fessi, e con angoscia | de la bocca e de li occhi uscì del petto' [the ice, so tightly stretched around my core, | turned now to breath and water, issuing, | at mouth and eye, in spasms from my heart] (*Purg.*, XXX. 97–99, and then further at XXXI. 19–21). But in general, the journeying Dante's lexicon of embodied actions is much more modest and less visually memorable than that of the souls, consisting largely, as I shall explore later, of *giving attention*: pausing, turning, looking.[15]

In Hell, as the shades can be perceived to interact with place only insofar as it constitutes part of their suffering, so, I propose, the infernal shades are *not* evoked in the narration as authentically interactive social beings. The question of whether they recognise the journeying Dante as an 'intelligent other' (Lee) is moot: certainly, we might observe that they recognise a *presence*. But this recognition often seems generic, or somehow biological.[16] Francesca senses a fellow being, classified not as individual nor even person but simply as *'animal'*, in its Dantean sense of *corpo animato*, or animated body — 'O animal grazïoso e benigno' (*Inf.*, V. 88); Farinata recognises an accent, 'O Tosco' [O Tuscan] (*Inf.*, X. 22). In stark contrast to the repeated expressions of amazement and curiosity in *Purgatorio*, few in *Inferno* recognise or seem to care that the journeying Dante is still mortal.[17] Indeed, as the journeying Dante penetrates further into hell, the illusion of any kind of reciprocity in the encounters collapses altogether. Prefigured perhaps in Ciacco's marionettish squint-and-collapse routine in *Inferno* VI ('Li diritti occhi torse allora in biechi; | guardommi un poco e poi chinò la testa: | cadde con essa a par de li altri ciechi' [His forward gaze now twisted to a squint. | He stared at me a little, bent his head, | then fell face down and joined his fellow blind] (91–93)), bodies in the bottom of hell seem to participate in what might be deduced to be an on-demand, unilateral display: the journeying Dante merely the object that trips the automated performances of Maometto, Pier da Medecina, Mosca.[18] Finally, even this parody of embodied utterance fails: locked under the ice, the shades weep without being able, physically, to weep: 'Lo pianto stesso lì pianger non lascia' [They weep. Yet weeping does not let them weep] (*Inf.*, XXXIII. 94).

This reading suggests that the shades of Hell are simply not able or equipped to recognise the journeying Dante (or any passing intelligent being) as an intentional other. Not only this, they lack the integrated human 'wiring' to have or express meaningful intention. Different to empathy-enabled real human bodies (including the journeying Dante's body), the *parole*, *mani* and *cenni* of infernal bodies are not consonant and generatively endorsing. Instead, I suggest, in *Inferno* the reader is directed by the mechanisms of the text to model *not* what the parodic bodies of the damned 'say', but instead to model how the journeying Dante mediates these encounters for the reader through his own body. This distinction is directed in the text, I shall propose, through different modes of narration: one mode, narration of gesture, that invites neural mirroring of a visceral body state and triggers semantic retrieval in the reader (deployed to narrate the journeying Dante's body language); and another, narration of semantically neutral action, that invites only a visual mental model (narration of the shades in Hell). Such an analysis raises the question of why many scholars experience certain of the encounters in *Inferno* as moving and pitiable, as for example in Auerbach's reading, with W. R. Trask, of *Inferno* X, which moves him to write that '[w]hen we hear Cavalcante's outburst: non fiere li occhi suoi il dolce lome? [And are his eyes not struck by bonny light?] [...] we experience an emotion which is concerned with human beings and not directly with the divine order in which they have found their fulfillment' (Auerbach and Trask 1952: 241). My understanding based on examination of the narratological devices at work is that whilst this is a very human interpretation, it is one that *exceeds* the reading as it is directed by the mechanisms of the text, as I seek to demonstrate in the next section. Cavalcante's rhetoric is powerful, but *mani* and *cenni* do not authenticate it. The purpose of modelling *only* the journeying Dante's body states in *Inferno*, rather than experiencing social presence directly with the shades is precisely, I suggest, to protect the reader from the cloudy reflex of pity that might inhibit her progress on the journey to clear-sighted desire for God.

Moving on into *Purgatorio* and *Paradiso*, my suggestion is that the reader is next progressively invited to participate in an illusion of social presence directly with the *souls* themselves, reflexively reading and ultimately sharing in their intentions. The journeying Dante remains available as mediating body, should the reader need or want it as a model for well-judged reading of and participation in the intentions of another, but with increasing intermittence.

In the next section, I offer an example of how an invitation to social presence is set up through the mechanism I describe as *narration through kinaesthetic empathy*, through a close reading of the encounter between the journeying Dante and Pier della Vigna in *Inferno* XIII.

3.2. Narration through kinaesthetic empathy

Pressing through the Wood of the Suicides in *Inferno* XIII, Dante becomes so bewildered by the apparently disembodied cries around him that his thoughts spiral into nested inferences of people hidden in the vegetation ('Cred'io ch'ei credette ch'io credesse' [Truly I think he [Virgil] truly thought that, truly | I might just have believed] (25)), and Virgil invites him to confront his thoughts by breaking off a twig, a 'ramicel' (32), from a hawthorn bush. But when the bush shrieks and bleeds, the journeying Dante quickly discovers that the twig belongs to the vegetative embodiment of a human soul, the suicide Pier della Vigna. Poised with the twig still in his hand as Pier speaks, Dante finally lets it fall to the ground, horrified, 'come l'uom che teme' [like someone terror-struck] (45). The event is narrated as follows:

> Allor porsi la mano un poco avante
> e colsi un ramicel da un gran pruno;
> e 'l tronco suo gridò: 'Perché mi schiante?'
>   Da che fatto fu poi di sangue bruno,   34
> ricominciò a dir: 'Perché mi scerpi?
> non hai tu spirto di pietade alcuno?

> Uomini fummo, e or siam fatti sterpi:
> ben dovrebb' esser la tua man più pia,
> se state fossimo anime di serpi.'
>   Come d'un stizzo verde ch'arso sia   40
> da l'un de' capi, che da l'altro geme
> e cigola per vento che va via,
>   sì de la scheggia rotta usciva insieme
> parole e sangue; ond' io lasciai la cima
> cadere, e stetti come l'uom che teme. (31–45)

> And so I reached my hand a little forwards.
> I plucked a shoot (no more) from one great hawthorn.
> At which its trunk screamed out: 'Why splinter me?'
>   Now darkened by a flow of blood, the tree   34
> spoke out a second time: 'Why gash me so?
> Is there no living pity in your heart?
>   Once we were men. We've now become dry sticks.
> Your hand might well have proved more merciful
> If we had been the hissing souls of snakes.'
>   Compare: a green brand, kindled at one end —   40
> the other oozing sap — whistles and spits
> as air finds vent, then rushes out as wind.
>   So now there ran, out of this fractured spigot,
> both words and blood. At which I let the tip
> drop down and stood like someone terror-struck.

There are six instances of embodied character action in the narration of this event: two pertaining to Pier, and four to the journeying Dante.[19] Under the schema outlined above, I suggest that both of Pier's embodied actions are semantically neutral, unqualified actions inviting no clear inference of an emotional association that might trigger semantic retrieval in the reader. The first action is the issuing of blood; second, the issuing of words and blood. Both are narrated as straightforward observations of visual phenomena: 'Da che fatto fu poi di sangue bruno' [now darkened by a flow of blood] (34); 'sì de la scheggia rotta usciva insieme | parole e sangue' [So now there ran, out of this fractured spigot, | both words and blood] (43–44). If the damage incurred by Pier della Vigna's vegetative body seems vivid and memorable it is not, I will suggest, because there is an invitation in the narration to kinaesthetic empathy. Further, the simile that is offered to help the reader elaborate Pier's condition — the bloody verbal issue that recalls a firebrand whistling with sap (43–45) — might aid the aural imagination of the onlooker, but is just not modellable as an inner experience for the reader possessed of a human rather than a vegetable body.[20] She might be able to imagine hearing it, but not to experience for herself how it feels to whistle with sap; just as being able to imagine *seeing* something is not the same as imaginatively *experiencing* an inner body state for yourself. Pier's words, too, bear no explicit emotional charge, even if the sympathetic human reader may be inclined to read into them emotional or physical pain. Instead, Dante's narration records two requests for information ('Perché mi schiante?' [Why splinter me?] (33), 'Perché mi scerpi?' [Why gash me so?] (35)); a rhetorical question ('non hai tu spirto di pietade alcuno?' [Is there no living pity in your heart?] (36)); and a sarcastic observation ('ben dovrebb' esser la tua man più pia, | se state fossimo anime di serpi' [Your hand might well have proved more merciful | if we had been the hissing souls of snakes] (38–39)). Consistent with all the damned, as I have proposed, Pier is not able to reflexively or directly invite empathic identification in the reader. Instead, I suggest, it is the journeying Dante who mediates the opportunity for social presence for the reader in this encounter, as I shall now seek to demonstrate.

The journeying Dante's four narrated embodied actions are: reaching out his hand a little, 'Allor porsi la mano un poco avante' (31); breaking off the twig, 'colsi un ramicel' (32); letting the twig fall, 'lasciai la cima | cadere' (44); standing like someone terrified, 'e stetti come l'uom che teme' (45). Two of these are unqualified actions: breaking off the twig; then letting the twig fall (reading as directed by the text in relation to the latter in particular — that is, if we separate this action from the subsequent contextual revelation of Dante's terror). The other two I classify as Kendon's embodied action as utterance: reaching out his hand a little (a gesture) and standing like a man terrified (a posture whose associative affect is rendered explicit by the qualifying simile). I will focus on the first of these, the gesture, to explore why the narrative choice to qualify the journeying Dante's action of reaching out his hand *a little*, 'un poco', is so significant, and why I propose it to be part of a wider narrative strategy in the poem.

What is described is a very small movement — 'Allor porsi la mano un poco avante' — but its very smallness is key: the modifier 'un poco' is what transforms an unremarkable action (reaching out, as we all do every day, to pick up a cup of coffee, to take a book from a shelf) into a *gesture* loaded with potential for associative interpretation — hesitance, anxiety, trepidation. Via Bolens's process of semantic retrieval, the reader may infer how the journeying Dante feels through kinaesthetic empathy, re-experiencing a moment when she, too, reached out a hand 'un poco', anticipating that the interaction will not end well.[21]

And, indeed, it does not. The reader's empathic trepidation is paid off in the narrative thirteen lines later when the journeying Dante finally lets the broken-off tip fall to the ground, transfixed and terror-struck, 'e stetti come l'uom che teme' (45). If the reader has accessed and explored her own feelings of trepidation she is rewarded: Dante was feeling the same. The reader has just, briefly, experienced social presence in the encounter with Pier della Vigna, sharing the same affective experience or body state as the journeying Dante, as if she were there responding to Pier on her own account, an active participant rather than an onlooker.

The sheer number of instances where an action is qualified such that it is transformed into an embodied utterance inviting kinaesthetic empathy (the majority of the eleven hundred instances of narrated embodied action in the poem) leads me to propose this to be a strategy rather than narrative accident on Dante's part. But I also focus here on the example of Pier for another reason that becomes clearer when we compare Virgil's own narration of Dante's source event. In Book III of the *Aeneid*, a text Virgil will claim in *Inferno* XX that Dante knows inside out, 'tutta quanta' (114), historical poet Virgil narrates a similar event when Aeneas tears up a number of saplings that turn out to be the remains of Polydorus.[22] After Dante's horrified reaction to the train of events he set off by plucking Pier's twig, Virgil addresses Pier, 'anima lesa' (47), in a kind of *captatio benevolentiae*, saying of the journeying Dante:

> 'S'elli avesse potuto creder prima',
> rispuose 'l savio mio, 'anima lesa,
> ciò c'ha veduto pur con la mia rima,
>   non averebbe in te la man distesa;
> ma la cosa incredibile mi fece
> indurlo ad ovra ch'a me stesso pesa'. (46–51)

> 'You injured soul!' my teacher (sane as ever)
> now replied. 'If he had only earlier
> believed what my own writings could have shown,
>   he'd not have stretched his hand so far towards you.
> This, though, is all beyond belief. So I was forced
> to urge a deed that presses on my own mind still.'

Virgil says that the journeying Dante could have predicted that would happen, had he only believed, 's'elli avesse potuto creder prima' (46), what he had read in Virgil's own 'rima' (48). But the 'cosa', the thing, continues Virgil, is beyond belief, so he had to induce Dante to do the deed so that he could see for himself. But what is this 'cosa' that is 'incredibile'? For early commentators such as Buti (gloss on ll. 46–54), it was fairly straightforwardly the notion that a twig could spurt words and blood: 'It is incredible that blood and words issue from the stump'. However, Teodolinda Barolini raises a different point rooted in a premise that supposes Pier to be just as much a fictional construct as Polydorus, and therefore questions why Dante thinks his reader should believe in *his* construct of the vegetal Pier but not in Virgil's sapling-man, Polydorus. 'Why', she asks, 'is Pier della Vigna less incredible than his prototype, Polydorus?' (Barolini 1984: 212).

My suggestion is that this credibility is rooted in *kinesic narrative style*. Narration through kinaesthetic empathy, and specifically in this instance through gesture, can be believable and transformational because it is experiential (through embodied simulation); narration through unqualified action, locating the reader firmly outside the exchange as spectator, is forgettable. This is the basic tenet of experiential learning: you remember better what you experience for yourself, even if that experience is virtual, than what you are told. This, as discussed earlier, is why the journeying Dante had to be shown the 'perdute genti' for himself (*Purg.*, XXX. 136–38). But whilst the journeying Dante's encounter with Pier is narrated through *gesture*, inviting kinaesthetic empathy, Aeneas' with Polydorus, I suggest, is narrated through *action*. Consider Aeneas' account (in Latin and then McCrorie's English translation below, picking out Aeneas' key verbs of action):

> forte fuit iuxta tumulus, quo cornea summo
> virgulta et densis hastilibus horrida myrtus.
> accessi viridemque ab humo **convellere** silvam
> conatus, ramis tegerem ut frondentibus aras,

25

horrendum et dictu video mirabile monstrum.
nam quae prima solo ruptis radicibus arbos
vellitur, huic atro liquuntur sanguine guttae
et terram tabo maculant. mihi frigidus horror
membra quatit gelidusque coit formidine sanguis.   30
rursus et alterius lentum **convellere** vimen
insequor et causas penitus temptare latentis;
ater et alterius sequitur de cortice sanguis.
multa movens animo Nymphas venerabar agrestis
Gradivumque patrem, Geticis qui praesidet arvis,   35
rite secundarent visus omenque levarent.
tertia sed postquam **maiore hastilia nisu**
adgredior genibusque adversae obluctor harenae,
(eloquar an sileam?) gemitus lacrimabilis imo
auditur tumulo et vox reddita fertur ad auris: 40
'quid miserum, Aenea, laceras? iam parce sepulto,
parce pias scelerare manus. non me tibi Troia
externum tulit aut cruor hic de stipite manat.
heu fuge crudelis terras, fuge litus auarum:
nam Polydorus ego. hic confixum ferrea texit   45
telorum seges et iaculis increvit acutis'.
tum vero ancipiti mentem formidine pressus
obstipui steteruntque comae et vox faucibus haesit.
                                    (*Aeneid* III, 22–48)

[By chance a nearby hilltop was covered with copses, | cornel trees and myrtle, bristling densely | with spikes. I approached, **tried uprooting** some saplings | to cover the altar with green branches and leaflets, | and saw an omen. I shudder and wonder to tell you: | the first sapling's roots that **I tore** from the humus | began to bleed — black-red drops had already | stained and clotted the soil. A shuddering, chilling | dread ran through my body — my own blood was congealing. | Yet I tried once more. **I tore up** a second | tough shoot, probing deep for the cause of the omen. | Black-red blood flowed from the bark of the second. | Profoundly stirred I prayed to the Nymphs of that woodland, | to Lord Grandivus, presiding in Thracian farmland, | to make the omen auspicious, to lighten our vision. | But after I came to a third shoot and **engaged it** | with **greater effort, my knees in that soil resisted** — | how can I say this? or stay silent? — I heard a pathetic | moan deep in the ground, a voice restored to my hearing: | 'Why do you tear my wretched body, Aeneas? | Spare my burial! Keep your hands from pollution. | They bore me: no foreign blood runs from your sapling. | Leave this cruel shore, run from the greed of this country! | I'm Polydorus. Here an iron harvest of weapons | covered and pierced me. Now they sprout into thorn points.' | My mind teetered. Awe completely possessed me, | my hair stood up, my tongue stuck in my throat, I was speechless.]

Aeneas' actions are consistently described by Virgil as unqualified actions. The repeated verb is that of tearing up, uprooting (*convellere, vellitur*): a large, physical action but with nothing equivalent to the 'un poco' to trigger the kinaesthetic empathy that gives the reader a window into Aeneas' inner body state or state of mind, through which she might, by semantic retrieval, simulate the experience mentally for herself. And importantly, while there *is* narration of affect (and lots of it), it is divorced from the verbs of action and is even explicitly diegetic: 'I shudder and wonder to tell you' (26); 'A shuddering, chilling | dread ran through my body' (29–30); 'My mind teetered. Awe completely possessed me, | my hair stood up, my tongue stuck in my throat, I was speechless' (47–48). Inner and outer body states are not integrated and made manifest in the gestures and postures that invite mental simulation in the perceiver. The reader of the *Aeneid* may listen and observe, but she has not been given the necessary data to *model* Aeneas' body states or experience for herself. It is no wonder then, I suggest, that the journeying Dante 'was not able to believe' what happened in Virgil's text ('S'elli avesse potuto creder prima | [...] | cio c'ha veduto pur con la mia rima' [If he had only earlier | believed what my own writings could have shown], as Virgil says in *Inferno* XIII); or that he has not retained a meaningful mental simulation of the experience; and that instead he is required to experience it for himself in the Wood of the Suicides.

And finally, in the encounter in the *Comedy* we might observe that Dante points to this directly in the words he puts in his Virgil-character's mouth. The journeying Dante's gesture is initially narrated using the verb 'porgere' ('porsi la mano un poco avante' (31)), a rich verb open to figurative interpretation in medieval texts in the context of praise or instruction (*porgere lode, porgere ammaestramento*), fear or belief (*porgere paura, porgere fede*), or in acting to connote a certain type of modulated delivery that can include gesture.[23] This densely associative gestural hand movement is re-cast, in Virgil-character's subsequent *captatio* to Pier, as unqualified *action*, Virgil-character being made to use the verb 'distendere', a stretching-out rooted in the physical, in muscle and nerves: 'non averebbe in te la man distesa' (49).[24] So, when Virgil-character is made to say, essentially, 'well, on the strength of my text, he should have known that was coming', he is made to point to a limitation in his own kinesic narrative style.[25]

Peter Hawkins suggests in his essay 'For the Record: Rewriting Virgil in the *Comedy*' that Dante's interest is in a rewriting of the *Aeneid* in a new context of Christian authority:

> The *Aeneid* provides Dante with the wonder of a bleeding stalk and a voice from the beyond. The author of *Inferno* XIII, however, takes that legacy and runs with it, increasing our sense of amazement, complicating the conversation with the dead [...], and projecting the entire encounter against the theological background of Last Things [...]. Reinterpretation is finally not enough: the *Aeneid* must be rewritten. (Hawkins 2003: 85, 88)[26]

I propose that Dante rewrites Virgil's narrative event in all the ways Hawkins describes but, additionally and crucially, transforms it from a *narrative of action* to a *narrative of gesture*. It is this fundamental shift in kinesic narrative style that invites the reader to *participate* in the illusion of social presence in the interaction with Pier, not only witnessing the journeying Dante's experience but simulating the protagonist's inner experience for herself. We are not just more amazed; we engage our own personal, idiosyncratic faculties of memory and imagination in a way that helps us learn how to participate, memorably, not solely by *observing* from without, empathising, maintaining an aesthetic distance — knowledge that depends on the intellect for retention — but by imaginatively *experiencing*, recruiting the integrated embodied mind, the semantic retrieval of experiential memory, and identifying with the protagonist's experience in an agential, participatory way by recreating an experience of our own.

3.3. Progression in *Purgatorio* and *Paradiso*

In *Inferno*, I suggested that the reader learns to appreciate the condition of the soul in Hell through intuitively reading and mirroring the responses of the journeying Dante as, guided by Virgil, he progresses in understanding. His early reflexive sympathy with the shades of the lustful is partially repeated in the interaction with Pier: he experiences such pity, 'tanta pietà m'accora' (84), that he has to ask Virgil to speak for him; but by the time he encounters the bush of the unknown Florentine suicide who has just been stripped of his leaves by black dogs ('e quel dilaceraro a brano a brano', 127), at the end of the canto, his emotional response is tempered. His gesture of gathering together the leaves is poignant but bears an explicit correction: it is for love of home that Dante makes this gesture, not blind sympathy:

> Poi che la carità del natio loco
> mi strinse, raunai le fronde sparte
> e rende'le a colui, ch'era già fioco. (*Inf.*, XIV. 1–3)

> Seized, in pure charity, by love of home,
> I gathered up those scattered leaves, then bore them
> to my countryman, his voice grown dim.

Experiencing social presence with the journeying Dante, then, permits the reader to learn in parallel with the protagonist in *Inferno*. However, in *Purgatorio* and *Paradiso* there are progressively more opportunities for the reader to experience social presence directly in relation to the souls of the penitents and the blessed.

The journeying Dante is (almost) always present throughout the entire poem to channel the reader's attention: stopping, turning, looking. He gazes fixedly at Manfred, for example, 'Io mi volsi ver' lui e guardail fiso' [I turned to him and fixed him with my gaze] (*Purg.*, III. 106); turns his feet to see another narrative in the *intagli* of the *visibile parlare*, 'I' mossi i piè del loco dov' io stava, | per avvisar da presso un'altra istoria' [I turned my feet away from where I'd stood | to note another story, close at hand] (*Purg.*, X. 70–71); looks at Beatrice looking up, 'Beatrice in suso, e io in lei guardava' [Beatrice looked up. I looked at her] (*Par.*, II. 22). This arguably designates his function, in part at least, and to borrow Elena Lombardi's comment on *Purgatorio* as whole, as 'a gigantic act of pointing' (2007: 153).[27] And he is also often present as a model for kinaesthetic empathy, as set out above in relation to Pier — that is, he supports the progressive refinement of the reader's capacity intuitively to read another's intention by explicitly modelling, step-by-step, his own responses of kinaesthetic empathy with the souls.

However, he also begins to step out of the way altogether, on occasion, leaving a gap in the text that, I propose, invites the reader to directly experience social presence with the souls in her own right. I offer here two short examples to illustrate this. The first sets out how on the terraces of Pride (*Purgatorio* X to XII), the reader is progressively assisted to participate in modelling the journeying Dante modelling Oderisi's outer posture that models, in turn, Oderisi's inner condition of humility as he practices repentance of his pride. The second considers what I propose to be an invitation to the reader independently and autonomously to participate — separately from the journeying Dante — in the flush of St Peter in *Paradiso* XXVII.

In *Purgatorio* X, the journeying Dante initially struggles to identify the prideful as human, 'non mi sembian persone' (113), but Virgil guides him to recognise the breast-beating bodies under the stones: 'Ma guarda fiso là, e disviticchia | col viso quel che vien sotto a quei sassi: | già scorger puoi come ciascun si picchia' [Look, though, and fix your gaze. Let sight untwist | the vines of what comes there beneath these stones. | You see already how each beats his breast] (118–20). Through application, the journeying Dante succeeds, to the extent that by the end of the canto, he is even able to explicitly intuit verbal speech in the actions of one of them, 'e qual più pazïenza avea ne li atti, | piangendo parea dicer: "Più non posso"' [The one who, from his actions, bore the most, | appeared in tears to pant: 'I can't do more'] (138–39). Significantly, in the narration of the sequence, the narrating Dante breaks the frame not once but twice. The first time is with a direct address to the reader to engage her imagination not in the physical manifestation or form of their suffering (109), but to find in this physical enactment an intention:

> Non attender la forma del martìre:
> pensa la succession; pensa ch'al peggio
> oltre la gran sentenza non può ire. (*Purg.*, X. 109–11)

> Don't dwell upon the form their sufferings take.
> Think of what follows, and that, come the worst,
> it can't go on beyond the Judgement Day.

The second metalepsis is an invitation to humility addressed to 'superbi cristian' [proud Christians] (121) to recognise themselves and the opportunity to practise rehearsal of their own penitence here. Through these invitations, the narration has explicitly set up a model of participation for the reader in relation to the terraces of Pride and what she will encounter there over the three cantos.

Next, in canto XI, the journeying Dante explicitly models the process of kinaesthetic empathy, mirroring Oderisi's bent posture:

> e videmi e conobbemi e chiamava,
> tenendo li occhi con fatica fisi
> a me che tutto chin con loro andava. (76–78)

> He saw and recognised, then called to me,
> holding his eyes, with effort, firmly fixed
> on me, bowed down, who went along with him.

He maintains this mirrored posture, the two of them yoked up like oxen, 'Di pari, come buoi che vanno a giogo' (*Purg.*, XII. 1), until Virgil (correctively) advises him that each must find their own mode of progress, 'Lascia lui e varca; | ché qui è buono con l'ali e coi remi, | quantunque può, ciascun pinger sua barca' [Leave him and go beyond. | The best thing is that each here drives along | his craft, by oar or sail, as best he can] (4–6). But the residue of the act of modelling the posture is made explicit in the narration: the journeying Dante's inner body state has followed his outer ('souls follow bodies', in Jean Gerson's fifteenth-century formulation: see in 1998: 293), and he mentally models humility:

> dritto sì come andar vuolsi rife'mi
> con la persona, avvegna che i pensieri
> mi rimanessero e chinati e scemi. (*Purg.*, XII. 7–9)

> I made myself (as walking, one must do)
> in person stand up straight. And yet my thoughts
> remained in me stripped bare, reduced, bowed low.

Physical enactment of kinaesthetic empathy has worked for the journeying Dante: he now briefly participates in Oderisi's humility, empathically sharing his intention not only outwardly but also reflected in a mental condition of humility in his thoughts.[28]

Finally, we might take this further, as Webb has invited us to, in considering whether there is even a very rare instance here of an invitation to the reader to enact *motorically* this empathy for herself. In relation to the acrostic contained in *Purgatorio* XII's narration of the examples of pride carved into the marble pathway of the mountain, Webb points out that the repeated initial letters of each tercet that progressively spell out the word 'man', VOM, over the space of twelve tercets from line 12 to line 60, invite the reader to 'bend our necks in order to look swiftly down the sweep of the page' (Webb 2016: 103). In this way, the reader mimics the attitude of humility — '[w]e will literally bow our heads' (103) — thus participating, independently of the journeying Dante, in a facsimile of the posture of the penitents on the terraces of Pride, making a space, potentially, in which her own soul may 'follow' its body.

Different to Oderisi's humility that is so powerfully written in his posture, in *Paradiso* there is, of course, no motor gesture or posture with which to empathise kinaesthetically in order to model the inner body states of the souls of the blessed. Instead, I propose, in *Paradiso* the reader is invited to model social presence through an experience of the viscera rather than a gesture or posture: an intensity, a vivacity, that in the early cantos speaks explicitly of pleasure or ardent attention, as for example in Justinian's increasing brilliance when he comes into relation with the journeying Dante, 'ond' ella fessi | lucente più assai di quel ch'ell' era' [And this itself now shone | with far more brilliance than it did before] (*Par.*, V. 131–32), or Carlo Martello's pleasure at their interaction, 'E quanta e quale vid' io lei far piùe | per allegrezza nova che s'accrebbe, | quando parlai, a l'allegrezze sue!' [How, with new happiness, in strength and kind, | that light, when I addressed it, now increased] (*Par.*, VIII. 46–48). St Peter too, I suggest, in canto XXVII offers an exemplary modelling of *viscerality* in the form of a flush that, as Dante explains in an initial visual simile, turns him from white (the white of Jupiter) to red (Mars) — or from red to white; the possibility is left open:

> e tal ne la sembianza sua divenne,
> qual diverrebbe Iove, s'elli e Marte
> fossero augelli e cambiassersi penne. (13–15)

> And now, in how it looked, this face became
> what Jove would be if he and Mars were birds,
> and both exchanged their plumage, white for red.

His flush is contagious. St Peter himself remarks, 'Se io mi trascoloro, | non ti maravigliar, ché, dicend' io | vedrai trascolorar tutti costoro' [If I change colour now, | don't be amazed at that. For all of these, | as I go on, you'll see change colour, too] (19–21). And, indeed, all of heaven flushes with him, as Dante narrates: 'vid' io allora tutto 'l ciel cosperso' [I saw, in every part, the heavens flush] (30); Beatrice flushes, 'così Beatrice trasmutò sembianza' [so Beatrice changed in countenance] (34). The flush is rendered imaginatively enactable for the reader through two further similes: a visual simile of the cloud that paints the evening or morning sun (28–31); and, in relation to the contagion that has affected Beatrice, a visceral simile of the female innocent who flushes empathically with another's fault, 'E come donna onesta che permane | di sé sicura, e per l'altrui fallanza, | pur ascoltando, timida si fane' [And as some innocent — herself quite clean | in conscience — when she notes another's fault | may still, on hearing this, grow chaste and shy] (31–33).[29] The only participant at the event who is *not* narrated as co-participant in this global flush is, in fact, the journeying Dante himself, and his absence liberates the reader: she is invited to experience participation in social presence with St Peter and the blessed on her own account, without mediating the experience through the journeying Dante's body as model.

Indeed, in *Paradiso*, the journeying Dante is intermittently absent (I return to this in Chapter 4). We are introduced to this propensity for the narration to veil his person to the reader early on in the canticle when it is narrated that he makes clear in gesture and word, 'con atto e con parola' (*Par.*, III. 94) that he wishes to hear more of Piccarda's story; but whilst Piccarda, notionally physically co-present with him in the Heaven of the Moon, directly witnesses his gestures and words, narrative ellipsis means the reader must imagine it for herself.[30] This absence of his body allows the reader to rehearse intuiting, and sharing in, the intention of the penitents and the blessed on her own account. But it also, I suggest, creates a *gap* for independent reader participation. If the reader truly wants to participate, reading and sharing the intentions of the blessed, she needs to become highly skilled at enacting presence at the encounters of the poem on her own account. In the next chapter, I will set out more fully exactly what constitutes such gaps, and the mechanisms by which the reader is invited to fill them, through a phenomenon I describe as *self-presence*.

3.4. *Coda*: The language of praise

There is a further point to which I would like to gesture in relation to social presence, and that is the question of *reciprocity*. I do not include this discussion in the body of this chapter because it is part of a different and much wider discussion of the language of *praise*, into which I do not enter here, but I would like at least to note it as offering considerable scope for further research on the *Comedy* in working with theories relating to AI, emergence and generativity in video game critical theory. In this chapter, I have focused on how a subject (the journeying Dante, or the reader) may intuitively recognise the intention of another person. But in real life, social presence is reciprocal: we expect not only to understand the other, but to have the other reciprocally engage in understanding us. Conversation — the turn-taking model of oral discourse — is the most obvious way in which this is achieved. And Calleja, as discussed in Chapter 2, defines true interactivity in an artefact as 'having one's [...] presence [...] acknowledged by the system itself' (2011: 22). In video game criticism terms, conversation is generative and is an emergent behaviour, different every time, in dynamic relation to the input of others, 'producing many outcomes, each conforming to the same overall guidelines', in Ian Bogost's words (2007: 4). The experience of social presence as I have set it out here takes account, then, of only half of the potential for participatory interaction in the social encounters of the text.

But how is the reader of a text to communicate reciprocally her intention in turn, if even AI cannot find a solution to this? Dante, I suggest, astonishingly, is able to offer us a model, one that requires a shift in thinking similar to that observed in relation to place in Chapter 2 — from place as fixed and material, to place as relational and emerging temporarily as the site of dynamic interaction. Singleton refers to a 'change in gravitation' in the reader's understanding, using the term (in his commentary) in relation to the description of the 'inverted snowstorm' in *Paradiso* XXVII: 'the swarm of bright lights [that returns] to the Empyrean — "just as our air flakes downward with frozen vapours" in midwinter when the sun is in Capricorn' (gloss on *Par.*, XXVII. 67–72). He continues: 'These inversions [...] are contributing to an experience which the reader will undergo as he passes, with the pilgrim Dante, from time to eternity, from the universe with earth at the centre to a universe that has God at its centre: a complex change in gravitation, from the material to the spiritual'.

In *Paradiso*, my suggestion is that such a 'change in gravitation' is required to reconceptualise a notion of human discourse. We may commonly conceive of speech as the locus of emergent meaning in communication: the subject expresses herself through a system of language that allows her to combine words in conventional ways such that she can set out what she means.[31] The oral verbal utterance — the combination of words — constitutes the emergent element of communication, being different every time. In the poem, Dante invites the reader — as video games do — to become more alert to *embodied* utterance. The external sign is economical (there is a smaller lexicon of embodied utterances than is supported in language), but the process of semantic retrieval in the reading of such utterances relocates the site of emergence, I suggest, inwards: my internal body state — how I feel when I read your embodied utterance — is unique to that specific interaction. Other observers will experience their own internal body state in response.

And in Paradise, other than when the condescended souls are exceptionally in conversation with the journeying Dante, the mode by which intention is shared is a generative, authenticating combination of the physical (dance), the visceral (generative *ardore*; 'caldo suo caler', *Par.*, XXXI. 140), and the verbal (choric praise: psalms, hymns, prayers).[32] In *Paradiso*, we communicate reciprocally by manifesting that we *share* the communal intention. Different to mortal speech, what the reader progressively comes to experience for herself in *Paradiso*, I suggest, is that whilst the utterances of praise are choric and scripted (psalms, hymns, prayers), it is the *inner* body state, the individual inner conversation with God, that is the locus of emergence: individual, dynamic, different every time, in every interaction with divine love.

Notes to Chapter 3

1. In relation to feeling 'electively' addressed (my term), Clark and Carlson suggest this is triggered in real life situations 'by the history of the ongoing conversation': if the subject has felt addressed in the past, and there is no indication to the contrary, 'they can assume' continuing participation (1982: 346). I discuss in Chapter 4 how this might work in relation to a virtual interaction, but for the purposes of my discussion here in relation to social presence I take advantage of an innovation by cognitive theologian Kirsten Marie Hartvigsen. She transforms Clark and Carlson's model from one of 'speaker intention' to one of 'elective audience participation' in her analysis of audience involvement in an oral performance of the Gospel of Mark. On the basic premise of audience participation, she writes: 'From the position they construct for themselves in the conceptual world, audience members are allowed to hear most speech acts [...] [and] will probably process them as if they are side-participants who are intended to hear these speech acts. Consequently, *they are informed by these speech acts, but they will not respond by attempting to carry out the suggested actions* [...]. Audience members who are not transported to the narrative world may also process speech acts uttered by characters as side-participants [...]. Because these audience members are not immersed in the narrative world, they will not consider the possibility that they are addressed by these speech acts' (Hartvigsen 2013: 64; my emphasis).

2. In *Persuasive Games*, Ian Bogost explains: 'To write procedurally, one authors code that enforces rules to generate some kind of representation, rather than authoring the representation itself. Procedural systems generate behaviours based on rule-based models; they are machines capable of producing many outcomes, each conforming to the same overall guidelines' (2007: 4). Further: '[the arguments of] procedural rhetoric [...] are made not through the construction of words or images but through the authorship of rules of behaviour, the construction of dynamic models' (29).

3. O'Neill writes: 'Unlike blended animation, all motion [for 'fully procedural characters'] is procedurally generated, so the engine never produces the repetitiveness seen in game engines that call the same mocap [motion capture] clips over and over. The small amount of performance randomness gives the character more of a sense of being alive, in that the same action will be performed differently every time' (2016: 239).

4. Kendon refers specifically to gesture but, in this chapter, I will seek to extend his definition to include other related phenomena: posture, carriage or gait, and facial expression. Further, Denys Turner writes that '[o]ur bodies are caught up into language whether we like it or not, which is why bodies are something we have to read' (2010: 291).

5. In their gloss (ll. 97–102), Durling and Martínez point to the openness of the simile (helpfully, for my later discussion of semantic retrieval), noting that '[s]ome commentators see a hooded

hawk or caparisoned horse implied, but Dante's language is generic'. Chiavacci Leonardi sets out the same argument in her own gloss (ll. 97–102, *nota integrativa*), concluding that 'in our opinion, the comparison is deliberately indeterminate', and that 'it is not a matter of a "bizarre simile" ['similitudine bizzarra'] (Sapegno), but in fact the most precise possible, as Poletto observes'; and precisely because, her interpretation seems to suggest, its indeterminacy requires the reader to focus on the movement itself and its effect rather than visualising the nature of the animal.

6. Webb has written extensively on the reading of gesture and posture in the poem, both in her 2013 essay 'Postures of Penitence', and in *Dante's Persons* (particularly Chapter 2, 'Gestural Persons'). In the latter she writes: 'I would suggest [...] that the gestures of persons as narrated in the *Comedy* are intended not only to be shown to act upon and together with the group that surrounds them within the frame of the narration; the gestures are intended to act upon us as readers in particularly compelling ways, bringing us into the space of the event' (Webb 2016: 35).

7. Dante follows Aquinas, who follows Aristotle, on natural perfection: 'Anima autem, cum sit pars humanae naturae, non habet naturalem perfectionem, nisi secundum quod est corpori unita' [Now the soul, as part of human nature, has its natural perfection only as united to the body] (Aquinas 1912: 256). In Virgil's terms as expressed in the poem (*Inf.*, VI. 94–111), this means feeling an absolute (good, pain) more intensely; in Solomon's terms, set out in *Paradiso* XIV, it means an intensification related to a generative expression and experience of love: 'Tanto mi parver sùbiti e accorti | e l'uno e l'altro coro a dicer "Amme!" | che ben mostrar disio d'i corpi morti: | forse non pur per lor, ma per le mamme, | per li padri e per li altri che fuor cari | anzi che fosser sempiterne fiamme [So ready and alert they seemed to me — | those double choirs — to add their plain 'Amen' | they showed their keen desire for long dead bones, | not only for themselves but for their mums, | their fathers, too, and others dear to them, | before they were these sempiternal flames] (*Par.*, XIV. 61–66); the souls desire their bodies not just for themselves but for those they love — that is, *in relation* (this is what Dante's mediated Virgil forgets).

8. But the sensible *forma* has no material substance as manifested in the failed embraces in *Purg.*, II. 78–81, and a limited capacity for autonomous motor agency (see Chapter 2). For a full exploration, see Manuele Gragnolati, who notes Dante's innovation in this respect: 'Dante goes further than Aquinas and does not wait for the resurrection in order to reactivate the "human" part of the person' (2003: 200).

9. See Webb (2016: 22–23) for more on her analysis of the aerial body. Kirkpatrick writes: 'In *Paradiso* [...], human beings are *being* human — displayed, that is, through their activities rather than in pseudo-monumental attitudes of self-aggrandisement' (2010: 24). See also Lombardi (2016: 170). On corporeal realism in *Paradiso*, see Hooper (2017: especially 292–95).

10. As discussed in relation to Bolens's semantic retrieval, there is often an element of subjectivity in classifying an embodied action as simply action or as 'utterance'. Singleton, gloss on *Purg.*, II. 11–12.

11. The journeying Dante, we might recall, makes explicit his reflexive pity for the shades, saying: 'Oh lasso | quanto dolci pensier, quanto disio | menò costoro al doloroso passo!' [Alas, | how many yearning thoughts, what great desire, | have led them through such sorrow to their fate?] (*Inf.*, V. 112–14).

12. 'Com' io nel quinto giro fui dischiuso, | vidi gente per esso che piangea, | giacendo a terra tutta volta in giuso. | "*Adhaesit pavimento anima mea*" | sentia dir lor con sì alti sospiri, | che la parola a pena s'intendea' [Now loosed out on to circle number five, | I saw there people all around who wept, | each turned face downwards, lying on the earth. | "*Adhaesit pavimento anima mea!*" | I heard them say this, but sighing deep | so what they said was hardly understood] (*Purg.*, XIX. 70–75). 'Ne li occhi era ciascuna oscura e cava, | palida ne la faccia, e tanto scema | che da l'ossa la pelle s'informava | [...] | Parean l'occhiaie anella sanza gemme: | chi nel viso de li uomini legge "omo" | ben avria quivi conosciuta l'emme' [Each one was dark and hollow round the eyes, | pallid in feature, and so gaunt and waste | their skin was formed to show the very bone | [...] | The sockets of their eyes seemed gemless rings, | and those who read Man's 'OMO' in Man's face | would clearly have seen 'M' in all of these] (*Purg.*, XXIII. 22–24 and 31–33).

13. The cross blazing out Christ is notably coincident with the narrating Dante's invocation to any

follower of Christ just two lines later, 'ma chi prende sua croce e segue Cristo' [But those who take their cross and follow Christ] (106), suggesting an invitation to the reader to electively identify with 'those who...', a principle of participation I discuss further in Chapters 4 and 5. The sky-writing, too, is arguably another metaleptic invitation to the reader to electively identify and participate. The many instances of the smile and laugh in *Paradiso* include that which is readable in Piccarda's laughing eyes, 'occhi ridenti' (*Par.*, III. 42); in Cacciaguida's otherwise-hidden person (*Par.*, XVII. 36); Mary's smile (*Par.*, XXXI. 134); Bernard's (*Par.*, XXXIII. 49); and, of course, Beatrice's (including *Par.*, II. 52, III. 24, VII. 17, X. 61, XV. 71, XVI. 14, XVIII. 19, XXV. 28, XXVII. 96, XXIX. 7, XXXI. 92).

14. The souls account for 40 per cent; Beatrice for 5 per cent; and the highly gestural Virgil for a further 9 per cent. The journeying Dante accounts for 46 per cent.

15. For a discussion of giving attention in the poem, see Webb (2016: 123–63).

16. This is a quality we might associate with the most elementary of Antonio Damasio's three levels of the self in human consciousness, the *proto-self*: 'a [temporarily] coherent collection of neural patterns which map, moment by moment, the state of the physical structure of the organism in its many dimensions' (Damasio 2000: 154). Damasio's model, I suggest, offers potentially interesting grounds for further exploration of selfhood and social presence in the poem in its contrasting of the proto-self with a 'core' and an 'autobiographical' self.

17. For example, in *Purgatorio*, the newly arrived souls on the shores of the mountain collectively blanche at the realisation that the stranger is a mortal man (II. 67–69), drawing back at the sight of his shadow (III. 88–91); or the 'Miserere' that turns to an 'oh!' of surprise (V. 22–27). In *Inferno*, Phlegyas is one of the few to acknowledge his condition, 'Chi se' tu che vieni anzi ora?' [So who — you come too soon! — are you?] (*Inf.*, VIII. 33), but immediately inauthenticates his apparent curiosity by showing no interest in reciprocal exchange, wanting to talk only about himself: 'Vedi che son un che piango' [Just look at me. I'm one | who weeps] (36). The narrating Dante reports that the protagonist is recognised by Brunetto Latini, 'fui conosciuto da un' [I now was recognised, as known, by one] (*Inf.*, XV. 23); Bertran de Born recognises (albeit without any curiosity) that Dante is still alive, 'tu che, spirando, vai veggendo i morti' [Breathing you go still, watching on the dead] (*Inf.*, XXVIII. 131).

18. Pertile seems to nod towards a similar idea: 'What is deeply disturbing is the relentlessness of the conditions in which victims and tormentors are *caught by the eye of the passing visitor*: the notion that, for instance, Count Ugolino will always gnaw at the skull of Archbishop Ruggieri' (2015: 499; my emphasis).

19. Consistent with my parameters throughout this chapter, I exclude from the analysis Pier's two *verbal* actions of shouting (33) and speaking (35); these, too, are unqualified actions.

20. Spitzer writes: 'The fact that Dante chose to describe a hissing, guttering fire-log by way of characterising the genesis of speech in his *uomini-piante* shows that he conceived this as representing a purely physical process: the issue of blood and cries is on the same low "material" level as is the issue of sap and hissing sound from a fire-log' (Spitzer 1942: 89).

21. For a further reading of the neurological impact of 'un poco' here, see Matthew Reynolds (2020: 121).

22. Virgil says: 'Euripilo ebbe nome, e così 'l canta | l'alta mia tragedìa in alcun loco: | ben lo sai tu che la sai tutta quanta' [By name Eurypylus, there is some verse | in my great tragedy that sings of him. | But you'll know where. You know the whole thing through] (*Inf.*, XX. 112–14). In the sequence with Pier, the journeying Dante is depicted explicitly in the narration as *reader* of Virgil's text, so we might want to pay very careful attention to how he models this process of reading for us. Spitzer observes that in fact Dante borrows here from both Virgil and Ovid; the transformation of man into sapling 'is not Virgilian: Polydorus does not become the myrtle tree' (1942: 83).

23. Definition of 'pòrgere' from <http://www.treccani.it/vocabolario/porgere/> (accessed 21 September 2021).

24. Definition of 'distèndere' from <https://www.treccani.it/vocabolario/distendere/> (accessed 21 September 2021).

25. Referring to the first meeting of Dante and Virgil in *Inferno* II ('tu duca, tu segnore e tu maestro'

[You are my lord, my leader and true guide], 140), Elena Lombardi writes of a 'submissive relation between pupil and guide [that] conceal[s] the sadistic dismantling of the old author by the new one' (2010: 143). The gesture of the outstretched hand may also invite the reader to find here a further telling intertextual resonance of the Gospel of John, when Jesus appears to Thomas and invites him to reach out his hand to experience for himself the tactility of the nail mark in his side (John 20: 24–29).

26. See also Marchesi (2011: 15–16). Further, Hawkins writes that Dante 'used an old world [Virgil's] to construct something new, something that answered the call of *moderno uso*' (2005: 184).

27. My own analysis suggests that in *Purgatorio* pointing evolves to indicate full relationality: from initial self-identification (Manfred pointing out his wound, III. 111), to recognition of the co-presence of an intelligent other (an unnamed soul points at the journeying Dante, realising he is mortal, V. 3), to triangulating one individual with another individual through a deictic form of joint attention (Guido pointing out Arnaut Daniel to the journeying Dante, XXVI. 116). For further discussion of joint attention, see Chapter 5 in this book.

28. Chiavacci Leonardi (gloss on l. 9): 'even if the body has straightened up, the thoughts, that is, the soul, remains bowed, that is, humbled and diminished [*scemi*], that is, devoid, emptied, of the vain pride with which it was previously filled [sic]'. Hollander (ll. 7–9) introduces the notion of *recognition* — that is, in my terms, a bringing to consciousness of a pre-rational phenomenon: '[i]n other words, even if he has finally straightened up and begun walking as a confident human being, his thoughts remain bowed under the burden of the recognition of his pridefulness'.

29. Hollander (gloss on l. 13) comments: 'What probably makes the passage more difficult than it really should be is the adjective *timido*, understood by the early commentators as "ashamed" (a word readily associated with blushing), while modern ones think it means "timid" (an adjective more likely associated with facial pallor).' His interpretation makes the empathic reading I suggest easier still, whilst an understanding of 'timida' as 'timid' would conflict more with a kinaesthetically empathic reading. Kirkpatrick's translation eradicates this problem for his reader.

30. 'Ma sì com' elli avvien, s'un cibo sazia | e d'un altro rimane ancor la gola, | che quel si chere e di quel si ringrazia, | così fec' io con atto e con parola, | per apprender da lei qual fu la tela | onde non trasse infino a co la spuola' [But then, as often happens over food | (though satisfied with one, we crave the next, | reaching for that while still we're saying 'thanks'), | so now in word and gesture I betrayed | an eagerness to hear from her what weave | her spool had not yet drawn out to the end] (*Par.*, III. 91–96).

31. Both expression and understanding are of course imperfect and approximate, since speech, being based in signs, is a mediated form of communication.

32. In relation to Justinian's explanation in *Paradiso* VI that 'diverse voci fanno dolci note' [As, differing, voices sing a sweet-tuned chord] (124), Lombardi writes: 'Being part of such a choir, the voices of the blessed are a mere recreation tool (a "trastullo") in heaven' (2016: 153).

CHAPTER 4

❖

Self-Presence

This chapter explores whether and how the poem actively seeks to make the mental model of the narrated journey particularly personal to the individual reader, setting out a number of narratological devices in the poem that in combination, I propose, invite an experience of the perceptual illusion of *self-presence*.

Self-presence has been defined in somewhat broad terms by presence theorist Kwan Min Lee as 'a psychological state in which a virtual [...] self/selves [is/]are experienced as the actual self' (2004: 46). Literary theory has traditionally engaged with a subjective experience of *identification* with a protagonist; but identification has also eluded tight definition, especially in terms of the mechanics that invite it, and its cognitive complexity is encapsulated in the observation of *Nouvelle critique* theorist Georges Poulet that 'whenever I read, I mentally pronounce an *I*, and yet the *I* which I pronounce is not myself' (1969: 54).

My interest in this chapter is to explore, in narratological terms, whether it is in some way possible to 'participate' in the 'io' of the text through the construction of a perceptual illusion of self-presence. In the absence of a clear definition of self-presence for textual literary theory, I seek to approach one through examination of the mechanics in the poem that, in my terms, invite a particular form of embodied reader identification. I identify two particular narrative strategies in the poem that I propose open the way for this.

The first explores the poem's treatment of *narrative perspective* that builds into the 'io' of the text a strategic mutability that, I suggest, opens up a space for the reader (my *narrating instances* model) and that further invites the reader to participate in the illusion that she can look around in the virtual space, receiving narrated visual data as though she were turning her own head (a mechanism I term *narration through mobile camera view*).

The second, exploring the handling of *narrative mediation* in the poem, is related to affective devotion's model of personal imaginative elaboration, as set out in Chapter 1 and, I propose, radically extends it. I consider a new reading of the *direct addresses to the reader* as constitutive of just one end of a continuum of invitations to participate that establishes a model of participation through conscious, guided cognitive activity invited in the second-person voice. Then, in line with Karnes's new reading of the gospel meditations as serving a *cognitive* function through recruitment of the imagination as a 'trainable tool', I suggest that such cognitive participation is rendered habitual and intuitive through a sequence of *narrative training* exercises that progressively refines a 'fully activated imagination' (2011: 177). At the other end of this continuum of invitations, I propose, is the vast network of gaps in the text constituted by the poem's similes and narrative ellipses, which the reader may *elect* to 'fill', or imaginatively elaborate, to a greater or lesser degree depending on her habit, motivation, and cognitive skill.

Again, I shall suggest that video game critical theory might be useful for thinking about self-presence in a text. I put forward two reasons. First, as noted in Chapter 3, in theoretical discussions of the avatar, or playable character, video game critical theory tends to foreground the notion of identification with the *body* of the protagonist as the interface through which the player participates in the events and interactions of the virtual space. I propose that this helps us separate the effects of embodied identification, explored here in my concrete focus on narratological mechanisms, from more slippery philosophical questions of selfhood and consciousness. Gee, as noted in my Introduction, proposes that the avatar 'is a surrogate body for the player in the game world [...], [determining] what and how the player can see and sense in the game world' (2015: 17). Cultural and literary theorist Kris Pint writes that by controlling the avatar, 'a gamer can "incarnate" in cyberspace, and is able to perform a set of actions in a world he cannot physically enter' (2012: 5). Through Gallese's *embodied simulation*, we understand the processes by which we can neurologically identify with another's body (experiencing a 'shared motor code', in Gallese's terms) in the medium of a narrative artefact, as already set out in relation to spatial and social presence in Chapters 2 and 3. I use this model again here to explore how a perceptual illusion related to the reader's visual sensory perception in the virtual space may help to invite an experience of self-presence.

The second reason is that video game theory helps us think about individual subjectivity as being not static and fixed but dynamic and ceaselessly constituted in relation to others. Debate has opened up in video game criticism around the question of whether the player somehow 'merges' her identity with the notional identity of the avatar (Gee's stance (2015: 94)), or whether in fact a gap is maintained between player and avatar, as Tom Boellstorff proposes (2011: 513). The key insight for my argument here is born of Boellstorff's suggestion that it is the 'movements across' this gap that constitute the player's virtual experience. He writes:

> There is a clear and ontologically foundational gap between an avatar and an actual-world person [...]. Ideas, metaphors, power relations, and even forms of materiality routinely move across this gap between the virtual and the actual, but it is the gap and attendant movements across it — works of *techne* — that make the virtual possible at all. (2011: 513)

My suggestion in this chapter is that the narration constantly invites precisely such movement between the virtual and the actual through the mechanism of the highly mutable 'io' of the poem, and that this is the basis of self-presence in the *Comedy*: an experience of the reader's own selfhood in the virtual space that is constantly in balance with embodied identification with the protagonist's experience as the text invites her to continuously switch between the two.

4.1. Narrative perspective

In this section, I set out two new narratological models relating to *narrative perspective*. The first is a new model of *narrating instances*, rooted in Genette's theory of the same name but designed specifically for the *Comedy*, that exposes four different 'faces' of the narrating Dante character. I propose that the constant cycling through this subtle multiplicity of standpoints prevents the reader from simply *identifying* with the journeying Dante and instead opens up, in a foundational way, a model of reader participation in the poem. The second is a mechanism of narrative perspective that I have borrowed and developed from film theory, and that I term *narration through mobile camera view*. I propose that through strategic direction of the reader's line of sight, and a periodic strategy of narration that constantly brings new objects into view, Dante intermittently invites the reader to participate in an illusion that she has the ability to turn her own head in the space of the virtual environment, powerfully reinforcing the illusion of an experience of personal agency.

In the 1970s, narratologist Gérard Genette distinguished within the mechanism of narrative perspective two central components, *voice* and *mood*, seeking to mitigate what he referred to as 'a regrettable confusion [...] between the question *who is the character whose point of view orients the narrative perspective?* and the very different question *who is the narrator?* — or more simply, the question *who sees?* and the question *who speaks?*' (1980: 186; emphasis in original).

The question in the *Comedy* of 'who speaks?' is relatively straightforward. The poem is narrated in the first person; in the terms of discourse analysts Labov and Waletzky, it is a 'personal experience narrative' (1967: 3). Along with many critics, we might note the immediate surprise of the poem's opening line that uses the first person plural — 'Nel mezzo del cammin di *nostra* vita' [Midway through the journey of *our* life] (my emphasis) — but this instantly resolves in the next line into the first person singular, '*mi* ritrovai' [I came around], that will sustain the trajectory of the poem. This is a resolution into authoritative personal testimony that is reinforced with a repeated 'io' and a spatially locating 'vi': 'ma per trattar del ben ch'i' vi trovai, | dirò de l'altre cose ch'i' v'ho scorte. | Io non so ben ridir com' i' v'intrai [...]' [But since my theme will be the good I found there, | I mean to speak of other things I saw. | I do not know, I cannot rightly say | how first I came to be here] (*Inf.*, I. 8–10).

This first-person voice is attached to a specific character, the narrating Dante, who has an identity (the returned journeying pilgrim, now scribing poet); a geographic location (somewhere in Italy) that constitutes an outer story world different to the inner story world of the three realms of the afterlife; a temporal location (beginning soon after his return from his journey in Easter 1300 and ending presumably before the author's historical death in 1321); and, intermittently, evidence of a sentient body as he imaginatively relives the emotional and physical rigours of his journey with the renewed visceral and cognitive reactions this engenders (for example, 'Ahi quanto a dir qual era è cosa dura | esta selva selvaggia e aspra e forte | che nel pensier *rinova la paura*!' [How hard it is to say what that wood was, | a wilderness, savage, brute, harsh and wild. | Only to think of it *renews my fear*] (*Inf.*, I. 406;

my emphasis)). The narrating Dante speaks a great deal (his narration accounts for almost half the verses of the poem) and he sometimes speaks metaleptically, addressing the reader, 'lettor', directly.[1]

Importantly, the narrating Dante is not identical in terms of voice with the journeying Dante. The journeying Dante never 'speaks' in Genette's sense of narrative voice. Instead, he can speak *only* through the medium of direct discourse when cited verbatim by the narrating Dante (for example, on meeting Virgil in *Inferno* I: '"Miserere di me", gridai a lui, | "qual che tu sii, od ombra od omo certo!"' [I screamed my *Miserere*: "Save me, | whatever — shadow or truly man — you be"] (65–66)) — and he does so relatively rarely, averaging only eleven lines of direct speech per canto.[2] (He can also 'speak' by inference through his readable body states, which he does much more commonly, as discussed in Chapter 3.) But whilst the journeying Dante protagonist is ostensibly identical with the narrator in terms of mortal human *persona* (the same person but pre-'evental', in William Burgwinkle's term (2012: 15)), the journeying Dante is *not* a first-person character; in common with all the souls in Dante's afterlife, he is narrated as a third-person character.

As discussed in the Introduction, this construction gives the author the device of a frame narrative, with its resulting temporal and spatial flexibilities. He has two story worlds between which to switch: the *outer* story world of the scribing location in Italy, and the *inner* story world of the three realms of the afterlife. There is both a *closed* event in the journey through the afterlife, now completed; and a *still-open* event, that of the narrating Dante imaginatively re-constructing those earlier events through the process of writing them down. And there are two 'Dantes': a post-evental Dante, who has seen and experienced everything involved in the journey to the divine encounter, and to whom I refer as the *narrating Dante*, and a pre-evental Dante, the travelling pilgrim or my *journeying Dante*, who as a mortal man, at any one point in time, is possessed of all and only the knowledge that it has been possible for him to accumulate on his journey. The strategic deployment of these varying sight and knowledge privileges is something Genette's notion of 'mood' — 'who sees?' — can help us better understand.

Mood is perhaps most readily understood as an effect of the 'eyes' in the narrative through which the reader is shown events and encounters. However, since all human perception, including the visual, is partial and subjective, the reader's perception of events is necessarily coloured at a reflexive or pre-rational level by the knowledge, beliefs, and assumptions of the character through whose eyes she is seeing. Mood, as described by Genette, is an *effect*; the mechanism by which it is achieved is focalisation, so, from here, consistent with my approach throughout this book, I refer not to the effect but to its mechanism, *focal view*.

In the *Comedy*, there is only one narrating voice (the narrating Dante's) but there are two focal characters: the narrating Dante and the journeying Dante. When the reader's gaze is mediated through the *narrating Dante* as focal character, she observes the narrated world, the journeying Dante protagonist, and his encounters, from an external position of apparent omniscience. A particularly powerful example of this focal view is the rare example of extended diegesis in the sequence that opens

Inferno XVIII where, from a God's-eye view, the narrating Dante sets out the plan of Malebolge, beginning: 'Luogo è in inferno detto Malebolge, | tutto di pietra di color ferrigno, | come la cerchia che dintorno il volge' [There is in Hell a place called Rottenpockets, | rock, all rock, its colour rusted iron, | as is the wall that circles all around] (1–3), and extending over six tercets, before a return to the present narrative action at line 20: 'e 'l poeta | tenne a sinistra, e io dietro mi mossi' [The poet | took the left-hand fork. I followed in his track] (20–21). But action is also focalised for the reader through the eyes of the *journeying Dante* protagonist himself, who has the restricted, subjective sight of a normal mortal human being, and whose focal view invites the reader to feel as if she is located inside his head, strongly identifying with his subjective perceptual experiences and internal feelings. For example, in *Inferno* III, as the journeying Dante hears the laments of the shades as he and Virgil pass through the gates of Hell, the reader has access to his inner state, through the evocative detail of his head feeling banded with the horror of his experience: 'E io ch'avea d'orror la testa cinta, | dissi [...]' [I turned, my head tight-bound in confusion, | to say] (31–32); or in *Paradiso* XV, when he encounters Cacciaguida and, on reading Beatrice's smile, feels his will strengthen: '[Beatrice] arrisemi un cenno | che fece crescer l'ali al voler mio' [She smiled me such a sign | that made the wings of will in me grow strong] (71–72). The reader, then, can see through the journeying Dante's eyes (journeying Dante focal view), but she can also observe him very powerfully from outside (narrating Dante focal view). This means that sometimes she can *identify* with him and his experience; but equally, sometimes she can maintain *her own* identity in the narrated space. Her opportunities to identify directly with the journeying Dante protagonist are essentially controlled, mediated through the narrating Dante.

Further, what the reader perceives in the virtual world of the narrative is dependent at any one time on what the specific focal character *knows* (*knowledge privileges*), what and how much the focal character can physically *see* (*sight privileges*), as well as how the focal character responds to or perceives what is encountered. Together, these elements subtly shape the reader's response to what is shown by affording different knowledge and sight privileges, but all mediated through the sole first-person voice of the narrating Dante.

And whilst a change in voice would be obvious and easy to identify — if Virgil or Beatrice were to take over the narration, say (which of course never happens) — switches in focal view generally go unnoticed by readers, at a conscious level at least, becoming perceptible only when their deployment is dissonant, as discussed in the Introduction in relation to Bernard's sign. But skilful handling of focal view shifts allows the writer to weave into the narration variations in privileges of sight, knowledge and tone, manoeuvring the reader into instinctively shifting, cognitively, into a corresponding relational space. It is this mechanism, I suggest, that allows Dante to convey both deep authentic, personal experience, and total authoritative omniscience through the same narrative voice.

So how can the authoritative omniscience of the focal view that, in the first line of *Inferno*, situates the protagonist as 'nel mezzo del cammin di nostra vita' be made to appear wholly identical with the intimate, emotional, subjective focal view for whom even the very thought of the experiences in the wood renews his fear, 'rinova la paura', just five lines later? Another of Dante's major innovations in the *Comedy*, as I shall argue in the next section, is to construct a seemingly coherent narrator character that is in fact possessed of multiple faces, achieved through the construction and deployment in the *Comedy* of a sophisticated model of *narrating instances.*

4.1.1. A new model of narrating instances for the *Comedy*

In Genette's terms, a narrating instance is an 'act of narration' that arises at the intersection of 'the entire set of conditions (human, temporal, spatial) out of which a narrative statement is produced' (1980: 31 n. 10). On the basis of my analysis for the *Comedy*, I suggest we can delimit Genette's notion of 'the entire set of conditions' to key strategic variables: *focal view*, incorporating *sight privilege* and *knowledge privilege*; *experiential location*; and *tone,* including idiosyncratic habits of speech. A model of narrating instances is particularly helpful in relation to the *Comedy*, I propose, because it allows us to define different 'faces' of the narrating Dante character (the sole voice of the narration) with different strategic functions, helping us to think in a new way about how we engage with the poem's 'io' and liberating us from discussions of intentionality and autobiography.

I have identified four narrating instances, set out below, through which I suggest the narration to move strategically and largely seamlessly throughout the poem. As a narrative strategy, this invites the reader to experience a plurality of views, or 'multiplicity of standpoints' to borrow Wolfgang Iser's term, that, I shall suggest, discourages the reader from simply *identifying* with the journeying Dante protagonist and instead invites active *participation*; a shift, in Iser's terms, from 'representative illustration of one view' towards an invitation to an 'experience of the self' (1974: 133–34).[3]

My model is a preliminary and pragmatic one developed for this book, based on a line-by-line analysis of the narration sequences — that is, excluding direct speech — in the first and last cantos of the poem, *Inferno* I (68 verses of narration) and *Paradiso* XXXIII (106 verses of narration).[4] Each of the four narrating instances is discrete, defined by a different focal view and therefore different sight and knowledge privileges, and each inviting a different effect in the reader. It is a model of *narration* so the journeying Dante — who never narrates but speaks only in direct discourse, as discussed above — is represented only as mediated by the narrating Dante, based on his focal view as remembered and retrospectively voiced by the narrating Dante.

I refer to the four narrating instances as follows: the *Experiencing I* narrating instance (retrospective narration of the journeying Dante's inner mental processes, or his feelings *then*); the *Embodied Narrator* narrating instance (narration of the narrating Dante's feelings in the outer story world *now*); the *Implied Author* narrating instance (omniscient authority); and the *Zero-Focalised Narration* narrating instance (neutral, often gappy, propulsion of narrative action).[5]

Narrating instance:	Experiencing I	Embodied Narrator	Implied Author	Zero-Focalised Narration
Description	Retrospective narration of the journeying Dante's mental processes (his feelings then)	Scribing poet persona	Authoritative *auctor* persona	Neutral propulsion of action
Voice (*Who speaks?*)	Narrating Dante			
Focal view (*Who sees?*)	Experiencing I (journeying Dante then)	Embodied Narrator (narrating Dante now)	Implied Author	(none)
Sight privilege (viewpoint)	Restricted	Restricted	Total omniscience	Omniscience within storyworld
Knowledge privilege	None (own perceptions only)	'Reasonable knowledge': glossed/*lectio*	Total, including prophetic: *auctoritas*	None (sees, does not interpret)
Experiential location	Inner storyworld	Outer storyworld	Unlocated (transhistorical)	Unlocated
Tone	Personal, subjective (intimate)	Personal (emotional)	Authoritative	Neutral
Other notable characteristics	Temporal locatives	Temporal locatives	Responsible for most metaphor and simile	Diegesis
	Doubt, uncertainty	References to body and memory	Apostrophe	Narration of that which can be externally observed
		References to being in a historical, material reality		
Function	Story engagement, epistemic immersion	Authenticating ('true story')	Authority and universalisation	Narrative action propulsion, realism, inviting inference in relation to causality
Incidence, as proportion of narrated content: *Inf.*, I	High	Low	Medium	High
Incidence, as proportion of narrated content: *Par.*, XXXIII	Medium	High	High	Very low
Disadvantage of only using this narrating instance	Invites spectatorship, not participation	Highly cognitively demanding of the reader (not immersive)	Risk of detachment and perceived didactism	Limited engagement of affect

TABLE 4.1. Narrating instances model for the *Comedy*, derived from analysis of *Inferno* I and *Paradiso* XXXIII

Table 4.1 offers a summary of the key differences between the four narrating instances for reference as I explore each in turn below. All narrating instances are present in both cantos examined. The epistemically immersive Experiencing I and Zero-Focalised Narration instances dominate in *Inferno* I, establishing reader engagement with the journeying Dante's personal experience narrative as spectator; whilst in *Paradiso* XXXIII the dominant narrating instances are the authoritative Implied Author and the Embodied Narrator, struggling to reconstruct in language his earlier experience of the encounter with God; and both of which narrating instances, I shall suggest, particularly powerfully invite the co-presence of the participatory reader.

Experiencing I

The *Experiencing I* narrating instance provides retrospective narration, as recalled and voiced by the narrating Dante, of the journeying Dante's internal mental processes — his thought and feelings — at the time of the events and encounters of the journey, *as if* the narrating Dante were still pre-eventual and did not know the outcome. It is a highly relatable narrating instance, offering the reader direct, intimate, highly personal access to the protagonist's internal thoughts, feelings and beliefs, and thereby supporting reader identification with the journeying Dante through the narration. However, used in isolation there is a danger that the reader becomes stuck in enjoyable spectatorship, rather than feeling invited to participate in the narrative in her own right. In a standard, unframed first-person narrative (common to many novels, for example), the Experiencing I will be the dominant, even sole, narrating instance, but Dante's frame device liberates him from this monocular focal view and allows him to introduce the other narrating instances that invite the potential for reader participation.

The journeying Dante protagonist is still a living human being, so in terms of sight and knowledge privileges, the Experiencing I narrating instance has access only to what the journeying Dante already knows and can gather along the way, and can see or perceive only what is physically available to the senses of a mortal human being in that space. He cannot see in the dark, for example, as is evident at the start of *Purgatorio* XVI, where the journeying Dante has to rely on Virgil to lead him:

> Sì come cieco va dietro a sua guida
> per non smarrirsi e per non dar di cozzo
> in cosa che 'l molesti, o forse ancida,
> m'andava io per l'aere amaro e sozzo,
> ascoltando il mio duca che diceva
> pur: 'Guarda che da me tu non sia mozzo'. (10–15)

> And, as a blind man goes behind his guide –
> for fear he'll wander or collide with things
> that might well maim him or, perhaps, could kill —
> I too went through acrid, filthy air,
> attending to my leader, who would say,
> 'Take care. Don't get cut off!' repeatedly.

The Experiencing I narrating instance is a vivid and highly engaging mode of narration, a narration of the protagonist's feelings *then*, as he experienced them in the space of the inner story world, inviting empathy and identification (we model how *he* feels). Characteristic features include expression of feelings, uncertainty, temporal locatives, repeated use of 'io', and sensory impressions (particularly *parere*). In *Inferno* I, for example, the statement 'tant' era pien di sonno a quel punto' [[I was] so full of sleep, | that moment] (11) offers the reader, by self-report, information about an inner state that could not be deduced by observation (unless narrated as a posture of somnolence, which is not the case here), narrating the protagonist's feelings *then*, not now (so not attributable to the Embodied Narrator), and is personal and subjective (so cannot be the authoritative, omniscient Implied Author narrating instance). Similarly, in *Inferno* I, 'ma non sì che paura non mi desse | la vista che m'apparve d'un leone' [Yet not so far that no fear pressed on me, | to see, appearing now, a lion face] (44–45), is narration of an inner experience of fear; it narrates the protagonist's feelings *then*, so cannot be the Embodied Narrator, and it narrates subjective perception ('m'apparve'), so cannot be the Implied Author. Further examples in the two cantos examined include:

> questa mi porse tanto di gravezza
> con la paura ch'uscia di sua vista,
> ch'io perdei la speranza de l'altezza. (*Inf.*, I. 52–54)

> [the wolf] so heavily oppressed my thought with fears,
> which spurted even at the sight of her,
> I lost all hope of reaching to those heights.

> E io ch'al fine di tutt' i disii
> appropinquava [...]
> l'ardor del desiderio in me finii. (*Par.*, XXXIII. 46–48)

> And drawing nearer [...]
> the end of all desires, in my own self
> I ended all the ardour of desire.

> [...] parvermi tre giri
> di tre colori e d'una contenenza;
>   e l'un da l'altro come iri da iri
> parea reflesso, e 'l terzo parea foco
> che quinci e quindi igualmente si spiri. (*Par.*, XXXIII. 116–20)

> [...] there appeared to me
> three circling spheres, three-coloured, one in span.
>   And one, it seemed, was mirrored by the next
> twin rainbows, arc to arc. The third seemed fire,
> and breathed to first and second equally.

> veder voleva come si convenne
> l'imago al cerchio e come vi s'indova (*Par.*, XXXIII. 137–38)

> I willed myself to see what fit there was,
> image to circle, and how this all in-where'd.

These narrate, respectively, loss of hope, ardour, a dynamic visual impression and a desire to make sense of that visual impression, delivering immediacy, intimacy, authenticity, a human warmth and, above all, identifiability. The journeying Dante protagonist is not so dissimilar to us; it will be enjoyable and meaningful for us to witness his experiences and his story. But if the reader is not to be seduced into simply spectating, the other narrating instances will be necessary to multiply her standpoints, to observe the journeying Dante from the outside, and to experience herself in the narrative space as different to, and separate from, him.

Embodied Narrator

The Embodied Narrator narrating instance represents the embodiment of the historical, flesh-and-blood scribing poet, self-consciously reconstructing, through his memory, the experience of his earlier journey to the encounter with the divine. Reliving the journey such that he can write it down revives affect that is typically expressed through body states: he re-experiences his fear at the thought of it ('nel pensier rinova la paura' (*Inf.*, I. 6)), but also retains the residual sweetness of his encounter ('e ancor mi distilla | nel core il dolce che nacque da essa' [even if, still, within my heart, | there drops the sweetness that was born from that] (*Par.*, XXXIII. 62–63)). Returned from his journey, he is now located in an outer story world back on earth, 'qua giù', at a point in historical time between Easter 1300 and the narrating Dante's inevitable death as a mortal human being.

This outer story world is, of course, itself a fictive construct separated from the reader's own real world by virtue of historical time and location. But a key function of the Embodied Narrator narrating instance is to authenticate the narrating Dante's account as at least 'truthful', if not necessarily 'true' in the sense of verifiable in empirical terms. Through repeated exposition of the narrating Dante's body states, this narrating instance invites the reader to identify with a real person who made the journey and has returned, a person who lives and breathes and is still affected by both the awfulness and the transformative value of his experience.

Still reflecting a mortal and human experience, this narrating instance has restricted sight: reasonable human knowledge (*lectio*) based on what he has learnt and felt. He is 'post-evental' but still subject nonetheless to the limitations of mortal human perception — memory and language will eventually fail him — rather than possessed of the total omniscience of the Implied Author. 'Io non so ben ridir' [I do not know, I cannot rightly say], he says (*Inf.*, I. 10); and 'pur a quel ch'io ricordo' [even of what I still can call to mind] (*Par.*, XXXIII. 107).

The first occurrence of the Embodied Narrator narrating instance, 'Ahi quanto a dir qual era è cosa dura' [How hard it is to say what that wood was] (*Inf.*, I. 4), immediately establishes the intimate, embodied presence of this face of the narrating Dante. The Embodied Narrator narrates the feelings *now* of the narrating Dante (not the feelings *then*, which is the Experiencing I narrating instance). The tone is emotional, subjective, and rooted in embodied sensation (different to the disembodied authority of the Implied Author).[6] Other examples of this narrating instance include:

che nel pensier rinova la paura! (*Inf.*, I. 6)

[Only to think of it renews my fear!]

cotal son io, ché quasi tutta cessa
mia visione, e ancor mi distilla
nel core il dolce che nacque da essa. (*Par.*, XXXIII. 61–63)

so I am now. For nearly all I saw
has gone, even if, still, within my heart,
there drops the sweetness that was born from that.

La forma universal di questo nodo
credo ch'i' vidi, perché più di largo,
dicendo questo, mi sento ch'i' godo. (*Par.*, XXXIII. 91–93)

This knotting-up of universal form
I saw, I'm sure of that. For now I feel,
in saying this, a gift of greater joy.

There is the re-experienced fear as he recalls the dark wood; the affective residue as he tries to retrieve his experience of the divine; and a sense of joy redoubled as he re-sees with certainty the 'volume' [single book] (86) manifest in his encounter with God. These all authenticate this personal experience narrative, inviting inference of autobiography; but very clearly, under this model, this is just one discrete strategic face of the narrating Dante character.

Implied Author

With a sight privilege of total omniscience, the Implied Author narrating instance supplies what *is*, or the universally 'true' (as opposed to subjective experience, the role of the Embodied Narrator and Experiencing I narrating instances), and what is universally *known* (as opposed to what can objectively be observed, the role of the Zero-Focalised Narration narrating instance). It takes the *lectio*, glossed knowledge of the Embodied Narrator, this latter's sight still restricted by his mortality and humanity, and re-frames it within *auctoritas*, an authoritative re-situating of one event, one journey to God, within what *perfetto veder* will finally reveal to be the universal event or journey. Unlike the Embodied Narrator narrating instance, the Implied Author narrating instance is disembodied and unlocated geographically and in time; it is transhistorical.

The Implied Author narrating instance is authoritative in tone, with total knowledge (including the ability to prophesy), and poetic *ingegno* (it is the narrating instance that constructs the similes that are so critical to the invitation to self-presence, as I discuss later, making it responsible for some of the most sustained lyrical sections of the *Comedy*). The Implied Author can tell us with certainty in *Inferno* I, for example, that the path the journeying Dante had abandoned was the '*verace* via' [the *true* way] (12; my emphasis); and that the sun leads all on the right path, 'mena dritto altrui per ogne calle' (18). And it is an important narrating instance in the final encounter with God in *Paradiso* XXXIII, where things are *known*, either because 'this is how it *is*' — in the perfect sight of the Implied Author; or because 'this is how it felt *for me*' — in the powerful subjective experience of the Embodied Narrator. The Implied Author reflexively intuits the meaning of the expression in Mary's eyes, for example: 'Li occhi da Dio diletti e venerati, | fissi ne l'orator, ne dimostraro | quanto i devoti prieghi le son grati' [The eyes — which God both loves and venerates — | attentive to these orisons, made clear | how welcome to her were these holy prayers] (*Par.*, XXXIII. 40–42); it knows that the 'alta luce' of itself, is true, 'da sé è vera' (54); and it engages directly with the divine: 'O somma luce che tanto ti levi | da' concetti mortali' [You raise yourself so far, O highest light, | above our dying thoughts!] (67–68).

For the reader, then, this narrating instance provides the standpoint that liberates the poem from being a single account of one person's journey (autobiography, or a personal experience narrative) and locates it instead within a frame — a *system* — of *all* journeys, across all time. With its authority, though, comes a risk of didacticism and detachment if used as sole focal view, since it does not offer the identifiability and immersive effect of the Experiencing I or the intimate authenticating function of the Embodied Narrator. But as one of the four faces of the narrating Dante character, it provides the eternal and universal setting within which the discrete and personal may meaningfully be situated.[7]

Zero-Focalised Narration

The last of the four narrating instances, *Zero-Focalised Narration*, provides neutral, omniscient narration of the action within the inner story world, serving to drive forward the events of the story. This narrating instance sets out events without inferring causality, thereby leaving open the possibility of interpretation by the reader herself. In Zero-Focalised Narration, only that which is objectively perceptible within the inner story world can be narrated; and this instance is possessed of no specific knowledge privilege, so there is neither personal interpretation (different to the Embodied Narrator and Experiencing I narrating instances) nor authoritative comment (different to the Implied Author). For example, in *Inferno* I: 'ripresi via per la piaggia diserta, | sì che 'l piè fermo sempre era 'l più basso' [I started up the lonely scree once more, | the foot that drives me always set the lower] (29–30). This is neutral description of action, inviting no identification and without subjective interpretation or description of allied affect (as we would see in the Embodied Narrator or Experiencing I narrating instances); nor is there any authoritative comment about the meaning of the event (as would be supplied in the Implied Author narrating instance). Of course, the reader's reflex may be to infer meaning in the leading foot being the lower, perhaps even piquing her curiosity to break off and explore whether there is intellectual significance in this, but the narration does not impose such a response on her.

Other examples of this narrating instance in the two cantos examined include:

> Temp' era dal principio del mattino,
> e 'l sol montava 'n sù (*Inf.*, I. 37–38)

> The time, however, was the hour of dawn.
> The sun was mounting

Allor si mosse, e io li tenni dietro (*Inf.*, I. 135)

He made to move; and I came close behind

indi a l'etterno lume s'addrizzaro (*Par.*, XXXIII. 43)

and then turned straight to the eternal light

This narrating instance is heavily used in *Inferno* I, particularly in relation to the sequence involving the three beasts where its neutrality is highly effective as a mode for the 'sketching' that leaves open the possibility of allegorical interpretation.[8] By contrast, it is almost absent in *Paradiso* XXXIII, when the sketch or frame inviting interpretation necessarily gives way, as I have proposed, to individual, personal, felt experience. But its neutrality does not mean that this narrating instance cannot be evocative and poetic. *Inferno* I's hill, for example, has 'spalle | vestite' [shoulders | [...] clothed] (16–17) by the sun's rays. The Zero-Focalised Narration narrating instance supports powerful mental modelling because it is usually mimetic rather than diegetic (so it is emphatically not a case of being hard to identify with because it is 'bad' writing, as can happen in some other texts).

But the core function of the Zero-Focalised Narration instance, in my analysis, is to liberate the reader from necessarily experiencing the virtual world as mediated through another's eyes, instead offering her an illusion of the real world in which objects come into view piecemeal and gappily and the reader's brain automatically makes inferences about their significance, exactly as it does in real life. This will be important, as I shall discuss later, in constructing the illusion of the reader's agency to turn her own head in the space. As the fourth face of the narrating Dante, then, Zero-Focalised Narration facilitates and underpins the reader's experience of autonomous participation.

Finally, it is also interesting to observe that, as the poem approaches its conclusion, it becomes increasingly possible to argue for allocation of a given narrative unit to more than one narrating instance, either because of ambiguities that are subsequently resolved in the text (such as the seemingly dissonant shift in focal view described in relation to Bernard's sign in the Introduction), or because Dante's touch is so light that it is sometimes possible to perceive a 'melding' of narrating instances.

In summary, the four faces or discrete narrating instances that constitute the narrating Dante focal character function to discourage the responsive reader from *identifying* solely with the journeying Dante character. The first-person narrating Dante character offers the reader a viewpoint of external observation on the journeying Dante and this viewpoint is constantly shifting between four discrete focal views: the immersive identifiability of the pre-eventual Experiencing I, the embodied authentication of the post-eventual Embodied Narrator, the omniscient authority of the Implied Author, and the gappy, inference-provoking realism of Zero-Focalised Narration. This constant shifting, I have suggested, invites the reader to inhabit a multiplicity of standpoints from the very start of the poem, from the 'nostra' that resolves to an 'io', including the freedom to introduce her own; and I suggest this to be the basis for the mutable 'io' of the poem, inviting both identification and participation.

In the next section, I shall suggest that Dante takes this one step further, reinforcing the invitation to the reader to inhabit her own standpoint by creating the illusion that, on occasion, she has the freedom to direct *her own* line of sight in the narrated space, and that this invites the reader to perfect a reflex of looking, when invited, not through a focal character but directly for herself.

4.1.2. Directing line of sight: narration through mobile camera view

In 2014, Vittorio Gallese co-authored an article with film scholar Michele Guerra entitled 'The Feeling of Motion: Camera Movements and Motor Cognition' that reported findings from empirical EEG (electroencephalogram) research exploring how camera movements are processed in the brain of a viewer of a film. Their research built on film theorist Vivian Sobchack's 1982 model of movement in moving pictures, focusing particularly on the difference between movement of the camera lens from a *fixed position* through use of zoom (pulling focus in and out) or dolly (movement on fixed tracks), by comparison with *naturalistic movement* of the camera in space through the technology of Steadicam, in which the camera is attached to the body of the camera operator and simulates his or her movement through space.

Gallese and Guerra discovered that Steadicam invited a 'stronger form of simulation' (2014: 106) for the viewer, effectively functioning as prosthetic eye that 'simulates human vision' (111), in the terms of Steadicam inventor Garrett Brown, whom they cite directly. This is because the naturalistic human movement of Steadicam (attached to its moving operator) means that new and/or previously missing visual and proprioceptive data is constantly supplied to the viewer's brain, mimicking the experience of visual processing in the physical world and triggering the mechanism of embodied simulation in the viewer. Gallese and Guerra write that:

> The [Steadicam] moving camera not only implements our experience by adding kinaesthetic, bodily, tactile cues as well as the sense of balance and gravity, [but] also gives the impression that the movie is to some extent *live*, that there is an intentionality which endows it with peculiar bodily functions and subjectivity. (106; emphasis in original)

They found that the same effect is *not* replicated in the fixed camera views of the zoom and dolly, which tend to be associated with 'fake [or] abstract' movement (112), by contrast with Steadicam's ability to optimise the viewer's sense of participation through 'the capacity of the camera to simulate the virtual presence of the viewer inside the movie' (103). The central element in achieving this, they propose, citing Brown again, is *movement*: 'In the movies, when the camera begins to move, we are suddenly given the missing information as to shape and layout and size. *We are there*' (107; my emphasis). By having her focal view mediated through

Steadicam's naturalistic movement, the viewer experiences the illusion of *presence* ('*we are there*') in the film space.

And not only is the viewer 'there': crucially, she also has the illusion of *agency*. Gallese and Guerra write of how the camera 'explores the profilmic space by turning its "head" and by focusing on details or accomplishing movements both related and unrelated to the characters' behaviour' (111). Reflexively mirroring this fluidity of ocular movement through embodied simulation, the viewer achieves, say Gallese and Guerra, the illusion of autonomous, 'free' movement, 'following both the characters *and his own curiosity*' (my emphasis):

> The sense of immersion is of course provided by the fluidity of the [camera] movement that conveys a very ecological approach to the scene [...], but it is provided as well by the motor engagement of the viewer, which has the impression to move freely inside the shot, following both the characters and his own curiosity. (111)

My suggestion is that Dante deploys focal view in the *Comedy* to a similar end: realistically *simulating human vision* through directing the reader's line of sight in such a way that the constant movement and updating of visual data can invite the realistic sense of presence (triggered by Gallese's embodied simulation). If the brain accepts this dynamic provision of visual data as realistic, it invites in the responsive reader the illusion — however brief — of free autonomous movement of her own line of sight in the virtual space of the narrative, or the sense that she can freely turn her own head to look around.

I shall briefly illustrate what I mean with four examples from the poem. Again, my focus is on establishing a principle and a progression. In this case the mechanism is relatively simple and self-evident in each instance, so I provide only a brief commentary whilst citing each text in full so that the interested reader can experiment with imaginatively modelling this behaviour themselves.

The first example is in *Inferno* IV, when the journeying Dante emerges onto the lawn of Limbo with Virgil and, finding a vantage point, 'loco aperto, luminoso e alto' [a space, | illuminated, open, high and airy] (116), takes in the souls beyond ('mi fuor mostrati' [were displayed to me] (119)) from a static wide angle. Note how little data is provided to the reader in this sequence for her to allocate each soul to a location in her mental model:

> Traemmoci così da l'un de' canti,
> in loco aperto, luminoso e alto,
> sì che veder si potien tutti quanti.
>
> Colà diritto, sovra 'l verde smalto, 118
> mi fuor mostrati li spiriti magni,
> che del vedere in me stesso m'essalto.
>
> I' vidi Eletra con molti compagni,
> tra ' quai conobbi Ettòr ed Enea,
> Cesare armato con li occhi grifagni.
>
> Vidi Cammilla e la Pantasilea; 124
> da l'altra parte vidi 'l re Latino
> che con Lavina sua figlia sedea.

Vidi quel Bruto che cacciò Tarquino,
Lucrezia, Iulia, Marzïa e Corniglia;
e solo, in parte, vidi 'l Saladino.
　　Poi ch'innalzai un poco più le ciglia,　　　　　　130
vidi 'l maestro di color che sanno
seder tra filosofica famiglia.
　　Tutti lo miran, tutti onor li fanno:
quivi vid' ïo Socrate e Platone,
che 'nnanzi a li altri più presso li stanno;
　　Democrito che 'l mondo a caso pone,　　　　　　136
Dïogenès, Anassagora e Tale,
Empedoclès, Eraclito e Zenone;
　　e vidi il buono accoglitor del quale,
Dïascoride dico; e vidi Orfeo,
Tulïo e Lino e Seneca morale;
　　Euclide geomètra e Tolomeo,　　　　　　　142
Ipocràte, Avicenna e Galïeno,
Averoìs che 'l gran comento feo.
　　Io non posso ritrar di tutti a pieno,
però che sì mi caccia il lungo tema,
che molte volte al fatto il dir vien meno. (115–47)

And so we drew aside and found a space,
illuminated, open, high and airy,
where all of these were able to be seen.
　　And there, across that bright enamelled green,　　　118
these ancient heroes were displayed to me.
And I within myself am still raised high
　　at what I saw: Electra, many round her.
Hector, I recognised. Aeneas, too,
and Caesar in arms, with his hawk-like eyes.
　　Camilla I saw, and Penthesilea,　　　　　　124
and King Latinus on the other side —
his daughter seated with him, his Lavinia.
　　Brutus (he drove proud Tarquin out), Lucrece
and Julia, Marcia, Cornelia — all these I saw,
and there alone, apart, the sultan Saladin.
　　And then — my brow raised higher still — I saw,　　130
among his family of philosophers,
the master of all those who think and know.
　　To him all look in wonder, all in honour.
And, closer to his side than all the rest,
I now saw Socrates, I saw now Plato,
　　and one, Democritus, who claims the world is chance,　136
Diogenes and Tales, Anaxagoras,
Empedocles, Heraclitus and Zeno.
　　Then one I saw who gathered healing herbs –
I mean good Dioscorides. Orpheus I saw,
and Seneca the moralist, Linus, Tully,
　　Euclid (geometer) and Ptolemy,　　　　　　142
Hippocrates, Avicenna and Galen,
Avveroes, too, who made the *Commentary*.

> I cannot here draw portraits of them all;
> my lengthy subject presses me ahead,
> and saying often falls far short of fact.

The reader is not asked to do much in the way of arduous spatial cognitive work here: there is a list of souls at which she is invited to look sequentially (and to whom she may dedicate greater or fewer cognitive resources of recognition), but there are virtually no associated spatial directions, just the odd indicator of spatial relationality: on the other side (125); seated with (126); alone, apart (129). Further, the narration is mostly Zero-Focalised Narration (neutral description of what can be seen), allowing the reader to dedicate her cognitive resources primarily to the act of looking for herself rather than through the eyes of the journeying Dante protagonist.[9] The result is that the reader has an opportunity to practise directing her own line of sight around the narrated space but, in this early instance, few demands are made of her in terms of following spatial choreography. She need only sequentially imagine each soul, rather than imagine and additionally place them spatially.[10] This is a good starter exercise for practising mentally populating a virtual space with a list of narrated objects.

The second example is in *Purgatorio* XII, in which the journeying Dante's line of sight is trained on successive dynamic scenes in the animated marble bas reliefs of the *visibile parlare*. In a kind of hyper-attentive slow motion, the protagonist turns his head one way, 'da l'un lato' (27), and then the other, 'da l'altra parte' (29), and, in the repeated 'Mostrava', a reinforcing rhythmic linear progression in time is indicated ('now was displayed' (52); 'now there appeared' (55); 'now [...] were shown' (58)):

> ed el mi disse: 'Volgi li occhi in giùe:
> buon ti sarà, per tranquillar la via,
> veder lo letto de le piante tue'.
>
>   Come, perché di lor memoria sia,   16
> sovra i sepolti le tombe terragne
> portan segnato quel ch'elli eran pria,
>   onde lì molte volte si ripiagne
> per la puntura de la rimembranza,
> che solo a' pïi dà de le calcagne;
>   sì vid' io lì, ma di miglior sembianza   22
> secondo l'artificio, figurato
> quanto per via di fuor del monte avanza.
>   Vedea colui che fu nobil creato
> più ch'altra creatura, giù dal cielo
> folgoreggiando scender, da l'un lato.
>   Vedëa Brïareo fitto dal telo   28
> celestïal giacer, da l'altra parte,
> grave a la terra per lo mortal gelo.
>   Vedea Timbreo, vedea Pallade e Marte,
> armati ancora, intorno al padre loro,
> mirar le membra d'i Giganti sparte.
>   Vedea Nembròt a piè del gran lavoro   34
> quasi smarrito, e riguardar le genti

che 'n Sennaàr con lui superbi fuoro.
        O Nïobè, con che occhi dolenti
vedea io te segnata in su la strada,
tra sette e sette tuoi figliuoli spenti!
        O Saùl, come in su la propria spada   40
quivi parevi morto in Gelboè,
che poi non sentì pioggia né rugiada!
        O folle Aragne, sì vedea io te
già mezza ragna, trista in su li stracci
de l'opera che mal per te si fé.
        O Roboàm, già non par che minacci   46
quivi 'l tuo segno; ma pien di spavento
nel porta un carro, sanza ch'altri il cacci.
        Mostrava ancor lo duro pavimento
come Almeon a sua madre fé caro
parer lo sventurato addornamento.
        Mostrava come i figli si gittaro   52
sovra Sennacherìb dentro dal tempio,
e come, morto lui, quivi il lasciaro.
        Mostrava la ruina e 'l crudo scempio
che fé Tamiri, quando disse a Ciro:
'Sangue sitisti, e io di sangue t'empio'.
        Mostrava come in rotta si fuggiro   58
li Assiri, poi che fu morto Oloferne,
e anche le reliquie del martiro.
        Vedeva Troia in cenere e in caverne;
o Ilïón, come te basso e vile
mostrava il segno che lì si discerne! (*Purg.*, XII. 13–63)

        And then he said: 'Just turn your eyes down there.
That will be good for you, to ease the way.
See there the bed on which your paces rest.'
        Compare: to serve as some memorial   16
for those entombed beneath, our earthly graves
bear signs of what they had been when alive —
        at which it often happens that we weep,
responding to the spur of memories
which only strike the heel of pious minds.
        I now saw carvings there — though finer, far,   22
considering the hand that crafted them –
along the path the mountain cliffs had left.
        Mark now, to this side I here saw the on
nobler-created than all creatures else,
thrown down in flashing thunder fire from Heaven.
        Mark this, I witnessed on the other side,   28
pierced by the spear celestial, Briareus,
heavy on earth, laid low in deathly chill.
        Mark this, I saw Timbreus, still in arms,
and Mars and Pallas round their father's side,
amazed to see the scattered Giantbones.
        Mark this, I saw, beneath the tower he'd made,   34

Nimrod, as in confusion. All the tribe
of Shinar — arrogant as him — gazed on.
　　Ah! Niobe I saw. With grieving eyes,
I traced your outline carved within that road,
among your children — seven, then seven — slain.
　　Ah! Saul, it seemed that you were there, as dead,　　40
pierced on Gilboa's hill with your own sword,
feeling no longer showers of rain or dew.
　　Ah! Mad Arachne, how I saw you there
half-turned to spider and the work in shreds
which, once attempted, brought you so much harm.
　　Ah! Rehoboam, as you're there portrayed,　　46
you're not, now, menacing, but full of dread.
A chariot bears you off, though none gives chase.
　　Now also shown on that hard floor was how
Almaeon made the fatal ornament
that cost his treacherous mother very dear.
　　Now was displayed how Sennacherib's sons　　52
flung themselves at him in the temple hall,
and how, once dead, they left him there alone.
　　Now there appeared the chaos, crude and cruel,
wrought by Thamyris, who to Cyrus said:
'You thirst for blood. With blood I'll feed you full!'
　　Now fleeing, the Assyrians were shown —　　58
routed when Holofernes met his death —
and showed the relics of his mortal pain.
　　Mark this, I saw Troy's ash and hollowed stone.
Ah, Ilion! How humbled and how vile,
Now picked out in those signs, you seemed to be!

The reader is invited to imagine these mini-narratives unfolding in a situated way, her line of sight tightly melded to that of the journeying Dante's, as set up in Virgil's explicit invitation to him to look: 'Volgi li occhi in giùe' [Just turn your eyes down there] (13). This melding of experience is highly characteristic of the mode of co-present mirroring in *Purgatorio* as a whole discussed in Chapter 3: the reader is in cognitive 'learning' mode, her line of sight tightly bound to the journeying Dante's as she simultaneously experiences the kinaesthetic cues that invite autonomous embodied participation, mentally turning her head in the space alongside him.

　　The last two examples are in *Paradiso,* and each invites independent participation in a different way. In *Paradiso* XVIII, Cacciaguida invites the journeying Dante to marvel at the cross, 'mira ne' corni de la croce' [look in wonder on this cross's horns] (34), as the lights of Joshua, Maccabeus, Roland, Charlemagne, William, Reynald, Godfrey, and Roberto Guiscardo make their dynamic appearances along its beams:

　　　　El cominciò: 'In questa quinta soglia
　　de l'albero che vive de la cima
　　e frutta sempre e mai non perde foglia,
　　　　spiriti son beati, che giù, prima　　31
　　che venissero al ciel, fuor di gran voce,

sì ch'ogne musa ne sarebbe opima.
    Però mira ne' corni de la croce:
quello ch'io nomerò, lì farà l'atto
che fa in nube il suo foco veloce'.
    Io vidi per la croce un lume tratto   37
dal nomar Iosuè, com' el si feo;
né mi fu noto il dir prima che 'l fatto.
    E al nome de l'alto Macabeo
vidi moversi un altro roteando,
e letizia era ferza del paleo.
    Così per Carlo Magno e per Orlando   43
due ne seguì lo mio attento sguardo,
com' occhio segue suo falcon volando.
    Poscia trasse Guiglielmo e Rinoardo
e 'l duca Gottifredi la mia vista
per quella croce, e Ruberto Guiscardo.
    Indi, tra l'altre luci mota e mista,   49
mostrommi l'alma che m'avea parlato
qual era tra i cantor del cielo artista. (28–51)

'In this, the fifth espalier of that tree
that thrives', so he began, 'from summit down,
bears constant fruit and never loses leaf,
    are spirits of the blessed who, there below,   31
won such renown before they reached these spheres
that any muse which sang of them would thrive.
    So look in wonder on this cross's horns.
Each one I name to you will act as does
the swift fire darting through a thunder cloud.'
    I saw, along the Cross-tree's beam, a light,   37
drawn all along that length by Joshua's name.
Nor did I note the name before the deed.
    Then at the name of great Maccabeus,
I saw another, wheeling as it moved,
a spinning top whipped round by happiness.
    Then, as the eye will track a falcon's flight,   43
my own attentive gaze now followed two,
seeking out Roland and great Charlemagne.
    And then along the Cross my sight was drawn
to William, Reynald, Godfrey of Bouillon,
and with them, too, Roberto Guiscardo.
    Then moving, mingling with the other lights,   49
the soul that first had spoken now displayed
his own great art with those who sang the skies.

The challenge to the reader is not only to model the significance of each name, but, simultaneously, to model its dynamic visual movement in space. Once again, Zero-Focalised Narration is the dominant narrating instance, with a switch into the Experiencing I at line 39, where the journeying Dante explicitly models his cognitive resources being occupied *first* by tracking the movement and only subsequently by recognition of the soul: 'né mi fu noto il dir prima che 'l fatto' [Nor did I note the name before the deed] (39).[11] Afterwards, the reward for such cognitive dexterity is modelled by the journeying Dante: he experiences a clarification both in sight, as he looks into Beatrice's eyes, 'e vidi le sue luci tanto mere, | tanto gioconde, che la sua sembianza | vinceva li altri e l'ultimo solere' [and saw the light within her eye so clear, | so full of laughter that her look and air | defeated all that these, before, had been] (55–57), and in understanding, indicated in the double use of 's'accorgersi', in lines 60 and 61.[12] He is seeing progressively more perfectly and autonomously, as too will be the reader, I propose, who fully participates in such demanding acts of dynamic imaginative reconstruction.

Lastly for this section, in *Paradiso* XXXI the journeying Dante observes the celestial rose, unbidden by Beatrice but instead autonomously and spontaneously, as pilgrims do, 'quasi peregrin' (43), when they reach the long-sought 'tempio' [temple]. Liberated, he directs his own line of sight through the blessed co-ordinates that constitute the rose, following his own dynamic path, 'mo sù, mo giù e mo recirculando' [now up, now lower, circling all around] (48), 'in nulla parte ancor fermato fiso' [fixing, though, firmly no particular] (54):

> E quasi peregrin che si ricrea
> nel tempio del suo voto riguardando,
> e spera già ridir com' ello stea,
>
>   su per la viva luce passeggiando,   46
> menava ïo li occhi per li gradi,
> mo sù, mo giù e mo recirculando.
>
>   Vedëa visi a carità süadi,   49
> d'altrui lume fregiati e di suo riso,
> e atti ornati di tutte onestadi.
>
>   La forma general di Paradiso   52
> già tutta mïo sguardo avea compresa,
> in nulla parte ancor fermato fiso. (43–54)

> As pilgrims gaze, enthralled at their new life,
> around the temple that they'd vowed to reach,
> hoping to tell, already, where they've been,
>
>   so, pacing upwards through the living light,   46
> I drew my eyes through every step and grade
> now up, now lower, circling all around.
>
>   I saw there faces swayed to *caritas*,   49
> arrayed in their own smiles and light not theirs,
> and all they did adorned with dignity.
>
>   The general form of Heaven had by now   52
> been grasped entirely as my glance swept round,
> fixing, though, firmly no particular.

The simile also appears to liberate the reader to identify electively as pilgrim in this space, freely turning her head to see *not* the precise analogue of what the journeying Dante sees — since what he sees is elided, 'menava ïo li occhi per li gradi, | mo sù, mo giù e mo recirculando' [I drew my eyes through every step and grade | now up, now lower, circling all around] (47–48) — but instead to do her own creative work, to participate in constructing her own vision of the rose. In this way, she is no longer bound to *identify* with the journeying Dante but instead is invited to *participate* on her own account — no longer imagining what *he* sees and how *he* feels, but looking for herself. Again, the journeying Dante models an outcome, as this freedom to 'move his own head' yields a re-inflaming of his will as he turns to Beatrice 'con voglia riaccesa' [my will once more on fire] (55).[13]

There is one final, extended, diagrammatic choreographing of focal view, by Bernard in *Paradiso* XXXII as he locates the blessed in the rose (*Par.*, XXXII. 1–39 and 115–51). I shall return to this in the final chapter. Before this, though, I set out the second set of mechanics that I propose to invite self-presence in the poem: the continuum of direct and indirect invitations to imaginatively fill in the gaps in the poem.

4.2. Narrative mediation: the continuum of invitations to participate

In this section, I set out three new models related to *narrative mediation*. First, a new reading of the mechanism of the *direct address to the reader*, radically extending the work of Auerbach, Gmelin, and Spitzer beyond a reading of intermittent reader involvement at key points to a reading that defines the addresses as a foundational strategy that catalyses a vast system of different types of invitations to cognitive participation. Second, I propose in the poem a systematic model of *narrative training,* a programme of nine exercises embedded in the text that I propose to invite rehearsal of the reader's cognitive skills in a heavily mediated way; a model already familiar in the second-person address of the medieval gospel meditation, as discussed in Chapter 1. Third, I suggest a strategy of *narration through gaps* in the text, rooted in invitations to the reader to import her own cognitive data in response to the manifold similes and narrative ellipses in the poem. This strategy of narration and its remarkable prevalence (similes alone occupy one fifth of all the verses of narration in the poem) is what underpins, I suggest, the extraordinary 'openness' of the poem.

4.2.1. The direct addresses to the reader

The device of the direct address, deployed around twenty times in the poem (the first in *Inferno* VIII, 'pensa, lettor' [think, reader] (94); the last in *Paradiso* XXII, 'S'io torni mai, lettore' [So may I, reader, sometime join once more] (106)), typically invites the reader to break off from her consumption of the narrative and to consciously and actively engage in a particular cognitive activity: thinking ('pensa'), remembering ('ricorditi'), imagining ('imagini'), reading ('leggi'), directing her gaze ('aguzza [...] li occhi', 'leva [...] la vista'), not asking ('nol dimandar'), or switching between cognitive modes (for example, 'non attender [...] | pensa [...]').[14]

But is the reader really to *act* on such exhortations? When the narrating Dante says to the reader, 'pensa per te stesso | com' io potea tener lo viso asciutto' [think, yourselves: | could I have kept my own face dry] (*Inf.*, XX. 20–21; note how supportive Kirkpatrick's translation is of the invitation, with his interrogative reinforcing the imperative), or 'leggi Ezechïele' [read Ezekiel] (*Purg.*, XXIX. 100), or triply instructs her in the construction of a dynamic virtual event involving certain of the stars of the northern hemisphere in *Paradiso* XIII (1–21), is she really to stop reading the poem and think for herself how Dante might have kept himself from weeping? Is she to actually go to her bookshelf and compare Ezekiel and John's accounts with Dante's? Is she really to stop, envision the night sky from memory, pick out the twenty-four stars Dante describes, and mentally set them into two counter-rotating circles around her, in order to experience for herself just a trace of how it feels to have the lights of the theologians dancing around you in the Heaven of the Sun?

I suggest this is precisely what the participatory reader will increasingly find herself impelled to do, and that it establishes a model of cognitive participation paid off in a vast programme of more subtle indirect and elective invitations to participate through the pre-rational cognitions in the rest of the poem. Whilst Franke raised the question of 'leverag[ing]' the direct address in order to discover 'an implicit address' (2000: 119), the question of how this might be achieved in the text, and of what might constitute an 'implicit address', has not previously been explored, including in Auerbach, Spitzer and Gmelin's three famous essays on Dante's direct addresses.[15] However, I would suggest that these three critics might inadvertently point us towards a resolution of Franke's question precisely through their failure to agree on the exact number of direct addresses in the poem.

The three scholars broadly agree on the functions and constitution of the direct addresses. The direct address is a rhetorical device designed to 'create a feeling of intimacy between author and reader', writes Spitzer (1955: 150); it disrupts the reader from the immersive spell, directing understanding or 'intensify[ing] [...] attention' and serving to reinforce the poet's authority (Auerbach 1953: 268). Further, I propose, this metalepsis sets up the illusion of the possibility of social interaction, or social presence, between the narrating Dante and reader. Of course, the reader is not able to respond through the normal turn-taking mechanism of direct speech as she would in a real-life conversation but instead, I suggest, the direct address invites reciprocal response through *action*: the reader reciprocates and participates in the exchange by *doing*: thinking, looking, imagining. In this regard, the narrating Dante's direct address to the reader constitutes an innovative model of social reciprocity in a text, complementary to my discussion of social presence in Chapter 3.

The direct address in the *Comedy* is typically constituted by a vocative (usually 'lettor') and an imperative (most commonly 'pensa', but also 'nol dimandar', 'aguzza [...] li occhi', 'non attender', 'ricorditi', 'leggi', 'leva [...] la vista', 'imagini').[16] It can be distinguished from the classical apostrophe, I propose — bypassing Auerbach's perhaps unnecessarily complex argument (1953: 270) for the terms of my analysis — on the simple basis that the reader does or might reasonably *electively* feel herself to be the addressee.

Where the critics really diverge is on the tally of direct addresses in the poem — Auerbach proposing 18, Spitzer 'nineteen sure examples' (1955: 146), and Gmelin 20. My suggestion is that the presence of certain inconsistencies in the characteristics of the direct addresses — evident across not only the disputed instances but even some of the cases on which there is consensus — invites us to think about a notion of a *continuum* of invitations to the reader, as I shall set out below. For reference, Table 4.2 summarises the tally as far as the qualitative nature of the three essays reasonably allows, including the core verse(s) of each sequence, the verb that forms the imperative, and — importantly — the vocative used.[17]

TABLE 4.2. Survey of addresses to the reader: Auerbach, Spitzer, Gmelin, compared (translations: Kirkpatrick)

		Classified as direct address?			
	Core of sequence	*Auerbach*	*Spitzer*	*Gmelin**	Vocative
	Inferno				
VIII 94-96	'Pensa, lettor, se io mi sconfortai' [Reader, imagine! I grew faint at heart]	Yes	Yes	Yes	lettor
IX 61-63	'O voi ch'avete li 'ntelletti sani, | mirate la dottrina' [Look hard, all you whose minds are sound and sane]	Yes	Yes	Yes	voi
XVI 127-30	'e per le note | di questa comedìa, lettor, ti giuro' [Reader, | I swear by every rhyme this comedy | has caused to chime]	Yes**	Yes	Yes**	lettor
XX 19-24	'Se Dio ti lasci, lettor, prender frutto | di tua lezione, or pensa per te stesso' [That God may grant you, as you read, the fruit | that you deserve, in reading, think, yourselves]	Yes	Yes	Yes	lettor
XXII 118	'O tu che leggi' [O you there, as you read]	Yes	Yes	Yes	lettor/tu
XXV 46-48	'Se tu se' or, lettore, a creder lento' [if you are slow, my reader, to receive]	Yes	Yes	Yes	lettor
XXXIV 22-27	'Com'io divenni allor gelato e fioco, | nol dimandar, lettor | [...] | pensi oggimai per te, s'hai fior d'ingegno, | qual io divenni, d'uno e d'altro privo' [How weak I now became, how faded, dry, | reader, don't ask | [...] | Just think yourselves, if your minds are in flower, | what I became, bereft of life and death]	Yes	Yes	Yes	lettor
XXXIV 32-33	'vedi oggima quant'esser dee quell tutto' [so now you'll see how huge the whole must be]	No	Yes	No	tu
	Purgatorio				
VIII 19-22	'Aguzza qui, lettor, ben li occhi al vero' [Reader, now fix a needle eye on truth]	Yes	Yes	Yes	lettor
IX 70-72	'Lettor, tu vedi ben com'io innalzo | la mia matera' [You, reader, can now see how here I raise | the theme my verse attempts]	Yes	Yes	Yes	lettor
X 106-11	'Non vo' però, lettor, che tut i smaghi | [...] | Non attender la forma del martire: | pensa la succession' [Yet, reader, I'd not have your minds bewitched | [...] | Don't dwell upon the form their sufferings take. | Think of what follows]	Yes	Yes	Yes	lettor

XVII 1-9	'Ricorditi, lettor, se mai ne l'alpe | ti close nebbia per la qual vedessi | [...] | e fia la tua imagine leggera | in giugnere a veder' [Reader, recall, if ever in the hills | a fog has caught you so you couldn't see | [...] | From this, you'll easily be brought to see]	Yes	Yes	Yes	lettor
XXIX 98-103	A descriver lor form più non spargo | rime, lettor; [...] | [...] | ma leggi Ezechiele [I'll scatter, reader, no more rhymes to trace | what these forms were [...] | [...] But read Ezekiel]	Yes**	Yes	Yes	lettor
XXXI 124-26	'Pensa, lettor, s'io mi maravigliava' [Reader, just think how great my wonder was]	Yes	Yes	Yes	lettor
XXXIII 136-39	'S'io avessi, lettor, più lungo spazio | da scrivere' [If, reader, I'd more space in which to write]	Yes	Yes	Yes	lettor
Paradiso					
II 1-21	'O voi che siete in piccioletta barca, | desiderosi d'ascoltar, seguiti | [...] | Voialtri pochi' [You in that little boat who, listening hard, | have followed | [...] | You other few]	Yes	Yes	Yes	voi
V 109-14	'Pensa, lettor' [Think, reader]	Yes	Yes	Yes	lettor
IX 10-12	'Ahi anime ingannate e fatture empie' [You self-deceiving souls! Mere things-gone-wrong!]	No***	No** Apostr-ophe	Yes	[voi] anime ingannate
X 7-27	'Leva dunque, lettore, a l'alte rote | meco la vista [...] | [...] | Or ti riman, lettor, sovra 'l tuo banco' [Lift up your eyes then, reader, and along with | me, look [...] | [...] | Now, reader, sit there at your lecture bench]	Yes	No ('hidden address' within simile)	Yes	lettor
XIII 1-21	'Imagini, chi bene intender cupe | quell ch'I' or vidi [...] | [...] e avrà quasi l'ombra de la vera | costellazione' [Imagine, if you truly want to know | what I saw now [...] | [...] | you'll have a shade, then, almost, of that true | constellation]	No***	Yes	Yes	chi bene intender cupe
XXII 106-11	'S'io torni mai, lettore, a quell divoto | triünfo [...] | [...] | tu non avresti in tanto tratto e messo | nel foco il dito' [So may I, reader, sometime join once more | that prayerful march of victory [...] | [...] | you'd not so swiftly have withdrawn and thrust | your finger in the fire]	Yes	Yes	Yes	lettor
		18	19	20	

* As recorded by Auerbach.

** But recorded with a line or canto typo.

*** Auerbach notes that Gmelin includes these two in his first footnote, giving Auerbach the 'some twenty' in total that he eventually claims.

There are four instances of apparent disagreement between the three critics, highlighted in shading on the figure. Two of the disputes, I suggest, can be bracketed for the purposes of this discussion on the grounds of clerical rather than strategic disagreement. In *Inferno* XXXIV, Spitzer treats 'nol dimandar' [don't ask] (23) and 'vedi oggimai' [now you'll see] (32) as separate addresses, whilst Auerbach and Gmelin count only one direct address here. In *Paradiso* X, Spitzer somewhat confusingly excludes 'Leva dunque, lettore, a l'alte rote | meco la vista' [Lift up your eyes, then, reader, and along with | me, look to those wheels] (7–8) on the grounds that it is a 'hidden address' within a simile; but since he classifies it as an address nonetheless, I do not count it here as truly disputed. There is a third, perplexing, exclusion, this time by Auerbach, of the proposed instance in *Paradiso* XIII, 'Imagini, chi bene intender cupe' [Imagine, if you truly want to know] (1). He simply fails to mention this sequence in his essay, but offers no apparent reason for its exclusion, so for the purposes of this analysis I conclude that this is an oversight.

This leaves one instance which is genuinely disputed in my view — that is, the instance in *Paradiso* IX:

> Ahi anime ingannate e fatture empie,
> che da sì fatto ben torcete i cuori,
> drizzando in vanità le vostre tempie! (10–12)

> You self-deceiving souls! Mere things-gone-wrong!
> Twisting your hearts away from that true good,
> you strain your brows direct to nothingness.

Following Carlo Martello's account in *Paradiso* VIII of how, in the journeying Dante's words, bitterness can issue from sweet seed, 'com' esser può, di dolce seme, amaro' (93), the narrating Dante reflects at the start of canto IX that grief will follow the harm 'you' wreak, 'pianto | giusto verrà di retro ai vostri danni' (5–6), then issues this metaleptic castigation to 'self-deceiving souls', 'anime ingannate'. Gmelin includes this as a direct address; Auerbach and Spitzer do not.

The first thing we might observe is that it does not use the vocative 'lettor' but instead addresses a second-person plural group, arguably directing us towards exclusion on the grounds that it is an apostrophe.[18] However, the three scholars allow other instances of addresses to a second-person plural group to be classified as addresses; in fact, the vocative 'lettor', reader, is used in indeed only 16 of the 20 instances included. An interesting question arises: how does the reader cognitively process the pronoun 'you' in a first-person narration? Is it always in the same way? When does 'you' actually mean 'you, reader'; and when does it mean 'other people outside this text but who aren't you'?

There are four instances in the sample of direct addresses collected between the three critics where the vocative 'you' ('voi' or 'tu') is used, rather than 'lettor'. The first is in *Inferno* IX, 'O voi ch'avete li 'ntelletti sani' [Look hard, all you whose minds are sound and sane] (61), which all three critics allow as a direct address. The second is in *Paradiso* II, with the double 'voi' vocative, 'O voi che siete in piccioletta barca' [You in that little boat] (2) or 'Voialtri pochi' [You other few] (10), which again all three allow as a direct address. There is the disputed one above, in

Paradiso IX. And lastly, there is the second-person singular instance in *Paradiso* XIII, 'Imagini, chi bene intender cupe | quel ch'i' or vidi' [Imagine, if you truly want to know | what I saw now] (1–2, and following), which only Auerbach, seemingly inexplicably, excludes.

But if the reader is to feel herself directly addressed as one of the 'intelletti sani' in *Inferno* IX, or one of either 'voi che siete in piccioletta barca' or 'voialtri pochi' in *Paradiso* II, why not as one of the 'anime ingannate' in *Paradiso* IX? Is the reader in this case to experience it as an apostrophe directed at a specific group of *others* of which she has no part?

Spitzer rejects it as an address on the grounds that it 'is in truth only an "apostrophe" in the ancient sense' (154). But Gmelin includes it; and whilst Auerbach does not include it in his own list, in fact Spitzer writes that Auerbach 'accepts' Gmelin's reading. Spitzer continues that:

> Dante is surely here not addressing his reader (whom it would be singularly tactless to identify with *anime ingannate e fatture empie*), rather is he using an apostrophe directed against persons who become 'present' only by his castigation. We may compare a similar invective of Dante's against earthly sinners, uttered at the moment when he sees the punishment of the proud in Purgatory (*Purgatorio* X, 121): 'O superbi cristian, miseri lassi | Che, della vista della mente infermi, | Fidanza avete ne'ritrosi passi; | Non v'accorgete voi, che noi siam vermin | Nati a formar l'angelica farfalla ...?' Surely no one in his senses would advocate the identification of Dante's readers with the *superbi*! (145–46)

Spitzer's argument rests on an appeal to politeness and tact that I would suggest to be a cultural over-reading.[19] Further, I would suggest the strategic function of the narrating Dante would never allow the imposition of any sort of identity on the reader, including a pejorative one, but rather would *invite* personal identification where appropriate. Of course, we might argue that the participating reader who has actively modelled the rehearsal of penitence in *Purgatorio* is unlikely to identify realistically at this point in *Paradiso* as an *anima ingannata*. But not all readers will have been reading in such a way (for example, any of the 'desiderosi d'ascoltar' who have not heeded the warning to turn back), and I suggest the text certainly leaves open the possibility for elective identification in this way at this stage.

I would argue, then, that in technical terms we could read it either way — as an address or as an apostrophe — but that the key factor is that, to be read as an address, it depends on the reader *electively identifying* as part of such a group. My suggestion is that the direct addresses, in their explicit and overt invitations to the reader actively to find herself present as subject in the text by virtue of her interlocutory relationship with the narrating Dante, function as a model to invite the reader to habituate herself to a practice of elective identification as subject even when the invitation is not explicit.

Elective identification within the context of the direct address then opens up my proposed notion of a *continuum* of invitations to the reader. The reader who has become accustomed to reciprocal engagement through *doing* in the outer story world may then feel primed to do the same in the inner story world, reciprocally engaging with the blessed not only when directly addressed but also by voluntary, elective inference. Might such a reader not then also find herself electively addressed in some of the many instances when Beatrice uses an imperative 'tu'? For example, 'Or drizza il viso a quel ch'or si ragiona' [Now fix your eye on what we're now to say] (*Par.*, VII. 34)? Or even imaginatively co-present in the narrating Dante's 'noi', as for example in the Heaven of the Sun in *Paradiso* XIII — 'Compié 'l cantare e 'l volger sua misura; | e attesersi a noi quei santi lumi, | felicitando sé di cura in cura' [The singing done, the measured round complete, | these holy lights stretched out their thought to us, | rejoicing in themselves as this new care] (28–30) — and in Bernard's 'noi' in his praise of Mary in *Paradiso* XXXIII — 'Qui se' a noi meridïana face | di caritate' [You are, for us, the noon-time torch of love] (10–11)?

In a participatory model of reading, then, perhaps the question more radically becomes: why, when the narrator addresses all of, or any subset of, the mortal and post-mortal human community, should we imagine we are *not* implicated, that we stand only as external observers to those guilty of sin or engaged in the journey to God as we encounter them in their present incarnation in the three realms of the afterlife? If we begin to think in this way, we might question why we as readers of this poem, here, now, would excuse ourselves from finding ourselves addressed in a present way in Dante's 'conversation'. Historical and temporal distance is no reason: the text invites us to consider post-mortal, transhistorical, transcultural connectivity, the penitents of *Purgatorio* XI praying across time for *us*, *now*: 'Quest' ultima preghiera, segnor caro, | già non si fa per noi, ché non bisogna, | ma per color che dietro a noi restaro' [This final prayer is made, O dearest Lord, | not for ourselves (we now have no such need). | We speak for those behind us, who've remained] (22–24).[20]

I return later to the continuum of invitations but first will consider how, having established a principle of cognitive participation, the poem invites the reader to reinforce this behaviour through a series of guided rehearsals in the text, a strategy I term *narrative training*.

4.2.2. Narrative training

Following Auerbach, I suggested earlier that one of the functions of the direct address to the reader is to disrupt epistemic immersion. My proposal in this section is that in certain instances of the direct addresses (around half, as I quantify later), such strategic disruptions precede sequences in which the narration of certain perceptual or cognitive events is radically slowed down such that the process of the successive mental models that constitutes the dynamic sequence of action becomes discernible.[21] This constitutes, I suggest, a narratological strategy I term *narrative training*, in which the frame-by-frame mode of narration invites the responsive reader to defamiliarise her reflexive mode of constructing a dynamic mental model, and to experiment with a different, more powerful, model of imaginative work.[22]

In literary and creative writing theory, we might traditionally have thought of the imagination in terms of skills particularly of *visualisation*, but my suggestion is that in fact Dante's innovation is to invite the reader not simply to become more expert in *pictorial* mental modelling — constructing a static image in the form of a picture — but in the mode cognitive neuroscience and cognitive poetics is beginning to define as *enactive*.[23] Enactive mental modelling seeks to construct not just a visual mental representation, but to embody it by incorporating the multiple senses, and to animate the representation mentally, sustaining it across time — a cognitive skill the narrative encourages most explicitly in its invitation to the reader to construct a complex dynamic mental model of the counter-rotating circles of the lights of the theologians in *Paradiso* XIII, as I shall discuss in a moment. Such an enactive model of representation mimics much more accurately than the pictorial the dynamic processes of human consciousness, supporting the illusion that the virtual input data is *realistic*, reinforcing the reader's experience of self-presence in the virtual space.

The practice of enactive mental modelling, or visceral imaginative elaboration, has a precedent in the medieval gospel meditation, as discussed in Chapter 1. However, whilst the narrative of the gospel meditation focuses on engagement of the rational cognitions through conscious direction of attention, I suggest that the *Comedy*'s innovation is to leave partially intact the immersive spell in these narrative training exercises, recruiting the pre-rational cognitions and thereby changing or honing reflexive or unconscious — intuitive — behaviours.[24]

Cognitive neuroscience is beginning to equip us with new understanding about how cognitive rehearsal can change not only rational behaviours (as used in, for example, elite sports coaching and cognitive behavioural therapy) but also pre-rational behaviours and intuitions. The term 'cultural neuroscience' has been used (Gallese et al. 2011: 395) to define a field of research that explores how such effects can be reproduced through the medium of an artefact, acknowledging a particular debt to Elaine Scarry who writes of a poem or novel as 'a set of instructions for mental composition [...]. The "instructional" character is key, because it allows the image to come into being by an agency not one's own' (2001: 244). Comparative literature scholar Joshua Landy published an applied analysis of a very similar phenomenon, writing of texts that function not to 'teach' but to 'train' (2012: 202) and proposing that in fact a minority of texts — 'only a relative handful' (182) — invite this level of cognitive transformation in the reader.[25] Certain texts, he writes:

> function as *training grounds for the capacities*: in engaging with them, we stand to become not more knowledgeable or more virtuous but more *skilled,* whether at rational thinking, at maintaining necessary illusions, at achieving tranquillity of mind, or even at religious faith. Instead of offering us propositional knowledge, these texts yield know-how; rather than attempting to instruct by means of their content, they hone capacities by means of their form; far from seducing with the promise of instantaneous transformation, they recognise, with Aristotle, that change is a matter of sustained and patient practice. (Landy 2012: 167; emphasis in original)

For Landy, as for my proposal, training is 'gradual'; 'skills are burnished through repeated exercise in a benevolent spiral' (194); and whilst 'we simply begin by reading and listening', with what he terms a *formative fiction,* 'there is always a moment at which the stakes become apparent, a moment at which we realise that we are not just being told a story, a moment at which a crucial offer is put before us' (195).

My proposal in relation to the *Comedy* is that, in each of the putative narrative training exercises, the discrete cognitive steps of the usually intuitive process of constructing a mental model are rendered perceptible, defamiliarising to the participatory reader her automatic habits of perception and interpretation; and subsequently providing her with a framework through the mechanism of an imaginative enactment exercise embedded in the narrative sequence, to hone her capacity to imagine narrated events so vividly, enactively and sustainedly that her brain may experience them as 'realistic'. The exercises are typically rendered in a kind of 'stop-motion' mode of narration, whereby the particular mental event — the thing seen, experienced or imagined by the protagonist — is narrated frame-by-frame in the text at a level of unusual detail or vividness. Such a mode requires that the reader slow down if she is to process the highly detailed data without becoming overwhelmed, to withhold her own imaginative habits and inferences, and that she construct instead a series of mental models based on the precisely observed data provided in the text. Over the course of the exercises in the poem, I suggest, the reader is trained to extend and refine her reflexive mode of imagining from a model of relatively straightforward *visualisation* (prevalent in *Inferno*), through multi-sensory embodied or *visceral* reconstruction (*Purgatorio*), and finally, to an expert intuitive model of dynamic, *enactive* imagination (*Paradiso*) that will equip her to cope with the extremely demanding requirements of imagining in the abstract essential in *Paradiso*; that is, without rooting everything in the data of the senses. Ultimately, I propose, this skill of imaginative enactment in the abstract will equip her to imagine things she has never seen and to viscerally and realistically experience for herself things that cannot be conveyed in words, a practice that will become essential if she is to complete the journey on her own account when words will finally fail the narrator.

I propose there to be nine such narrative training exercises in the poem: four in *Inferno*, two in *Purgatorio* and three in *Paradiso*. To summarise these briefly: in *Inferno*, the first two exercises occur in the second and third of the three serpent–shade transmutations in *Inferno* XXV, each radically slowing the reader's pace of reading and inviting sustained and detailed attention to an algorithmic reconstruction of complex visual events. Next, there is the extended simile of the battlefield body parts in *Inferno* XXVIII (1–21), inviting the reader to visualise and composite a count of body parts from five battles in Southern Italy. Finally, in *Inferno*, there is the protagonist's loss of bodily sensation in canto XXXIV (22–27), which is uncharacteristically brief but constitutes, I suggest, a preliminary exercise in enactive imagining from abstraction, because there *is* no sensory input data — Dante is completely numb. There are two exercises in *Purgatorio*, both mental acts that recruit *embodied* experience: Virgil's visual compositing exercise in *Purgatorio* IV (58–84) which offers a guided inversion of common perception; and an invitation in *Purgatorio* XVII (1–12) to re-construct, through the simile of a mole, a synaesthetic embodied experience of 'seeing' through the skin as the sun gradually penetrates the hill-fog. In *Paradiso*, each of the three consists of a guided rehearsal in constructing a *dynamic, enactive* mental model: first, Beatrice's discussion of the science of optics in *Paradiso* II (91–111); then the constructed simile of the universe at *Paradiso* X (7–21) that deploys natural phenomena to guide the imaginative construction and animation of a model of the universe; and lastly, in *Paradiso* XIII (1–21), the most demanding, requiring near-simultaneous engagement of all the higher cognitive functions in a guided enactment imagination exercise. In this last, rather than simply visualising descriptive data, the reader is invited to imaginatively construct for herself, from the constituent stars in the night sky, a multi-dimensional, dynamic, embodied simile against which she might then understand, by analogy, the contemporaneous experience of the journeying Dante as the lights of the theologians circle him in the heaven of the Sun.

It may be argued that most of the similes in the poem similarly carry an invitation to cognitive rehearsal, and also that much of the narration of *Paradiso* consists of exercises in abstract reasoning, but I suggest that two key elements differentiate the narrative training exercises. The first is the direct address to the reader that signals each exercise, disrupting epistemic immersion and strategically priming the reader's cognitions, I propose, for a shift into a more active, participatory engagement with the text. The second is their algorithmic construction that in computational theory of mind would signal a *learner* mode (and makes the exercises typically longer than the three to six verses of the majority of Dante's similes).[26] My focus here is to establish the principle and mechanics of the narrative training model, so I explore as an example the last of the shade–serpent transmutations in *Inferno* XXV.

In the seventh bolgia, where the thieves are punished, in a narration that spans *Inferno* XXIV and XXV, the journeying Dante and Virgil look on from their vantage point on the arch that straddles the seventh ditch as the shades are subjected to repeated physical ambush by serpents and serpent-derivatives.[27] Each ambush catalyses a relentless cycle of transmutation, either of degeneration and regeneration through fire into ash that spontaneously reanimates (described in the first short sequence in canto XXIV, lines 97–105), or by progressive mutual transformation into one another's form, as in the second and third transmutations, evoked at greater length and with much greater demands on the cognitive functions, in canto XXV (lines 46–78 and 79–137, respectively).

The full narrative event of the third transmutation extends across 58 lines, of which the central frame-by-frame narration sequence occupies over half (33 lines, from line 103 to 135). The event begins when a tiny *serpentello*, a 'snakelet', 'livido e nero come gran di pepe' [livid as a peppercorn] (84), punctures the belly-button of the last of the three shades, triggering the algorithmic procedure of the transmutation that is explicitly signposted in the narration, 'Insieme si rispuosero a tai norme' [Each answered each in working through this rule] (103), and then enacted in the narrative as the reader's visual frame is directed metronomically from *serpentello* to shade to mentally model each step in turn. The schema in Table 4.3 illustrates the dexterity necessary in the reader's mental modelling of visual perception, sometimes switching between frames even in the middle of a line:

Visual frame directed at...
Serpent — Both — Shade

Insieme si rispuosero a tai norme,	Each answered each in working through this rule:
che 'l serpente la coda in forca fesse,	the serpent fashioned (from his tail) a fork;
e 'l feruto ristrinse insieme l'orme	the wounded human dragged his footprints to.
Le gambe con le cosce seco stesse	The legs, now fastening at their inner thighs,
s'appiccar sì, che 'n poco la giuntura	adhered so well that soon the join between
non facea segno alcun che si paresse.	gave no clear sign of ever having been.
Togliea la coda fessa la figura	The cloven tail assumed the figure now
che si perdeva là, e la sua pelle	of that which, over there, was lost to view.
si facea molle, e quella di là dura.	Hide softened here, but hardened over there.
Io vidi intrar le braccia per l'ascelle,	I saw each arm retract and reach its pit.
e i due piè de la fiera, ch'eran corti,	The paws, conversely, of that stubby newt,
tanto allungar quanto accorciavan quelle.	lengthened as much as human feet grew short.
Poscia li piè di rietro, insieme attorti,	The hindmost toes then curled around and clinched;
diventaron lo membro che l'uom cela,	these formed the member that a man conceals.
e 'l misero del suo n'avea due porti.	The other wretch wrenched his own part in two.
Mentre che 'l fummo l'uno e l'altro vela	As now, around this pair, the fumes still hang,
di color novo, e genera 'l pel suso	A gauze of stranger colours – causing hair
per l'una parte e da l'altra il dipela,	to sprout fresh here, while there it plucks it sleek –
l'un si levò e l'altro cadde giuso,	the one rose up, the other fell down flat,
non torcendo però le lucerne empie,	yet, peering out, as this snout changed for that,
sotto le quai ciascun cambiava muso.	neither could wrest from either evil eye beams.
Quel ch'era dritto, il trasse ver' le tempie,	Upright, the one dragged jowl across to temple.
e di troppa matera ch'in là venne	And then, from leakages of surplus pulp,
uscir li orecchi de le gote scempie;	a pair of ears appeared, on thinned-out jowls.
ciò che non corse in dietro e si ritenne	Whatever residue did not run back
di quel soverchio, fé naso a la faccia	now gelled, and gave that face its human nose.
e le labbra ingrossò quanto convenne.	The lips, plumped up to meet the need, gained bulk.
Quel che giacëa, il muso innanzi caccia,	The other, lying flat, extends his muzzle.
e li orecchi ritira per la testa	Then, just like snails when pulling in their horns,
come face le corna la lumaccia;	he draws his ears back, flush along his skull.
e la lingua, ch'avèa unita e presta	And now the tongue – once whole and quick to speak –
prima a parlar, si fende, e la forcuta	divides in two. The other finds his fork
ne l'altro si richiude; e 'l fummo resta.	has closed right up. The furls of smoke now cease.

Table 4.3. *Inferno* XXV. 103–35: narrative training exercise

Over the course of these 33 lines, 25 individual processes are described — a vast amount of data for the reader to process. We start by watching the serpent bifurcate his tail; then are invited to look across to see the shade, ''l feruto' (105), dragging his legs together; we continue looking to see his legs knit together at the thigh; then look back to see the serpent's bifurcated tail complete its morphing into human lower limbs. And so on, through the arms/front limbs, the mid-section, the growth/loss of hair, the sudden exchange of stance from prone to erect and vice versa ('l'un si levò e l'altro cadde giuso', 121), through the nose/snout, the facial flesh, the ears, and finally the tongue.

The repeated swinging of the reader's visual frame across the horizontal plane makes the sequence uncomfortable to read, like watching a tennis match from overly close quarters at the net; and once the lateral motion has been established, a series of swings through the vertical axis is added, sending the reader's eye up and down, up and down (121, as the creatures switch postures, then at 124 and 130), and then a zoom, from wide shot to close-up as their heads morph (124–26 and 130–32). Different to the authentic verisimilitude offered by a technique such as Steadicam, discussed earlier, this is akin to the distancing effect of the fixed-track camera using the zoom or the overly enthusiastic amateur camera operator using a hand-held camera to relentlessly pursue action and response with no thought for the viewer's experience. The journeying Dante protagonist is explicitly left with a sense of visual confusion: 'E avvegna che li occhi miei confusi | fossero alquanto e l'animo smagato' [And though my vision was a bit confused | (spirit quite drained of all its energies)] (145–46). The reader may very well feel the same, particularly if she has tried to read the sequence at the same apparently real-time pace at which it is narrated.[28]

However, the overload of information, I propose, is designed precisely to invite the reader to radically slow her pace of reading. If she reads at real-time pace (as became common in silent reading), the sheer volume of visual data makes it very hard to engage anything but her suppositional imagination, sketching only an outline, getting just an approximate idea of the specific processes of the transmutation, and relying on a propositional pay-off at the end to explicitly *tell* her what it all means. But by slowing her pace and modelling each data point frame-by-frame, taking time to visualise, to look properly, to see what is really there, she experiences a different way of imagining, one more likely to trigger the embodied simulation necessary for a realistic illusion of self-presence in the narrated space. In inviting the reader to practise the construction of her own realistic illusion of self-presence in a highly-mediated way on these nine occasions in the text, the poem prepares the reader, I suggest, to learn how to participate independently and autonomously in the construction of meaning in the abstract space of *Paradiso*. In addition to these nine 'learner mode' exercises, the poem is full of other elective opportunities to spontaneously deploy her new cognitive skills, in the manifold gaps in the text, as I shall explore next.

4.2.3. Narration through gaps in the text: similes and ellipses

Iser's indeterminacy hypothesis, quoted in my Introduction, proposes that 'the written part of the text gives us the knowledge, but it is the unwritten part that gives us the opportunity to picture things; indeed, without the elements of indeterminacy, the gaps in the text, we should not be able to use our imagination' (1974: 283). All narrative texts are inherently 'gappy' to a certain extent, because it is neither possible (in terms of volume of description) nor desirable (in terms of reader engagement) to describe every detail of the people, places and events evoked; so, in any text, readers must constantly make inferences to fill in these gaps in order to establish logical coherence.[29] However, in this section I shall propose that Dante's deployment of two particular types of 'gap', the *simile* and the *narrative ellipsis*, goes radically beyond this narrative convention of essential readability and instead reveals itself to be a strategy that invites progressively more agential and creative reader participation, supporting the exceptional 'openness' of the *Comedy*.[30]

To understand why we may be able to consider the narration of gaps in the *Comedy* in a new light, I borrow from cognitive theorist Emily Troscianko on recent developments in the so-called 'imagery debate' to consider how this might change our understanding of how readers construct mental models. Troscianko (2013: 181–83) writes that mental models have traditionally been assumed to be either 'pictorial' (Kosslyn 1980) or 'propositional' (Pylyshyn 2003). Pictorialists such as Stephen Kosslyn, writes Troscianko, pursued 'a theory of mental imagery based on pictorial, or analogue representation' (2013: 181) — that is, a 'depictive' model (182); Propositionalists like Zenon Pylyshyn proposed instead that the content of visual and imaginative experience is encoded in a language-like, rather than analogous, form. However, an emerging line of thought in cognitive poetics, attributed to Nigel Thomas and rooted in the embodied models of cognition discussed in Chapter 1, now suggests instead that mental models also carry perceptual and motoric information, making them *embodied* and *dynamic* in form, or *enactive*, in Troscianko's terms.[31] This leads Troscianko to conclude that 'we need to get away from the notion of representation — pictorial or propositional — as the explanatory medium and think about imagining as enactive — that is, as a way of acting' (2013: 181). In this enactive account, 'the role of representation is reduced to the neural encoding of instructions for exploring the world, with knowledge of [...] how the visual input would change if I or the object I'm looking at were to move' (184). 'Imagining isn't about building up a picture in the head, but is a form of ongoing exploration just as is seeing' (186).

This is consistent with contemporary thinking in neuroscience. Crucially, '[i]mages are not just visual', writes neuroscientist Antonio Damasio, nor static; nor are they always conscious (2000: 318–19).[32] Rather than conceiving of a mental model primarily as something we *see* — a kind of projected image or picture in the mind that we view as external observer (like the Cartesian theatre model) and come to understand through deciphering its meaning — we might conceive of it instead as something we experience or *feel*: a dynamic, multi-sensory, multi-modal series of cognitive operations that in combination support the re-presentation or simulation of a particular 'body state', or feeling in the body.

Troscianko noted in 2013 that the enactive view 'has so far failed to break the deadlock' (181) of the imagery debate, probably because the historical primacy of visual representation in (Cartesian) culture has created a 'folk-psychological understanding of vision and imagination as working pictorially' (187). But I would suggest that in terms of cognitive narrative theory, this is precisely where the notion of embodied simulation takes us, towards an understanding of an interaction with the text based on a dynamic, enactive simulation, rather than mentally representing a sequence of static images.

Further, I suggest that precisely such a progression from pictorial to enactive mental modelling is one that the poem invites the reader to make over the course of the narrative, through the mini-frameworks instantiated by the hundreds of similes and ellipses in the poem that invite progressively more dynamic work, and support a capacity to sustain an increasingly realistic internal model of the interactions with the blessed.[33] The 'gappiness' that Dante's similes and ellipses constitute in the *Comedy*, I suggest, invites the brain to do the work of making inferences dynamically, just as we do in real life, and in this way underwrites the illusion of realistic self-presence in the virtual space of Dante's afterlife.[34]

In the next two sections, I set out the principle and a quantification of the instances of such gaps in the poem to indicate the scale of Dante's narrative strategy of inviting the reader to import her own cognitive data into the space of the poem from both memory and imagination, examining first how Dante deploys the *simile* as invitation to participate, and second the *narrative ellipsis*.

Similes

A simile is a figure of speech that invites the reader to compare one thing with another, whereby 'A remains A and B remains B' in Spitzer's phrase (1955: 153).[35] In the *Comedy* similes are typically signposted by such connecting words as 'come [...], così [...]', 'qual è [...], cotal [...]', 'sì [...], così [...]' and occasionally 'similmente' or 'non altrimenti'.[36] Such connectors are mildly disruptive, much less forcefully so than the mechanism of the direct address but sufficient nonetheless to signal a switch in cognitive mode in the reader's brain.

A simile serves to make a phenomenon vivid, recognisable and imaginable, facilitating the construction of a mental model by giving the reader components she can composite from memory: if she has seen a ferry backing out from a quay, if she has been up a hill in the fog and witnessed a watery sun breaking through, if she has ever pulled, or thought about pulling, her finger from a fire, she can begin, respectively, to visualise the movement of Geryon as he prepares for downward flight, to feel how the journeying Dante felt as he re-emerged into the sun from the darkness of the terrace of Wrath, to experience what it means to ascend the celestial ladder.[37] The reader is beginning to populate the simulation of Dante's narrated events with her own recreated experiences and her own embodied knowledge — not only in terms of the visual, but also the sensory, the motor, the visceral and, ultimately, the fully experiential in a virtual sense. In inviting the reader to hold in balance two concepts in her mind, using one to imaginatively construct the other, the simile constitutes another kind of 'gap' in the tissue of the text, inviting the reader to use things she knows — body states, experience of events, phenomena witnessed — to enrich her grasp of phenomena or experiences she does not, or cannot, know directly in material reality.

The simile has traditionally been characterised in narrative theory as a *comparison statement* (Aristotle's *Rhetoric*; I. A. Richards's *Philosophy of Rhetoric*), but it has proven remarkably difficult to establish from a literature review for the purposes of my analysis of the *Comedy* how readers actually understand or make meaning from similes (by comparison with an extensive body of work on metaphor including conceptual metaphor theory and embodied theories of metaphor), and how similes invite an effect in the reader.[38] My hypothesis in relation to the *Comedy* is that similes are deployed (as already discussed in relation to narrative training) to invite and hone in the reader the skill of dynamic, enactive mental modelling, but also to support the reader in learning to incorporate the cognitive data from her own experiences into the model, thereby re-experiencing old memories in a new context or creating new memories. I propose this because I find evidence, as I shall outline below, of a progression in Dante's narration from a prevalence of similes rooted in natural phenomena that are observable but not directly modellable (the *vehicle* — the figurative expression — is not an entity the human protagonist can fully simulate — for example, a whistling fire-brand), to an increasing presence of similes based in visceral human body states that the reader can directly reproduce in her own right.[39] I suggest that Dante achieves this by deploying a particular mode that I refer to as *narration through simile*, evidenced both through the quantity and deployment of similes and the progression in the type of imaginative work they invite the reader to do.

Whilst there is a rich history of commentary and scholarship relating to individual similes in the *Comedy* and some important work classifying different perceived categories of similes, there does not appear to have been any assessment of the cumulative and progressive effect of deployment of the simile as mode of narration or an analytically productive quantification (rather than the straightforward census popular with some late nineteenth-century critics).[40] However, the vast quantity of similes in the poem — they occupy more than a fifth of all the verses of narration in the poem — makes narration through simile such an extraordinarily prevalent mode in the *Comedy* that it seems essential (and arguably remarkable in its omission in scholarship hitherto) to explore whether there is a strategy at work.

The poem, as mentioned earlier (see n. 1), consists of some 14,000 verses, of which narration occupies just under half (the balance accounted for by the direct speech of the interacting souls and infernal 'staff', and of Virgil, Beatrice and the journeying Dante). Similes occupy almost 1,300 verses, or about 20 per cent of all the poem's verses of narration.[41] In *Inferno* and *Purgatorio,* the single-tercet simile is more prevalent (accounting for 44 per cent of all cases across the poem in total); in *Paradiso,* the double-tercet simile is more common (37 per cent); and in one in five cases (19 per cent), the comparison is extended over three or more tercets (found at similar levels across all three canticles).[42] This equates to a total of more than 200 similes in the poem (229, by my count), meaning the reader encounters on average between two and three similes per canto.[43] Such prevalence, I suggest, means that the way the reader habitually engages with the simile as narrative device — with greater or lesser cognitive effort and with more or less imaginative skill — will have a substantial impact on her overall interaction with the poem, and it seems surprising, then, that such relatively little attention seems to have been paid to how the reader 'reads' a simile.

In his analysis of the 'curious comparison' relating to the speed of the sky in *Paradiso* II, Singleton alludes to the highly concentrated cognitive effort of the visual imagination, of counter-factual reasoning (imagining how things could be otherwise), and of dynamic enactive imagination, that can be required to truly grasp the comparison in many of Dante's similes. In the single-tercet simile that ends the lengthy direct address to the reader in *Paradiso* II, Dante narrates that his thirst to arrive at the encounter with God bears him on almost as rapidly as the movement of the skies seen down here on earth:

> La concreata e perpetüa sete
> del deïforme regno cen portava
> veloci quasi come 'l ciel vedete. (19–21)

> In-born in being, our perpetual thirst
> to reach the deiform domain now bore us on
> as rapid, almost, as the spheres you see.

Singleton observes in his gloss (l. 21) that:

> we are not ordinarily conscious of the sky's motion. If, however, we follow the position of a heavenly body from hour to hour, we discover that in a very brief period it traverses an immense distance. The sky, without seeming to move at all, is really travelling with inconceivable velocity; and so we were doing.

Like the embodied enactment of a different standpoint discussed in Chapter 2 in Beatrice's reminder to the journeying Dante that 'tu non se' in terra' (*Par.*, I. 91), if the reader is to grasp the true nature of this simile she will need to pause and visualise dynamically this phenomenon of the apparently moving sky — which may involve cognitive activities of remembering, thinking about, or going out and observing for herself in real time, 'follow[ing] the position of a heavenly body from hour to hour' — in order to enact the necessary adjustment in perception that will enable her to imaginatively construct the analogy by which she can understand the journeying Dante's experience of vection in this space.[44] To do so fully requires no small investment of cognitive resource and time and this, I suggest, is what the strategy of narration through simile both invites and rewards.

Further, whilst we do not see a sizeable increase in the *number* of similes in *Paradiso* compared with *Inferno* (as perhaps may have been expected), there *is* an important way in which the reader's interaction with them is invited to change radically as the poem progresses. This progression is consistent with that seen in the narrative training exercises — that is, from a relatively straightforward model of visualisation, or what is observable, in *Inferno*, to a dynamic, enactive model in *Paradiso* that hones

and rewards a capacity for enactive imagination based in a reproduction of the
generative processes of consciousness that underpin the experience of realistic self-
presence, even in the abstract interaction with the divine.[45] Amongst the powerful
visual images of observable phenomena in *Inferno*, for example, we might consider
the Minotaur in the first circle of hell, described as jerking about — 'qua e là
saltella' — like a mortally wounded bull:

> Qual è quel toro che si slaccia in quella
> c'ha ricevuto già 'l colpo mortale,
> che gir non sa, ma qua e là saltella,
>   vid' io lo Minotauro far cotale. (*Inf.*, XII. 22–25)

> A stunned bull, stricken by its mortal blow,
> wrenches, that instant, free from noose and rope.
> It cannot walk but skips and hops about.
>   The Minotaur, I saw, behaved like that.

The reader, I suggest, is invited to model *not* the experience of either *vehicle* or
tenor (direct modelling — that is, to experience for herself what it feels like to be a
wounded bull or a jerking minotaur), but instead to model the journeying Dante's
experience of *seeing* this sight: spectating — that is, experiencing how such a sight
might make her feel. Further, there is the extended simile in *Inferno* XXI of the
busy scene of Venetian shipbuilders boiling up pitch (vehicle) and working away
on boat hulls that is used to convey — with an arguably deliberately obfuscating
superfluity in the data of individual industry — the detail of the thick black
substance, the 'pegola spessa' (17) (tenor), that bubbles and splashes onto the banks
in Malebolge.[46] The journeying Dante is reduced to simply staring, mesmerised ('la
giù fisamente mirava' [In mesmerised amazement I just gazed] (22)), his cognitive
resources too occupied with the visual data before him to pay attention to the
approaching threat of the 'diavol nero' [black devil] (29). Further, in *Inferno* XXI,
the dog unleashed to chase a thief, the chefs' boys forking simmering meat, the dogs
rushing on a pleading beggar; and in the very pit of Hell, Antaeus' posture that
has its analogue in the optical illusion of the Garisenda tower that looks like it is
falling when a cloud passes behind, the Danube that was never so thickly frozen as
Hell's ice lake, the experience of the first sight of Satan compared with seeing the
looming appearance of a windmill turning in thick fog or black night: all powerful
images inviting deployment of and burnishing the reader's visual imagination, all
supporting the illusion of spatial presence, but not yet fully exercising the reader's
capacity to experience herself as *tenor* and to directly model the *vehicle* in her own
right.[47]

   I propose that proficiency in the skill of visual imagination is an essential first step
in becoming adept in the more challenging skill of *enactment* (dynamic, embodied)
imagination. In *Paradiso*, I suggest, the emphasis shifts towards directly modellable
and enactable similes. Some of the more self-evident cases of such similes include,
for example, the compound simile of the paralysing effect of making a choice
between two comparable options that opens *Paradiso* IV, as the journeying Dante is
prevented from speaking by an inner tension of doubt and desire:

Intra due cibi, distanti e moventi
d'un modo, prima si morria di fame,
che liber' omo l'un recasse ai denti;
    sì si starebbe un agno intra due brame
di fieri lupi, igualmente temendo;
sì si starebbe un cane intra due dame:
    per che, s'i' mi tacea, me non riprendo,
da li miei dubbi d'un modo sospinto,
poi ch'era necessario, né commendo. (IV. 1–9)

Between two equidistant portions, equally
moving, if free to choose, you'd starve to death
before you'd carried either to your teeth.
    So, too, some lamb might stand between the bite
of hungry wolves, fearing them both alike.
So, too, a hound would stand between two does.
    If, therefore, I kept silence now, I neither
criticise nor praise myself. Driven by doubts
of equal measure, this was necessity.

Even distinguishing what is tenor and what is vehicle here is not straightforward. The usual order — vehicle, tenor — is inverted, and there appear to be two vehicles, which in combination express the inner conflict and the complexity of the paradox: the vulnerable lamb that stands between two wolves; the hound rendered powerless between two does. The tenor, then, is the impersonal 'si' (2), qualified in the next verse with 'omo' (3), a person: 'prima *si* morria di fame, | che liber' omo l'un recasse ai denti' (2–3). Through the twin vehicles, the reader is invited to model a complex visceral experience (an inner conflict of doubt and desire), requiring enactment imagination rather than visualisation alone; but, importantly, the tenor, the universal 'omo' [man], opens a space into which she can directly project her own identity. She is invited to imagine *for herself* how it would feel to starve to death through paralysis of choice; then to elaborate this visceral feeling imaginatively through modelling the lamb and the hound; and only then is she invited to project this back onto the journeying Dante in order to empathise with and participate in his experience. We might consider, too, in *Paradiso*, the invitation to visceral enactment through the simile of the dancers, whose exultation momentarily quickens their gestures, that evokes the intensified movement of the lights of the Christian philosophers in the Heaven of the Sun when Beatrice speaks (canto XIV); or the speed at which a lady's blush subsides that expresses the journeying Dante's experience of his sixth ascent (canto XVIII); or the instinctual stretching upwards of the lights in the Heaven of the Fixed Stars with love towards Mary that is compared to the suckling baby who, replete, holds out its arms to its mother (canto XXIII); or, in the Empyrean, the 'barbari' [barbarians] stupefied at seeing the treasures of Rome, the pilgrims that gaze freely around the temple and the Croatians come to view the Veronica (canto XXXI).[48] In each case, I suggest, the narration invites the reader to independently model the associated visceral body state for herself, but this takes real cognitive work, time and skill.

My suggestion, then, is that the strategy of narration through simile in the *Comedy* is deployed to repeatedly open up spaces in the text for increasingly enactive acts of imaginative participation, maximising the reader's 'personalisation' of the journey.

Finally, I turn to the second major component in Dante's strategy of narratological 'gappiness' as an invitation to self-presence: the narrative ellipsis.

Ellipses

With deceptive simplicity, Mieke Bal has characterised the narrative ellipsis as 'that which has been omitted' (2009: 101). In this section, I propose that Dante's deployment of narrative ellipses in the *Comedy* is complex: some ellipses invite and reward participation (yielding greater understanding or opportunities for participation with a community); others are distractions or blind alleys (a Ulyssean pursuit of knowledge for its own sake).[49] To engage well with the ellipsis, then, the reader must also deploy her skills of judgment and reasoning.

As discussed previously, all texts, by necessity, deploy narrative ellipsis in the interests of readability. The human brain, being adapted to storytelling as a means of making meaning, is adept in handling the gaps that narrative ellipses frame without disrupting immersion in the narrative, making inferences as required in order to support what cognitive psychologists McKoon and Ratcliff have termed 'local coherence' (1992: 440), or, in other words, an essential understanding of narrated events. However, I would suggest that Dante frequently *points* to his ellipses, to the extent that on many occasions the ellipsis highlights or draws attention to the very thing it ostensibly excises. Consequently, we may infer a strategy to be at work.

In *Inferno* IX, for example, Virgil reveals the astonishing information that he has travelled through Hell before. But his account is cut short by a narrative ellipsis: 'E altro disse, ma non l'ho a mente' [He said much more. But what I can't recall] (34), writes the narrating Dante, turning instead to the fire leaping from the top of the gates of Hell that is now occupying the journeying Dante. Such a transition could have been effected with minimal disruption with a simple jump-cut, as occurs elsewhere in the poem.[50] It is the announcement of the ellipsis that disrupts the reader's automatic processes of cognitive assimilation, rendering present — and thereby significant — the narrating Dante's silencing of Virgil, inviting questions. What did Virgil say? Why is the narrating Dante — Virgil's former pupil in the afterlife and now returned and re-presenting his experience — so casually dismissive of the significance of Virgil's earlier journey? There are some 300 ellipses that draw attention to themselves in some way in the poem.[51]

I suggest that narrative ellipses are usually deployed in the *Comedy* for two purposes. The first is the simple reinforcement of a principle that imaginative participation in an artefact is more powerful than spectatorship, since any first-person narrative account will be necessarily selective, subjective and partial — as set up from the very beginning of *Inferno*: 'ma per trattar del ben ch'i vi trovai, | dirò de *l'altre cose* ch'i v'ho scorte' [But since my theme will be the good I found there, | I mean to speak of *other things* I saw] (*Inf.*, I. 8–9; my emphasis). Of necessity, things will be excluded. This is a standard failure of convention to which all mediated narrative accounts are subject. Encountering something in person, as discussed in the Introduction in relation to the journeying Dante's own necessary physical interaction with the 'perdute genti', will always yield a more powerful form of experience; this is the principle upon which I have proposed invitations to presence in the *Comedy* to rest. In *Inferno* XIV, Virgil enacts this principle himself, explicitly excising his own words, stopping himself from describing to the journeying Dante how the three rivers of hell all pool together in Cocytus, on the grounds that Dante will *see it for himself*, 'tu lo vedrai, però qui non si conta':

> 'infin, là ove più non si dismonta,
> fanno Cocito; e qual sia quello stagno
> tu lo vedrai, però qui non si conta.' (118–20)

> 'until (since there is no way further on)
> they all collect as Cocytus. But you yourself
> will see that pool. So I'll not tell the tale.'

By becoming skilled at and habituated in deriving inferences from narrative ellipses, the reader supports her own capacity to experience the illusion of realistic presence, liberating her from the spectatorship of the 'desiderosi d'ascoltar'. This cognitive skill becomes progressively more important in *Paradiso* as the journeying Dante's internal experience is increasingly elided in the narration, inviting the reader to construct more by inference than by mirroring, or modelling, his narrated body states herself. In *Paradiso* IV, for example, the narrating Dante reports that the journeying Dante's desire is displayed on his face, ''l mio disir dipinto | m'era nel viso' (10–11); but crucially, because his face is not (visually) perceptible to the reader as it is (intuitively) perceptible to the blessed, the reader must rely on him to tell us how he feels. But in an explicit ellipsis, he is silent: 'Io mi tacea' (10). The reader must imaginatively model his desire independently.

Second, I suggest the ellipsis in the *Comedy* invites the reader to refine her skill in making judgments about the 'gaps' into which she will invest cognitive resource.[52] Not every invitation to participate will be benign or productive, and blanket cognitive participation — in the virtual world of the narrative as in the real world — would be overwhelming. Instead, the reader can learn to allocate attention and cognitive resource *with judgment*. In *Inferno* IX again, for example, we observe the destructive nature of unrestrained imaginative inference, or speculation, when the ellipsis (Virgil's 'parola tronca') that follows his failure to gain access to the City of Dis sends the journeying Dante into imagining the worst without due cause, as he now acknowledges: 'io traeva la parola tronca | forse a peggior sentenzia che non tenne' [And so, from these truncated words, I drew | a meaning worse, perhaps, than he had meant] (14–15).[53] *Inferno* is rich in such opportunities to dally, be sidetracked or lose the capacity for rational judgment as thoughts spiral out of control.

By contrast, *Purgatorio* repeatedly offers a model of the ellipsis that invites and actively rewards cognitive investment, including one particular type in the form of citations of openings to the psalms, hymns and prayers of the liturgy. As Helena Phillips-Robins has written in relation to the singing of the first psalm encountered in *Purgatorio* II, cited below, Dante repeatedly invokes and then immediately elides the content of these familiar texts in *Purgatorio*:

'In exitu Isräel de Aegypto'
cantavan tutti insieme ad una voce
con quanto di quel salmo è poscia scripto.
       Poi fece il segno lor di santa croce;
ond' ei si gittar tutti in su la piaggia:
ed el sen gì, come venne, veloce. (46–51)

'In exitu Isräel de Aegypto':
they sang this all together, in one voice,
with all the psalm that's written after this.
       Then, over them, he made the holy cross,
at which they flung themselves upon the shore.
And he, as fast as he had come, went off.

Whilst the singing of only the first line of the psalm is explicitly and mimetically narrated in the text, the event of the singing of the entirety of the psalm is implied in the summary narration of line 48, 'con quanto di quel salmo è poscia scripto', constituting for Phillips-Robins 'an implicit invitation to call to mind the rest of the psalm' (2016: 12). Observing that 'the shades are blessed and set foot in Purgatory as soon as they have finished the psalm', she asks: 'What happens if we pause our reading of the canto to recite, sing, or open a Bible and read the whole of the psalm?' (12). Her conclusion is that 'we are given a space in which to perform the psalm, to arrive at the souls' blessing with the same words on our lips, and to experience corporeally the shades' processional movement' (16). The reader, then, who 'fills' this gap by breaking off reading to rehearse for herself the psalm in full will return to the poem, contemporaneous with the other penitents, at the same point of blessing, mentally receiving the same sign of the cross from the angel, 'Poi fece il segno lor de la santa croce' (49). The ellipsis has opened a very particular space for the reader's direct participation, inviting her to mentally simulate her own experience of this element of the journey, imaginatively co-present with the other newly arrived penitential souls.

Many texts deliver a vivid empathic experience of identification with a protagonist, the sense of 'your own heart beating inside their clothes', to use Flaubert's formulation in *Madame Bovary*. In the *Comedy*, the reader has access to the thoughts and feelings of the journeying Dante (and occasionally those of the narrating Dante too) through self-report, and additionally through the mechanism of embodied simulation that invites empathic identification with the journeying Dante's personal experience through the interface of the body. Through the mechanisms of spatial presence, the poem invites the reader to experience the perceptual illusion of realistic presence in the narrated space; through those of social presence, it invites her to experience the illusion of presence at the encounters that take place there. In this chapter, I have suggested that the illusion of presence can be taken even further, with the reader invited to experience an illusion of personal agency in the virtual space. She can look *at* the journeying Dante, from outside, as she would in real life, but also directly through his eyes in an act of identification, switching constantly between focal views (the *narrating instances* model). She may on occasion experience the illusion that she can turn her own head in the narrated space, through narration of new objects constantly coming into her line of sight (*narration through mobile camera view*). She can experience the illusion of a reciprocal social relationship across virtual worlds (the mechanism of the *direct address to the reader*). She can hone her skills of imagination to transform the virtual into a powerful and sustained experience of an alternative reality (the *narrative training exercises*). And, in response to the massive network of gaps in the text, she can constantly deploy components from her own memories and imagination, reframing and reformulating her own cognitive data to enrich and personalise her virtual experience.

Defining an experience of *selfhood*, presence theorists Waterworth and Riva propose that:

> the basis for a conscious self is a feeling state that arises when organisms represent a largely non-conscious proto self in the process of being modified by objects [...]. This gives the feeling, not just that something is happening, but that something is happening *to me*. (2014: 14; my emphasis)

My suggestion is that the reader who responds to the invitations in the poem to self-presence maximises her likelihood of feeling 'modified' in some way or of experiencing a *change to the self* as a result of her interaction with the poem: a change in understanding, perhaps, or behaviour; or, perhaps most powerfully, a change in belief.[54]

So far, I have suggested that opportunities for participation in the *Comedy* are always mediated by the writer through the deployment of narratological devices used strategically to invite participation at a particular point in the narrative and in a particular way. In the next and final chapter of the book, I suggest that the poem, in fact, offers the reader the opportunity to take participation one stage further: not waiting for an invitation to participate, but reflexively and electively identifying as personally implicated in the narrative, not just in the 'noi', 'voi' and 'tu' of the direct addresses, but even, ultimately, in the poem's 'io'.

Notes to Chapter 4

1. The poem consists of 14,233 verses. By my count, narration occupies 6,590 verses, or 46 per cent of the total verses of the poem. For a brief discussion of earlier quantitative analyses of narrative vs. dialogue in the poem, see Paolo De Ventura (2007: especially 87–94).
2. Mean number of verses per canto of journeying Dante direct speech, within each canticle: *Inferno*, 13 verses; *Purgatorio*, 9; *Paradiso*, 10.
3. In *The Implied Reader*, Iser characterises Thackeray's *Henry Esmond* as 'the autobiography of a fictional character', whose 'various [narratological] perspectives [...] are constantly interacting throughout Esmond's narrative' (1974: 130). This interaction, writes Iser, 'brings about an almost kaleidoscopic succession of mobile standpoints, from which there emerges the gradual self-illumination of subjectivity [...]. It is only the plurality of views which can give rise to an adequate picture of subjectivity. A single standpoint would merely transform the life recorded here into the representative illustration of one view formed almost independently of experience, whereas the multiplicity of standpoints shows that possibilities of judgment must arise first and foremost out of experience of the self, which must come to terms with its own subjectivity' (133–34).
4. These cantos have been selected as likely to be indicative of the range of narrating instances afforded to both the newly arrived reader and the reader who has undertaken the entire journey of the poem.

5. The term 'Experiencing I' is borrowed from Franz Stanzel's *Theory of Narrative* (1984). 'Embodied Narrator' is my own term. 'Implied Author' and 'Zero-Focalised Narration' are reception commonplaces.

6. In 'Dante and his Reader', Beall points towards an identification of such a narrating instance in relation to the early authorial intrusion of this 'Ahi', but without then making the (for me) crucial additional distinction between an Embodied Narrator and an Implied Author narrating instance. He writes: 'This second terzina (so little noticed in the commentaries) not only introduces the author's voice, which we shall hear frequently, but also his all-important memory, with the temporal dimensions and the aesthetic distances that it implies' (Beall 1979: 300).

7. The necessary separation of the Implied Author and the Embodied Narrator may, I propose, offer a new way of thinking about the question of *auctoritas* in the *Comedy* as set out by Albert Ascoli in *Dante and the Making of a Modern Author*. Ascoli finds it so frustratingly difficult to find evidence to prove his own theory of Dante's desire to lay claim to a status of *auctor*, noting that in the *Comedy* Dante 'never applies the words *autore* and *autorità* to himself' (2008: 303). I would suggest that an understanding of the constant switching between narrating instances, particularly the having and not-having authority instances of the Implied Author and the Embodied Narrator, may form the basis for some kind of new resolution of Ascoli's question, by opening the possibility that Dante's narrative strategy precludes the stability in narrator character necessary for the attribution of a quality of *auctoritas*. The Implied Author narrating instance stands 'outside time', with its global omniscience and its authoritative, unequivocal tone that gestures towards Ascoli's 'transhistorical truths'. Compare this with the flesh and bone fictive construct of the Embodied Narrator narrating instance, situated *within* time, and which for this reason alone can have no claim to *auctoritas*.

8. Zero-Focalised Narration is responsible for the swift depiction of the journeying Dante's attempted ascents of the mountain in *Inferno* I, providing rapid movement through the action.

9. Switching into the Embodied Narrator at lines 120–21 and 145–47, the Experiencing I at 122 and 130, and (arguably) the Implied Author at 132–33.

10. The one exception is the spatial detail that Socrates and Plato are the closest to Aristotle: 'quivi vid' ïo Socrate e Platone, | che 'nnanzi a li altri più presso li stanno' [And, closer to his side than all the rest, | I now saw Socrates, I saw now Plato] (134–35).

11. There is also a brief switch into the Implied Author narrating instance with the simile at line 45.

12. 'E come, per sentir più dilettanza | bene operando, l'uom di giorno in giorno | s'accorge che la sua virtute avanza, | sì m'accors' io che 'l mio girare intorno | col cielo insieme avea cresciuto l'arco, | veggendo quel miracol più addorno' [And as we recognise from day to day | that we, in doing good, have now advanced | when, doing good, we feel a greater joy, | so, too, as with the skies I circled round, | I knew the arc through which we swung had grown, | seeing that miracle yet more adorned] (*Par.*, XVIII. 58–63).

13. Only to find, of course, that Beatrice has been replaced by Bernard ('Uno intendea, e altro mi rispuose' [I'd looked for one thing. Something else replied], 58). As discussed in my Introduction, this is one of the great narrative surprises of the poem. Pertile has written of this surprise that it 'does not seem to be narratologically cogent', going on to 'conjecture' that 'Saint Bernard may not have been in Dante's original plans for the conclusion of his poem' (2003: 111). My reading of Bernard's sign offers a different possible model to that of Pertile, suggesting a specific narratological strategy to be at work.

14. 'pensa': *Inf.*, VIII. 94, *Inf.*, XX. 20, *Purg.*, X. 110, *Purg.*, XXXI. 124, *Par.*, V. 109; 'ricorditi': *Purg.*, XVII. 1; 'imagini': *Par.*, XIII. 1, 7, 10; 'leggi': *Purg.*, XXIX. 100; 'aguzza': *Purg.*, VIII. 19; 'nol dimandar': *Inf.*, XXXIV. 23; 'non attender' [don't dwell]: *Purg.*, X. 109.

15. On an expansion of the category of the direct address, see also Beall (1979). More generally, on the context of scholarship relating to the direct addresses, see Paolo De Ventura's analysis of this previously 'neglected aspect' (2007: 66) of Dante scholarship in *Dramma e dialogo nella* Commedia *di Dante* (particularly 61–84). For De Ventura's summary of Dante scholarship in this field — limited, until the mid-twentieth century, to 'brief beats, encyclopaedia entries, and footnotes' (2007: 64) — see pp. 63–64; on the question of the 'varietà del pubblico' who may have engaged with the poem, see pp. 61–62, 66–69, and 80; on the relation of the addresses and apostrophes, see pp. 70–74; on an overlap with preaching and homiletics, see p. 78.

16. Note there is no imperative in the addresses at *Inf.*, XXV. 46, *Purg.*, XXXIII. 126 and *Par.*, XXII. 106.

17. Tallying each critic's counts is unfortunately made somewhat more difficult by their highly qualitative approaches, together with one or two typographical errors regarding line and canto numbers.

18. On apostrophe and the direct address, see De Ventura (2007: 70–79).

19. So too, it seems, would Beall, writing of the 'anime ingannate', or the 'miseri lassi' (*Purg.*, X. 121): 'But such passages often carry a message of indignation or contempt which Dante, being Dante, surely meant to be received through reading his text' (1979: 302).

20. See Vittorio Montemaggi's essay, 'Afterword: Forgiveness, Prayer, and the Meaning of Poetry' (2014: particularly 139–41).

21. There is further interesting work to be done to determine if there are any patterns in the cognitive responses invited by the direct addresses that do not precede a narrative training exercise.

22. I have chosen the term 'narrative training' because it most clearly reinforces the link I wish to make between narratological device and reader outcome. However, from the general standpoint of participation, I am sensitive that 'training' might imply intentionality. We might also say 'cognitive rehearsal' or think in terms of Joshua Landy's notion of 'formative fictions' — that is, 'texts whose function it is to fine-tune our mental capacities' (2012: 10).

23. Alvin Goldman distinguishes a visceral, embodied, dynamic 'enactment imagination' from a more sketchy 'suppositional imagination', defining enactment imagination as 'enacting, or trying to enact' the mediated or narrated content itself, whilst suppositional imagination involves 'merely supposing' that particular content obtains without trying to 'create a mental surrogate' of it. He gives as an example of content the notion of elation, so in suppositional imagination we would retrieve a grasp of what we understand 'elation' to *mean*, but it would only be through enactment imagination that we might actually re-experience *how it feels:* that is, through a visceral simulation (Goldman 2008: 47–48). See also Gallese and Goldman 1998). In literary theory, Emily Troscianko (2013) has summarised and continues to extend an analysis of the state of play of the so-called 'imagery debate' in the early twenty-first century, separating pictorial, propositional, and enactive theories of mental modelling. I explore this more fully in the next section in this chapter, on indirect invitations.

24. We know that something we see, hear, or experience can make us change our minds at a conscious level, modifying our understanding or beliefs. But we can also experience modification of our *unconscious* reflexes that support our habitual behaviours and beliefs. Philosopher of psychology Tamar Gendler terms these *aliefs*, writing: 'Alief is a more primitive state than either belief or imagination: it directly activates behavioural response patterns (as opposed to motivating in conjunction with desire or pretended desire)' (2008: 634). Waterworth and Riva refer to a similar principle but define it in terms of a *rendering intuitive* of the reflexes: giving the example of the way in which we internalise the steps necessary to drive a car, they suggest that 'intuition is not only innate [as it has long been considered]. Research on perceptual-cognitive and motor skills shows that they are automatised through experience [and practice] and thus rendered intuitive' (2014: 37).

25. Most usefully for my purposes here, in Mark's Gospel, Landy explores the 'ostentatiously figurative language [of Jesus's speech]' that trains the receiver's capacity to 'dwell in metaphor', 'train[ing] one's mind to pass from letter into spirit, from immanence into transcendence, from human concerns to the point of view of God' (2012: 60).

26. Phenomenologist Hubert Dreyfus discusses a 'learner' mode (1972: xxii) in *What Computers Can't Do: A Critique of Artificial Reason,* in terms of the different cognitive tasks implied in learning a skill and deployment of that skill as expert.

27. A reptilian six-legged variety in the second transmutation ('un serpente con sei piè', XXV. 50); a miniature serpent in the third ('un serpentello', XXV. 83).

28. Of course, the narrator himself is *not* confused, fully able to re-create, from memory and with tremendously detailed observation, the entire experience. Interestingly, whilst 'abborra' is normally considered in its sense of 'to wander' or 'to be confused', this evidence perhaps lends

support to E. G. Parodi's etymological tracing of 'abborra' to the dialect word *abbarrucciare*, meaning 'to throw things around in confusion', with its emphasis on wilful and deliberate obfuscation (as noted in Singleton's gloss on l. 144). This might lend, I suggest, further support to my proposal that this authorial attention to the reader's cognitions is strategic.

29. I borrow the term 'gappy' from Ellen Spolsky (1993) who herself develops this notion and terminology of 'gappiness' in relation to the construction of meaning from a text from Dennett's work on consciousness. Further, on inference and coherence, see Arthur Graesser et al. (1994).

30. Nicola Gardini writes of an 'abundance of lacunae' (2014: 46) in the *Comedy*, finding in the creative work invited by such 'lacunosity' a readerly pleasure acknowledged since Aristotle (48), and identifying two key reasons for their deployment: a 'realism effect' (50), conventional to narrative discourse ('rendering concrete that which is not there', 50) and, of course in *Paradiso*, a not-saying because 'it is not sayable' [il poeta non dice perché non è in grado di dire] (51). He concludes: 'I am of the opinion that in Dantean rhetoric, these two reasons — the pragmatic and the metaphysical — are one. Saying you will not say from a pure and simple inability *to* say is a way of expanding the fiction and giving it the status of truth. Whatever the cause of not saying — the art or nature of speech itself –, not saying suggests a totality which, precisely in the name of this not-saying, is assumed to be authentic, incontestable and worth listening to' (53). For Gardini, then, lacunae are characteristic of Truth ('Dante [...] dice la Verità', 55): 'Lacunosity impels the reader to these two things: to trust the poet and — and here are the extremes to which Dante's metaphysical realism pushes you — to want to relive for yourself (sooner or later) that same experience that the text can only partially depict' (54).

31. See Thomas (1999).

32. Damasio writes: *'Images Are Not Just Visual*: By the term images I mean mental patterns with a structure built with the tokens of each of the sensory modalities — visual, auditory, olfactory, gustatory, and somatosensory. The somatosensory modality [...] includes varied forms of sense: touch, muscular, temperature, pain, visceral, and vestibular. The word "image" does not refer to visual image alone. There is nothing static about images either. The word also refers to sound images such as those caused by music or the wind, and to the somatosensory images that Einstein used in his mental problem solving [and refers to as 'muscular' images]. Images in all modalities "depict" processes and entities of all kinds, concrete as well as abstract. | Images may be conscious or unconscious. It should be noted, however, that not all the images the brain constructs are made conscious. There are simply too many images being generated and too much competition for the relatively small window of mind in which images can be made conscious — the window, that is, in which images are accompanied by a sense that we are apprehending them and that, as a consequence, are properly attended' (2000: 318–19; formatting in original).

33. The *Comedy* may be a particularly interesting text to explore in these terms, not only because of the way it may help us understand reader reception and how this has changed over time from oral to print to screen and now to digital cultures, but also because we need more properly to understand how a Cartesian habit of thinking critically in pictorial terms may have influenced scholarship.

34. I would propose that as a strategy, 'gappiness' really works when deployed with the requisite skill: consider the 'preposterousness' (Hollander's term) of the descent on Geryon that convinces nonetheless (see Chapter 2).

35. 'It may be noted that Dante's favourite device is not the metaphor in which A becomes B, but the simile in which A remains A and B remains B; indeed, the whole *Comedy* could be said to be one great simile in which A (the Beyond) is explained in terms of B (this earth)'. Of metaphor, Mazzeo comments: 'Both poetry and philosophy use metaphor to express truths which would be otherwise inexpressible. There is a considerable difference between this view and the conception in the *Convivio* of poetic metaphor as a beautiful lie embellishing a truth, sweetening some abstract moral idea' (1958: 41).

36. Kirkpatrick explains his motive for frequently translating 'come' as 'compare' as follows: the word compare 'may seem an unjustifiably free translation since all we have in the original is *come*; but I use "compare", here and throughout, for a particular reason — which you must judge

for yourselves to be right or wrong. In my view, where metaphor is often taken to be a defining characteristic of poetry, *simile* is the central feature in Dante's palette. And the implications of this bear upon the poet's philosophy or theology and also upon the way in which his poem invites us to read it [...]. Metaphor transforms our perceptions. By contrast, simile invites us to sharpen our appreciation of the inter-related plenitude of existence [...]. And through attending to the comparison, however humdrum this might appear, we as readers may orient ourselves in the order of creation, participating directly in its choreography. "Compare", I would like to think, invites one to see things, to trust one's eyes and to enter into the dance. In this regard as in others, we cannot read Dante passively as onlookers or only as dispassionate scholars. We need — even at the risk of translating him poorly — to perform his words for ourselves, in the visual imagination, on the tongue and larynx, down to our very nerve ends' (Kirkpatrick 2019: 145–46; emphasis in original).

37. The descent on Geryon in *Inferno* XVII (100–01); the journeying Dante's experience of emerging from the darkness of the terrace of Anger into the sun again, in *Purgatorio* XVII (1–12), and the journeying Dante's experience of his ascent up the celestial ladder in *Paradiso* XXII (109–11), respectively.

38. An unpublished doctoral thesis by Adam Gargani on this subject, 'Poetic Comparisons: How Similes are Understood', finds that 'there has yet to be a monograph published in English on the topic of how similes are understood' (2014: 1), suggesting that '[t]here is some confusion in the field of figurative language studies over the definition of simile. Moreover, metaphor is often conflated with simile. I claim that these two factors have led to a situation which is not conducive to research on how similes are understood' (2). Gargani concludes that there is a requirement for simile theory to better understand the effects of specifically *poetic* language (as opposed to literal comparisons). There is certainly further work that could be done in relation to similes in the *Comedy* to explore some of Gargani's ideas and to seek to add to discussions about the differing effects of metaphor and simile on reader understanding and participation in the *Comedy*.

39. I borrow the term *vehicle* here from I. A. Richards's work on metaphors (1965), in which the *vehicle* is the thing, or figurative expression, which constitutes the comparison, and the *tenor* is the subject. For example: 'Come le rane *[vehicle]* innanzi a la nimica | biscia per l'acqua si dileguan tutte, | fin ch'a la terra ciascuna s'abbica, | vid' io più di mille anime distrutte *[tenor]*' [Like frogs *[vehicle]* that glimpse their enemy the snake, | and vanish rapidly across the pond — | diving till each sits huddling on its bed — | I saw a thousand ruined souls or more *[tenor]*] (*Inf.*, IX. 76–79).

40. Important studies include those by Madison Sowell who rues 'the paucity of books relating to this subject' (1983: 170); James Applewhite's essay that opens with a series of remarks about the peak in scholarship in 'tabulation of the similes' at the end of the nineteenth century, including Giovanni Franciosi's 'compilation', and Luigi Venturi's more elaborate 'explication' that 'arrives at an indication of the newness of many of Dante's similes, as well as the accuracy of the descriptive power of the poet' (1964: 294); C. S. Lewis's essay, 'Dante's Similes' (1965), which defined four types of Dantean simile, 'Virgilian or Homeric', 'pictorial', 'psychological' and 'metaphysical'; Richard Lansing's study, *From Image to Idea*, in which he concludes that 'Dante's similes present images that are immediately comprehensible in a visual sense, but at the same time their full significance cannot be comprehended without reference to a wider context' (1977: 168); and Eric S. Mallin (1984) that explores a notion of a type of simile — his eponymous 'false simile' — which, he suggests, effectively compares A with A; a type of simile he proposes to be identical with Lansing's 'pseudosimile' and C. S. Lewis' 'psychological simile' (although I read the function of Mallin's 'pseudosimile' in a different way). For a review of a wider bibliography on similes in the *Comedy* since Venturi, see Nicolò Maldina (2008). See Maldina (2008 and 2017) also on the important role of rhetoric and medieval preaching in Dante's use of similes.

41. More precisely, as previously discussed: the poem consists of 14,233 verses; narration occupies 6,590 lines, compared with 7,643 verses of direct discourse. If similes occupy 1,285 lines of the poem, this equates to 21 per cent of the poem's narration, or 9 per cent of the total poem. As

with all quantitative analysis of narrative devices in the *Comedy*, necessary judgments have been imposed on, for example, the precise point at which a simile starts and finishes. It is interesting to note that Dante uses similes only very rarely in direct speech, with only eight instances of this, seven of which occur in *Paradiso*: Gerard (*Purg.*, XVIII. 58–59); Beatrice (*Par.*, I. 133–35, IV. 82–84, XVIII. 35–36); Cacciaguida (*Par.*, XVII. 46–48); the Justice Eagle (*Par.*, XIX. 58–63); the journeying Dante protagonist to St Benedict (*Par.*, XXII. 55–57); and St Bernard (*Par.*, XXXII. 139–41). Further research is needed to explore why this is the case, but we might make a preliminary inference that, in conversation, we immediately and directly simulate how something feels through present and reciprocal interaction via mechanisms such as kinaesthetic empathy (see Chapter 3), whilst in retrospective narration this is not possible, so this present simulation is aided by recruiting the reader's own previous lived experience. In fact, 97 per cent of all the instances of similes noted in this analysis occur in the poem's narration, and primarily in the Implied Author narrating instance (see the section on narrating instances in this chapter): when the reader participates in the construction of similes, she is principally interacting with the omniscient, lyrical, authoritative creator of the poem as system.

42. We might infer that the increase in double-tercet similes in *Paradiso* more explicitly invites the reader to award equal weight to each component of the simile, both the material analogue and the after-life subject. This establishes, I propose, a mental oscillation between the two phenomena that supports a sense of holding two concepts simultaneously in the mind, honing a capacity for rapid cognitive switching that is so important in balancing the reader's sense of identification with the journeying Dante protagonist with her own experience of participation in the events of the virtual space.

43. I have included only those comparisons where Dante clearly sets out the qualities of the phenomenon with which he is inviting comparison; I have excluded for now those cases (of which there are only a handful and which normally do not extend beyond a single verse) where the qualities are not explicit and must be inferred. I exclude here the compact lyrical evocation of metaphor, such as Charon's 'occhi di bragia' [hot-coal eyes] (*Inf.*, III. 109), or the 'tristo sacco' [grim bag] that is Maometto's colon (*Inf.*, XXVIII. 26).

44. It is worth noting here that the narration explicitly separates the reader(s) from not only the journeying Dante but also the narrating Dante through the plural vocative 'voi' [you] ('vedete' [you see], 21), rather than 'noi' [we]. Of course, there is already a choice of 'voi's with which the reader might electively identify: the 'voi' in the 'piccioletta barca' (1), counselled to turn back; or 'voialtri pochi' (10) who are fit to set out across the waters of *Paradiso*. We may infer that the participatory reader may put greater cognitive resources behind imaginatively enacting this comparison, the more fully to simulate the journeying Dante's experience for herself; the spectating reader, by contrast, may be more anxious simply to sketch the meaning and turn the page to know where Dante's journey will take him next.

45. The progression is by no means wholly linear: there are instances of each of the different modes of simile in all cantos, and there are opportunities for enactment imagination throughout the poem.

46. 'Quale ne l'arzanà de' Viniziani | bolle l'inverno la tenace pece | a rimpalmare i legni lor non sani, | ché navicar non ponno — in quella vece | chi fa suo legno novo e chi ristoppa | le coste a quel che più vïaggi fece; | chi ribatte da proda e chi da poppa; | altri fa remi e altri volge sarte; | chi terzeruolo e artimon rintoppa –: | tal, non per foco ma per divin' arte, | bollia là giuso una pegola spessa, | che 'nviscava la ripa d'ogne parte. | I' vedea lei, ma non vedëa in essa | mai che le bolle che 'l bollor levava, | e gonfiar tutta, e riseder compressa' [Compare: Venetians in their Arsenal, | in winter when their ships cannot set sail, | brew up a viscous pitch which they then smear | on ailing boards, or else lay down new hulls. | Others will plug the ribs of hulks that have, | by now, made many a long-haul trip. | Some hammer at the prow, some at the poop, | some whittle oars, where others plait the rig. | Some mend the mainsail, others patch the jib. | So here — though more by art of God than fire — | a dense black gunge was brought to boiling point, | and splashed on all the banks in sticky smears. | I saw this stuff but nothing else within | but bubbles as the boiling bubbled on, | swelling to roundness, glue-ily sinking in] (*Inf.*, XXI. 7–21).

47. *Inf.*, XXI. 43–45, 55–57 and 67–71, respectively. In the pit of hell: *Inf.*, XXXI. 136–40, XXXII. 25–30 and XXXIV. 4–7, respectively.

48. *Par.*, XIV. 19–24, XVIII. 64–68 and XXIII. 121–25, respectively. In the Empyrean, all in XXXI, 31–40, 43–48 and 103–11, respectively.

49. Beyond the scope of my discussion here but of related interest is Hooper's observation of the 'elliptical' nature of Dante's characterisation (2019: 46). Hooper introduces, from medieval rhetorical theory, the distinction between the sketch (*effictio*), the description (*notatio*) and dialogue (*sermocinatio*) (46–47).

50. Compare, just a few tercets later, the much more conventional jump-cut between the *Messo*'s departure and the re-commencement of the journey: 'Poi si rivolse per la strada lorda, | e non fé motto a noi, ma fé sembiante | d'omo cui altra cura stringa e morda | che quella di colui che li è davante; | e noi movemmo i piedi inver' la terra' [He then turned back along the filthy road. | He spoke no word to us. He had the look | of someone gnawed and gathered up by care — | though not the cares that here confronted him. | And now we set our tread towards that land.] (*Inf.*, IX. 100–04).

51. My count suggests a total of 336, distributed across the canticles as follows: *Inferno*, 35 per cent; *Purgatorio*, 45 per cent; *Paradiso*, 20 per cent. We might hypothesise that the peak in *Purgatorio* is consistent with a mode of communal participatory learning in this canticle.

52. As Barański remarks, '[w]henever Dante leaves things vague, it is because he wants us to employ our "intelletti sani" (*Inf.*, 9. 61)' (2014: 167).

53. '[Virgil:] "Pur a noi converrà vincer la punga," | cominciò el, "se non ... Tal ne s'offerse. | Oh quanto tarda a me ch'altri qui giunga!" | I' vidi ben sì com' ei ricoperse | lo cominciar con l'altro che poi venne, | che fur parole le prime diverse; | ma nondimen paura il suo dir dienne, | perch' io traeva la parola tronca | forse a peggior sentenzia che non tenne' ['This contest, even so, we're bound to win. | If not ...' he began. 'Yet granted such a one ... | How long to me it seems till that one comes!' | I saw quite clearly how he covered up | his opening thoughts with those that followed on — | words inconsistent with the first he spoke. | Yet fear came over me at what words he had said. | And so, from these truncated words, I drew | a meaning worse, perhaps, than he had meant] (*Inf.*, IX. 7–15). See also Gardini on this ellipsis, specifically on the contagion of doubt and anxiety (2014: 46–48). De Ventura proposes that the use of interruption or pause in direct discourse, more generally, marks a 'cambio di progetto' (2007: 161–63).

54. In digital culture terms, we might think of this as an event of 'modding' (modifying) and in terms of 'hacking' our own unconscious.

CHAPTER 5

❖

First-Person Participation

'First-person participation', as I have conceived it in relation to the *Comedy*, is a *mode of reading* in which the reader responds to invitations to a particular form of enactive, or neurally embodied, imaginative elaboration; an elaboration that leads to an unusually 'realistic' experience of the virtual world and the encounters within it, and potentially yielding a powerful affective residue and a retrospective sense of some degree of personal transformation. We might recognise this effect as being similar to the dynamic and visceral imaginative participation in Christ's suffering observed in the practice of medieval affective devotion. My thesis in this book is that the *Comedy* is full of explicit propositional cues and implicit visceral triggers to model the narrated body states and cognitive behaviours that emerge at the site of the encounters in the poem and increase the desire in the individual for God.

Modelling is a powerful mode of experiential learning. Moevs, as I have noted, writes of the *Comedy* that 'the point [...] is that understanding *is* practical' (2005: 171; emphasis in original). I have argued that, in a text, this effect can be triggered by particular models of narration that evoke not only a visual representation, but that also, crucially, invite the reader to represent in her own body how a particular experience *feels*.[1] In the responsive reader investing cognitive effort in imaginative elaboration as directed by the mechanisms of the text, such narrative strategies invite the neural mirroring that triggers the same body state in the reader, opening a space for her to feel what the subject feels.[2] The poem further invites her to personalise that experience through importing into the vast network of gaps in the text her own cognitive memorial and imaginative data.

First-person participation, I have suggested, is a complementary mode of reading. It is not a substitute for, but is in interplay with, other modes of reading, including the classic immersive storytelling mode of identification with a protagonist, and with analytical and scholarly modes of reading. It is an elective, not mandatory, mode of reading. The propositional content of the poem — what it 'means' — can be grasped without reading in this mode; first-person participation layers upon this propositional understanding a grasp of how it feels to *experience* the journey, cognised directly through the viscera and the intuitive certainty of embodied knowledge (Wojciehowski and Gallese 2011: 12).

This mode of reading requires a sensitivity to the possibility of a personal productive interaction with a text: that is, an openness to finding oneself individually implicated in the poem's explicit invitations to model specific cognitive behaviours ('think', 'imagine', 'remember', and so on), and a willingness to invest creative cognitive effort in imaginative elaboration of the experiences and encounters set out in the text. It is a mode of reading that is not commonplace in the modern humanities with its habituation towards 'a distanced, measured hermeneutics' (Ritchey 2012: 342), but in late medieval culture a similar practice of reading became established and widespread through the model of 'affective meditation' on spiritual texts (Bestul 1996: 38). Such devotional texts invited active and personal cognitive engagement with the manifold gaps in the gospel narratives, yielding a notion of text as 'mnemonic' (Yates 1984: 95) or system for retrieval of the individual's own memorial data in support of the creation of new, individuated, 'realistic' virtual experiences of the imagination. For medieval readers (as also for modern readers dishabituated to such a practice), this was a mode of cognitive engagement that had to be actively cultivated, requiring a conception of the imagination as a highly plastic 'trainable tool', the 'greatest potential' of which is unleashed in making the absent present and the virtual personally transformational at the level of affect and behaviour (Karnes 2011: 20, 177).

In this book, I have suggested that Dante's innovation exceeds the model of affective devotion, since the *Comedy* rests not on the second-person address of the gospel meditations — although it deploys this mechanism in the direct addresses — but additionally incorporates the model of an immersive first-person 'personal experience narrative' (Labov and Waletzky 1967: 3). This narrativised model, further with its frame device, offers the reader the opportunity to experience deeply and empathically other standpoints in a sustained and present way. In addition to recruiting the cognitions at a conscious rational level (burnishing the will through propositional learning), the poem is also able to invite thereby the participation of the cognitions without rupturing the reader's immersion in the narrative of the poem, shaping desire, and preparing those for grace to whom grace will ultimately be granted.[3]

First-person participation is a mode of reading that is strategically invited, not accidental: it depends on a consistent and cumulative strategy of invitations to the reader to read in this way. The key to realistic simulation of body states in the reader, I have proposed, is an experience of the perceptual illusion known as *presence*: a familiar concept in video game criticism, where presence is understood as an embodied form of immersion (IJsselsteijn's 'experiential counterpart of immersion' (2004: 136)), and also expressed in medieval affective devotion's goal of *praesentia* (Ritchey 2012: 349). I have suggested that there are three types of presence at work in the poem: spatial, social and self-presence.

Spatial presence, understood as the perceptual illusion of 'being there', is invited through a strategy I describe as *narration through situated body states*. This involves evocation of the narrated subject's body states in dynamic relation to the phenomena of his or her environment, and is constructed in the poem, I suggest, through a cumulative sequence of narrative effects. Most immediately evident is the narration of perceptual data through the multiple senses (sight, sound, smell, touch, taste and proprioception), a strategy common to many well-written narrative texts. The poem's innovation, I have suggested, is to layer on top of this perceptual data the effects of the dynamic interaction of the body with the phenomena of the space: by narrating sensorimotor correspondence data (how the protagonist's body responds to the perceptual data, evoking a perception–action loop) and by narrating dynamic environmental feedback data, as, for example, in the narration of vection, foregrounded in the narration of the descent on Geryon and the ascent of the celestial ladder.

Social presence, in the sense of a perceptual illusion of being with other selves in a shared environment, staging the possibility of reflexive understanding of another's intention, is invited in the poem by *narration through kinaesthetic empathy*. By consistently narrating gesture or posture that 'utters' (Kendon 2004: 2), rather than omniscient description of feeling, the text invites 'semantic retrieval' (Bolens 2012: 2) of a similar experience in the (reading) observer, triggering the possibility of body state simulation in the reader. This leads to 'direct' understanding of the subject's affective state or intention (Wojciehowski and Gallese 2011: 12), mimicking in the mechanisms of the poem's narration the dynamic neural processes of empathy in real life. Bolens has identified a similar model of invitations to kinaesthetic empathy in Proust. Dante's innovation, I suggest, is to have constructed a strategy of invitations to social presence as just one part of a wider strategy to invite active reader participation.

The final form of presence I have identified is *self-presence*, characterised as the sense that something is happening *to me* (Waterworth and Riva 2014: 14) — that is, that the reader is changed in some way by the virtual experience in which she is invited to participate. In relation to self-presence, I have identified five narrative strategies in the *Comedy* that underpin the exceptional openness of the poem and that, in combination with the invitations to spatial and social presence, render the poem an exceptionally participatory text. The first strategy is a model of *narrating instances* specific to the *Comedy* that reveals four different 'faces' of the narrating Dante's 'io'; in combination, these four faces prevent the reader from simply identifying with the journeying Dante protagonist and instead establish a possibility of participation through multiple subjectivities. Second, a mechanism of *narration through mobile camera view*, in which the reader's line of sight is intensively directed around the narrated space, yielding an illusion of new objects constantly moving into view that invites the brain to infer personal agency in the virtual world through a capacity to turn the head. Next, I define a new continuum of invitations to the reader, marked at one end by the *direct addresses* that establish a model of social reciprocity between reader and narrator. The direct addresses additionally signpost a series of *narrative training* exercises, whose invitations to frame-by-frame reconstruction of the narrated event enable the reader to develop and rehearse advanced cognitive skills of sustained enactment imagination. Finally, at the other end of the continuum of invitations to participate, I have located a vast system of indirect and elective invitations that includes both the many similes that account for a fifth of all the narration in the poem, and the often auto-indexing device of the narrative ellipsis. Together, these two phenomena underpin a strategy I describe as *narration through gaps in the text*, inviting the reader to personalise radically her experience of the journey to desire for the divine. The combination of direct and indirect invitations to cognitive participation in the poem appears to offer a *system* for the progressive finessing of the reader's capacity for enactive imaginative elaboration of the protagonist's journey; a system that supports her to refine her desire for God through imaginative projection of her own mortal body into the virtual space of Dante's narrated afterlife, successfully combining different orders of reality.

An awareness of having experienced instances of reading in the mode of first-person participation would seem to be conferred through retrospective recognition: the reader feels personally changed in some intuitive way, as if, to adapt Waterworth and Riva, 'something [has] happen[ed] *to me*' (2014: 14). Indeed, such an experience is modelled by the narrating Dante himself, when he recounts his own experience of the sweetness that remains in his heart following the imaginative reconstruction of his journey, comparing it with the affective residue of a dream:

> Qual è colüi che sognando vede,
> che dopo 'l sogno la passione impressa
> rimane, e l'altro a la mente non riede,
>   cotal son io, ché quasi tutta cessa
> mia visïone, e ancor mi distilla
> nel core il dolce che nacque da essa. (*Par.*, XXXIII. 58–63)

> Like those who see so clearly while they dream
> that marks of feeling, when their dreaming ends,
> remain, though nothing more returns to mind,
>   so I am now. For nearly all I saw
> has gone, even if, still, within my heart,
> there drops the sweetness that was born from that.

The content of the dream — another kind of virtual experience — has become elusive, 'e l'altro a la mente non riede', but an affective residue remains, 'e ancor mi distilla | nel core il dolce che nacque da essa'. The dreamer, like the post-evental narrating Dante, has been *transformed* by his experience.

In my view, it is the strategic interplay of this total of seven strategies — in several cases, narratological innovations in their own right — that supports the innovation of the particularly mobile 'io' of the *Comedy* and constitutes the poem's status as exceptionally participatory text. The key to this mobile 'io' lies in the invitation to both spectate on the journeying Dante's narrated journey and to participate in her own — a process of constant oscillation between personal and collective subjectivities.

In narratological terms, the end effect of this mode of reading is to invite spontaneous elective self-identification in a plural narrative 'io'. Instead of waiting for the explicit invitation to participate indexed in the 'tu' of the direct addresses, the reader, I propose, instead begins reflexively to identify spontaneously as implicated in the 'tu', the 'voi' and even the 'noi' of the utterances of the blessed. Eventually, she may even glimpse herself in certain of the 'io's of the poem, participating as first-person protagonist in her own right — as perhaps in the sequence of the de-coupling of the reader's gaze from the journeying Dante's in response to Bernard's sign in *Paradiso* XXXII, as I set out next.

In the Empyrean, in *Paradiso* XXXI and XXXII, Bernard points out the identities of the blessed in the celestial rose in an explicit diagrammatic choreographing of the journeying Dante's line of sight. This is the last of the extended sequences of narration through mobile camera view (discussed in Chapter 4), in which repeated dynamic movement through vertical and lateral axes in the narration means that new 'objects' (in the form of the named blessed) are constantly coming into view. The sequence starts in canto XXXI at the point of Bernard's lyrical invitation to the protagonist to fly with his eyes through the garden before him, 'vola con li occhi per questo giardino' (97), and continues with two further extended sections in canto XXXII (1–39 and 115–51). The reader who invests sustained cognitive effort in imaginatively elaborating the succession of mental images for herself is invited by the text to simulate neurally a constant dynamic re-orientation of her line of sight on the basis of Bernard's directions, thereby participating, across media, in the phenomenon of joint attention with the journeying Dante and Bernard.[4]

This sustained experience of joint attention makes the sudden decoupling of the reader's line of sight from that of the journeying Dante all the more shocking when Bernard makes his narratologically dissonant sign, as I set out in the Introduction:

> Bernardo m'accennava, e sorridea,
> perch' io guardassi suso; ma io era
> già per me stesso tal qual ei volea:
>   ché la mia vista, venendo sincera,
> e più e più intrava per lo raggio
> de l'alta luce che da sé è vera. (*Par.*, XXXIII. 49–54)

> Now Bernard, smiling, made a sign to me
> that I look up. Already, though, I was,
> by my own will, as he desired I be.
>   My sight, becoming pure and wholly free,
> Entered still more, then more, along the ray
> of that one light which, of itself, is true.

The reader turns her eyes upwards just a split second after the journeying Dante, triggering an instance of perceptual dissonance as she experiences the decoupling of her gaze from his.

But the decoupling, I propose, reveals the gap in the text for the reader's own 'io' or 'I'; a momentary distillation of her own 'io' from all the other narrating instances that constitute the plural 'io' of the text. My suggestion is that, in the half-tercet that describes the moment when the reader finds she is looking the wrong way, we can discern a division of the repeated 'io' into two discrete and distinct 'io's, each with a different subject.

The first 'io', invited by Bernard to look up, 'perch' *io* guardassi suso', is the reader, electively identifying as Bernard's interlocutor, reading in a mode of first-person participation, and ready to look up on her own account. The second 'io', 'ma *io* era | già per me stesso [...]', already looking up, is the journeying Dante protagonist, in the flow of his experience. Momentarily, in that first case, 'the *I* which I pronounce' *is* 'myself' (to subvert Poulet) and the plural 'io' of the narrative first-person fleetingly perceptible in its constituent parts: 'Bernardo m'accennava, e sorridea, | perch' io guardassi suso; ma io era | già per me stesso tal qual ei volea' (49–51). Bernard's choreographing of the protagonist's gaze through the celestial Rose in *Paradiso* XXXI and XXXII binds protagonist's and reader's lines of sight unusually tightly. The sudden rupturing of this conjoined perspective, in the shock decoupling of the reader's gaze from the protagonist's that is triggered by Bernard's sign, momentarily exposes the reader's own 'io' written into the text. Such a recognition, I suggest, invites a radical re-reading of the poem, instantiating an intuitive new sensitivity to invitations to electively identify as one of a kaleidoscope of 'io's that constitutes the agency of the first-person subject in the text.[5]

Notes to Chapter 5

1. Pertile has written that: 'Having placed Paradise beyond the confines of human memory and language, what the poet claims to describe is not the reality of perfect bliss, but *his experience of approaching it*, the desire that propels him from the heaven of the Moon to the Empyrean — for the fulfilment that lies beyond that desire is also beyond the limits of poetry' (2015: 500; my emphasis).
2. Lakoff and Johnson link such an experience of imaginative projection with a notion of *transcendence*. They write that a 'major function of the embodied mind is empathic. From birth we have the capacity to imitate others, to vividly imagine being another person, doing what that person does, experiencing what that person experiences. The capacity for imaginative projection is a vital cognitive faculty. Experientially, it is a form of "transcendence". Through it, one can experience something akin to "getting out of our bodies" — yet it is very much a bodily capacity' (Lakoff and Johnson 1999: 565).
3. 'Trasumanar significar *per verba* | non si poria; però l'essemplo basti | a cui esperïenza grazia serba' [To give (even in Latin phrase) a meaning | to 'transhuman' can't be done. For those whom grace | will grant experience, let my case serve] (*Par.*, I. 70–72).
4. Psychologists Peter Mundy and Lisa Newell propose that 'joint attention' is an innately social behaviour that promotes fellowship: 'Joint or shared attention is a foundational skill in human social interaction and cognition. It is defined as re-orienting or re-allocating attention to a target because it is the object of another person's attention. Shared attention plays a critical role in a wide range of social behaviours: it sets the stage for learning, facilitates communication, and supports inferences about other people's current and future activity, both overt and covert' (Mundy and Newell 2007: 269). Further: 'Hominid binocularity entails limited visual field, but humans typically spend time around conspecifics. This affords the expansion of our field of vision by proxy, as it were. When one human orients to a new target or location, others who see the action tend to become interested, and reorient to that region' (270).
5. Alastair Minnis and A. B. Scott point to what might be another instance of a perceptibly participatory 'io' in *Paradiso* I, writing of the tercet 'Nel ciel che più de la sua luce prende | fu' io, e vidi cose che ridire | né sa né può chi di là sù discende' [High in that sphere which takes from Him most light | I was — I was! — and saw things there that no one | who descends knows how or ever can repeat] (4–6), that: 'Perhaps these lines, with their dramatic juxtaposition of the fantastically fictive ("In the heaven [...]") and the bluntly factual ("fu' io", a past historic of untranslatable force), mount the most urgent and tantalising challenge to interpretation that Dante ever threw out' (Minnis and Scott 1988: 444). My suggestion is that the 'untranslatable force' of the 'fu' io' [I was!] is linked to its status as participatory 'io'.

BIBLIOGRAPHY

❖

Printed or textual works

ALDERMAN, NAOMI. 2016. 'Why Can't We Talk to the Characters in Games? Careful What You Wish for …', *Guardian*, 11 January 2016 <https://www.theguardian.com/technology/2016/jan/11/games-computers-conversation-characters> [accessed 15 June 2021]

AMSLER, MARK. 2012. *Affective Literacies: Writing and Multilingualism in the Late Middle Ages* (Turnhout: Brepols)

APPLEWHITE, JAMES. 1964. 'Dante's Use of the Extended Simile in the *Inferno*', *Italica*, 41.3: 294–309

AQUINAS, THOMAS. 1912. *The Summa Theologica of St Thomas Aquinas, Part 1*, trans. by Fathers of the English Dominican Province (London: Washbourne)

ARISTOTLE. 1924. *Metaphysics, Book I*, trans. by W. D. Ross (Oxford: Oxford University Press)

ASCOLI, ALBERT RUSSELL. 2008. *Dante and the Making of a Modern Author* (Cambridge: Cambridge University Press)

—— 2019. 'Starring Dante', in *Teaching Dante*, ed. Christopher Metress (= *Religions*, 10.5): 319: 1–14

AUERBACH, ERICH. 1953. 'Dante's Addresses to the Reader', *Romance Philology*, 7: 268–78

—— 2001. *Dante: Poet of the Secular World*, trans. by Ralph Manheim (New York: NYRB)

AUERBACH, ERICH, and W. R. TRASK. 1952. 'Farinata and Cavalcante', *The Kenyon Review*, 14.2: 207–42

BACHELARD, GASTON. 1969. *The Poetics of Space*, trans. by Maria Jolas (Boston: Beacon Press)

BAILENSON, JEREMY. 2018. *Experience on Demand: What Virtual Reality Is, How It Works, and What It Can Do* (New York: Norton)

BAL, MIEKE. 2009. *Narratology: Introduction to the Theory of Narrative*, 3rd edn (Toronto: University of Toronto Press)

BARAŃSKI, ZYGMUNT G. 1989. 'Dante's (Anti-)Rhetoric: Notes on the Poetics of the *Comedy*', in *Moving in Measure: Essays in Honour of Brian Moloney*, ed. by Judith Bryce and Doug Thompson (Hull: Hull University Press), pp. 1–11

—— 1995. 'Dante's Signs: An Introduction to Medieval Semiotics and Dante', in *Dante and the Middle Ages*, ed. by John C. Barnes and Cormac O. Cuilleanáin (Dublin: Irish Academic Press), pp. 139–80

—— 2000. *Dante e i segni: Saggi per una storia intellettuale di Dante Alighieri* (Naples: Liguori)

—— 2002. 'Canto XXII', in *Lectura Dantis Turicensis. Paradiso*, ed. by Georges Güntert and Michelangelo Picone (Florence: Cesati), pp. 339–61

—— 2005. 'Dante Alighieri: Experimentation and (Self-)Exegesis', in *The Cambridge History of Literary Criticism*, II, ed. by Alastair Minnis and Ian Johnson (Cambridge: Cambridge University Press), pp. 559–82

—— 2014. 'The Temptations of a Heterodox Dante', in *Dante and Heterodoxy: The Temptations of Thirteenth Century Radical Thought*, ed. by Maria Luisa Ardizzone (Newcastle: Cambridge Scholars Publishing), pp. 164–96

—— 2017. 'On Dante's Trail', *Italian Studies*, 72.1: 1–15

—— 2018. 'Dottrina degli affetti e teologia: la rappresentazione della beatitudine nel *Paradiso*', in *Dante poeta cristiano e la cultura religiosa medievale. In ricordo di Anna Maria Chiavacci Leonardi. Atti del Convegno internazionale di Studi (Ravenna, 28 novembre 2015)*, ed. by Giuseppe Ledda (Ravenna: Centro Dantesco dei Frati Minori Conventuali), pp. 259–312

BAROLINI, Teodolinda. 1984. *Dante's Poets: Textuality and Truth in the 'Comedy'* (Princeton: Princeton University Press)

—— 1992. *The Undivine Comedy: Detheologising Dante* (Princeton: Princeton University Press)

—— 2006. *Dante and the Origins of Italian Literary Culture* (New York: Fordham University Press)

—— 2013. 'Dante and Reality/Dante and Realism (*Paradise*)', *Spazio Filosofico*, 8: 199–208

BEALL, CHANDLER B. 1979. 'Dante and his Reader', *Forum Italicum*, 13.3, 299–343

BELLOMO, SAVERIO. 2004. *Dizionario dei commentatori danteschi. L'esegesi della* Commedia *da Iacopo Alighieri a Nidobeato*. Biblioteca di Lettere italiane. Studi e testi, 62 (Florence: Olschki)

BESTUL, THOMAS H. 1996. *Texts of the Passion: Latin Devotional Literature and Medieval Society* (Philadelphia: University of Pennsylvania Press)

BIERNOFF, SUZANNAH. 2002. *Sight and Embodiment in the Middle Ages* (New York: Palgrave)

BIOCCA, FRANK. 2003. 'Can We Resolve the Book, the Physical Reality, and the Dream State Problems?', draft paper presented at 'EU Future and Emerging Technologies Presence Initiative Meeting' (Venice, 5–7 May 2003) <http://citeseerx.ist.psu.edu/viewdoc/download?doi=10.1.1.545.7706&rep=rep1&type=pdf> [accessed 15 June 2021]

BLATT, HEATHER. 2018. *Participatory Reading in Late-Medieval England* (Manchester: Manchester University Press)

BOELLSTORFF, TOM. 2011. 'Virtuality: Placing the Virtual Body: Avatar, Chora, Cypherg', in *Companion to the Anthropology of the Body and Embodiment*, ed. by Frances Mascia-Lees (Oxford: Wiley-Blackwell), pp. 504–20

BOGOST, IAN. 2007. *Persuasive Games: The Expressive Power of Videogames* (Cambridge, MA: MIT Press)

BOLENS, GUILLEMETTE. 2012. *The Style of Gestures: Embodiment and Cognition in Literary Narrative* (Baltimore: Johns Hopkins University Press)

BOTTERILL, STEVEN. 1994. *Dante and the Mystical Tradition: Bernard of Clairvaux in the 'Comedy'* (Cambridge: Cambridge University Press)

BRANTLEY, JESSICA. 2007. *Reading in the Wilderness: Private Devotion and Public Performance in Late Medieval England* (Chicago: University of Chicago Press)

BROWN, BILL. 2005. 'The Dark Wood of Postmodernity (Space, Faith, Allegory)', *PMLA*, 120.3: 734–50

BROWN, GARRETT. 2003. 'The Moving Camera. Part One', *Zerb*, 58: 32–35 <https://edition.pagesuite-professional.co.uk/html5/reader/production/default.aspx?pubname=&edid=922f748e-12d2-4926-84ab-4b72800e29af> [accessed 11 September 2021]

BURGWINKLE, WILLIAM. 2012. 'Modern Lovers: Evanescence and the Act in Dante, Arnaut, and Sordello', in *Desire in Dante and the Middle Ages*, ed. by Manuele Gragnolati, et al. (Oxford: MHRA; Leeds: Maney), pp. 14–28

BURROW, JOHN A. 2002. *Gestures and Looks in Medieval Narrative* (Cambridge: Cambridge University Press)

CALLEJA, GORDON. 2011. *In-Game: From Immersion to Incorporation* (Cambridge, MA: MIT Press)

CARRUTHERS, MARY J. 2008 [1990]. *The Book of Memory: A Study of Memory in Medieval Culture* (Cambridge: Cambridge University Press)

CARTOCCI, GIULIA, ET AL. 2016. 'The "NeuroDante Project": Neurometric Measurements of Participants' Reaction to Literary Auditory Stimuli from Dante's *Divina Commedia*',

Symbiotic Interaction: 5th International Workshop, Symbiotic 2016 (Padua, 29–30 settembre 2016), pp. 52–64 <https://doi.org/10.1007/978-3-319-57753-1_5> [accessed 15 June 2021]

CERVIGNI, DINO. 1982. 'Dante's Poetry of Dreams', *Pacific Coast Philology*, 17.1–2: 24–30

CHANCE, JANE. 2012. 'Cognitive Alterities: From Cultural Studies to Neuroscience and Back Again', *Postmedieval: A Journal of Medieval Cultural Studies*, 3.3: 247–61

CHATMAN, SEYMOUR. 1980. *Story and Discourse: Narrative Structure in Fiction and Film* (Ithaca: Cornell University Press)

CLARK, ANDY. 1999. 'Embodied, Situated, and Distributed Cognition', in *A Companion to Cognitive Science*, ed. by William Bechtel and George Graham (Oxford: Blackwell), pp. 506–17

CLARK, HERBERT H., and THOMAS B. CARLSON. 1982. 'Hearers and Speech Acts', *Language*, 58.2: 332–73

CLOUGH, PATRICIA, and JEAN HALLEY (eds). 2008. *The Affective Turn: Theorising the Social* (Durham, NC: Duke University Press)

COLEMAN, JOYCE. 2017. 'Reading Practices', in *The Encyclopaedia of Medieval Literature in Britain*, IV, ed. by Sian Echard, Robert Rouse, Jacqueline Fay, Helen Fulton, and Geoff Rector (Oxford: Wiley-Blackwell), pp. 1573–74

CONSTABLE, GILES. 1996. *Culture and Spirituality in Medieval Europe* (Aldershot: Ashgate Variorum)

CONTINI, GIANFRANCO. 1969. 'Philology and Dante Exegesis', *Dante Studies*, 87: 1–32

—— 1976. *Un'idea di Dante: saggi danteschi* (Turin: Einaudi)

COPELAND, RITA. 1991. *Rhetoric, Hermeneutics, and Translation in the Middle Ages: Academic Traditions and Vernacular Texts* (Cambridge: Cambridge University Press)

COPELAND, RITA, and INEKE SLUITER (eds). 2009. *Medieval Grammar and Rhetoric: Language, Arts, and Literary Theory, AD 300–1475* (Oxford: Oxford University Press)

CORBELLINI, SABRINA. 2013. 'Introduction', in *Cultures of Religious Reading in the Late Middle Ages: Instructing the Soul, Feeding the Spirit, and Awakening the Passion*, ed. by Sabrina Corbellini (Turnhout: Brepols), pp. 1–12

CORNISH, ALISON. 1999. 'I miti biblici. La sapienza di Salomone e le arti magiche', in *Dante: Mito e poesia. Atti del secondo seminario dantesco internazionale: Monte Verità, Ascona, 23–27 giugno 1997*, ed. by Michelangelo Picone and Tatiana Crivelli (Florence: F. Cesati), pp. 391–403

DAMASIO, ANTONIO. 1994. *Descartes' Error: Emotion, Reason, and the Human Brain* (New York: Putnam)

—— 2000 [1999]. *The Feeling of What Happens: Body, Emotion, and the Making of Consciousness* (London: Vintage)

DENNETT, DANIEL C. 1991. *Consciousness Explained* (London: Little, Brown)

DESCARTES, RENÉ. 2013. *Meditations on First Philosophy: Latin-English Edition*, ed. and trans. by John Cottingham (Cambridge: Cambridge University Press)

DE VENTURA, PAOLO. 2007. *Dramma e dialogo nella Commedia di Dante. Il linguaggio della mimesi per un resoconto dall'aldilà* (Naples: Liguori Editore)

DIJKSTRA, KATINKA, MICHAEL P. KASCHAK, and ROLF A. ZWAAN. 2007. 'Body Posture Facilitates Retrieval of Autobiographical Memories', *Cognition*, 102.1: 139–49

DONALD, MERLIN. 1991. *Origins of the Modern Mind: Three Stages in the Evolution of Culture and Cognition* (Cambridge, MA: Harvard University Press)

—— 1993. 'Précis of *Origins of the Modern Mind*', *Behavioural and Brain Sciences*, 16: 737–91

DREYFUS, HUBERT. 1972. *What Computers Can't Do: A Critique of Artificial Reason* (New York: Harper and Row)

DRONKE, PETER. 1986. *Dante and Medieval Latin Traditions* (Cambridge: Cambridge University Press)

ECO, UMBERTO. 1979. *The Role of the Reader: Explorations in the Semiotics of Texts* (Bloomington: Indiana University Press)

ESSARY, BRANDON K. 2019. 'Dante's *Inferno*, Video Games, and Pop Pedagogy', *Parole Rubate. Rivista internazionale di studi sulla citazione*, 20: 59–82

FARROW, ROBERT, and IOANNA IOCAVIDES. 2013. 'Gaming and the Limits of Digital Embodiment', *Philosophy & Technology*, 27: 221–33

FESTINGER, LEON. 1962. *A Theory of Cognitive Dissonance* (Stanford: Stanford University Press)

FRANKE, WILLIAM. 2000. 'Dante's Address to the Reader in Face of Derrida's Critique of Ontology', *The Poetry of Life in Literature, Analecta Husserliana*, 69: 119–31

—— 2012. *Dante and the Sense of Transgression: 'The Trespass of the Sign'* (London: Bloomsbury Academic)

FRECCERO, JOHN. 1986. *The Poetics of Conversion*, ed. by Rachel Jacoff (Cambridge, MA: Harvard University Press)

GALLESE, VITTORIO. 2011. 'Mirror Neurons and Art', in *Art and the Senses*, ed. by Francesca Bacci and David Melcher (Oxford: Oxford University Press), pp. 455–64

GALLESE, VITTORIO, and LUCIANO FADIGA, LEONARDO FOGASSI, and GIACOMO RIZZOLATTI. 1996. 'Premotor Cortex and the Recognition of Motor Actions', *Cognitive Brain Research*, 3: 131–41

GALLESE, VITTORIO, and MORTON ANN GERNSBACHER, CECILIA HEYES, GREGORY HICKOK, and MARCO IACOBONI. 2011. 'Mirror Neuron Forum', *Perspectives on Psychological Science*, 6: 369–407

GALLESE, VITTORIO, and ALVIN GOLDMAN. 1998. 'Mirror Neurons and the Simulation Theory of Mind-Reading', *Trends in Cognitive Sciences*, 2.12: 493–501

GALLESE, VITTORIO, and MICHELE GUERRA. 2014. 'The Feeling of Motion: Camera Movements and Motor Cognition', *Cinema et Cie*, 14: 103–12

GARDINI, NICOLA. 2014. *Lacuna. Saggi sul non detto* (Turin: Piccola Biblioteca Einaudi. Saggistica letteraria e linguistica)

GARGANI, ADAM. 2014. 'Poetic Comparisons: How Similes are Understood' (unpublished doctoral thesis, University of Salford) <http://usir.salford.ac.uk/31952/> [accessed 22 April 2020]

GEE, JAMES PAUL. 2015. *Unified Discourse Analysis* (Abingdon: Routledge)

GENDLER, TAMAR SZABÒ. 2008. 'Alief and Belief', *The Journal of Philosophy*, 105.10: 634–63

GENETTE, GÉRARD. 1980 [1972]. *Narrative Discourse: An Essay in Method*, trans. by Jane E. Lewin (Ithaca: Cornell University Press)

GERSON, JEAN. 1998. *Jean Gerson: Early Works, On Mystical Theology, Second Treatise*, trans. by Brian McGuire (New York: Paulist Press)

GIBBS, RAYMOND. 2006. *Embodiment and Cognitive Science* (Cambridge: Cambridge University Press)

GMELIN, HERMANN. 1951. 'Die Anrede an den Leser in Dantes *Göttlicher Komödie*', *Deutsches Dante-Jahrbuch*, 29–30: 130–40

GOLDING, JONATHAN M., DEBORAH L. LONG, MARK R. SEELY, and BRIAN J. OPPY. 2014 [1996]. 'The Role of Inferential Processing in Reading Ability', in *Models of Understanding Text*, ed. by Bruce K. Britton and Arthur C. Graesser (New York: Psychology Press), pp. 189–214

GOLDMAN, ALVIN I. 2008. *Simulating Minds: The Philosophy, Psychology, and Neuroscience of Mindreading* (Oxford: Oxford University Press)

GRAESSER, ARTHUR, ET AL. 1994. 'Constructing Inferences during Narrative Text Comprehension', *Psychological Review*, 101.3: 371–95

GRAGNOLATI, MANUELE. 2003. 'From Plurality to (near) Unicity of Forms: Embryology in

Purgatorio 25', in *Dante for the New Millennium*, ed. by Teodolinda Barolini and H. Wayne Storey (New York: Fordham University Press), pp. 192–210

GUMBRECHT, HANS ULRICH. 2004. *The Production of Presence: What Meaning Cannot Convey* (Stanford: Stanford University Press)

—— 2012. *Atmosphere, Mood, Stimmung: On a Hidden Potential of Literature*, trans. by Erik Butler (Stanford: Stanford University Press)

'HAL 90210'. 2016. 'Oculus Miffed: When VR is so Immersive You Fall Flat on Your Face', *Guardian*, 30 November 2016 https://www.theguardian.com/technology/2016/nov/30/oculus-vr-immersive-fall-face-plant-virtual-reality [accessed 11 September 2021]

HARTVIGSEN, KIRSTEN MARIE. 2013. *Prepare the Way of the Lord: Towards a Cognitive Poetic Analysis of Audience Involvement with Characters and Events in the Markan World* (Berlin: De Gruyter)

HAVELY, NICK. 2007. *Dante* (Oxford: Blackwell)

HAWKINS, PETER S. 1999. '"By Gradual Scale Sublimed": Dante and the Contemplatives', in *Dante's Testaments: Essays in Scriptural Imagination* (Stanford: Stanford University Press), pp. 220–43

—— 2003. 'For the Record: Rewriting Virgil in the *Comedy*', *Studies in the Literary Imagination*, 36: 75–97

—— 2005. '*Moderno Uso*', *Arion*, 13.1: 161–84

—— 2015. 'Religious Culture', in *Dante in Context*, ed. by Zygmunt G. Barański and Lino Pertile (Cambridge: Cambridge University Press), pp. 319–40

HEFFERNAN, THOMAS J., and THOMAS E. BURMAN (eds). 2005. *Scripture and Pluralism: Reading the Bible in the Religiously Plural Worlds of the Middle Ages and Renaissance* (Leiden: Brill)

HOFFMANN, DAVID. 1998. *Visual Intelligence: How the Mind Creates Visual Worlds* (New York: Norton)

HONESS, CLAIRE. 2013. 'The Language(s) of Civic Invective in Dante: Rhetoric, Satire, and Politics', *Italian Studies*, 68.2: 157–74

HOOPER, LAURENCE E. 2017. 'Characterization and Eschatological Realism from Dante to Petrarch', *The Italianist*, 37.3, 289–307

—— 2019. 'Characterization', in *The Cambridge Companion to Dante's 'Commedia'*, ed. by Zygmunt G. Barański and Simon Gilson (Cambridge: Cambridge University Press), pp. 43–60

HUME, DAVID. 2013. *Essays and Treatises on Philosophical Subjects*, ed. by Lorne Falkenstein and Neil McArthur (Peterborough, Ontario: Broadview)

HURLEY, SUSAN. 1998. *Consciousness in Action* (Cambridge, MA: Harvard University Press)

HUTTON, PATRICK H. 1993. *History as an Art of Memory* (Hanover, NH: University Press of New England)

IJSSELSTEIJN, WIJNAND. 2003. 'Presence in the Past: What Can We Learn From Media History?', in *Being There: Concepts, Effects, and Measurement of User Presence in Synthetic Environments*, ed. by Giuseppe Riva, Fabrizio Davide, and Wijnand A. IJsselsteijn (Amsterdam: Ios Press), pp. 17–41

—— 2004. 'Presence in Depth' (unpublished doctoral thesis, Eindhoven: Technische Universiteit Eindhoven) <https://doi.org/10.6100/IR581425> [accessed 15 June 2021]

—— 2005. 'Towards a Neuropsychological Basis of Presence', *Annual Review of CyberTherapy and Telemedicine: A Decade of VR*, 3: 25–30

INGOLD, TIM. 2008. 'Bindings against Boundaries: Entanglements of Life in an Open World', *Environment and Planning*, 40.8: 1796–810

INTERNATIONAL SOCIETY FOR PRESENCE RESEARCH. 2000. 'The Concept of Presence: Explication Statement' <https://ispr.info/about-presence-2/about-presence/> [accessed 15 June 2021]

ISER, WOLFGANG. 1974. *The Implied Reader: Patterns of Communication in Prose Fiction from Bunyan to Beckett* (Baltimore: Johns Hopkins University Press)

KEYSERS, CHRISTIAN, and VALERIA GAZZOLA. 2010. 'Social Neuroscience: Mirror Neurons Recorded in Humans', *Current Biology*, 20.8: R353–54

JEANNEROD, MARC. 2001. 'Neural Simulation of Action: A Unifying Mechanism for Motor Cognition', *NeuroImage*, 14.1: 103–09

JOHNSON-LAIRD, PHILIP N. 1983. *Mental Models: Towards a Cognitive Science of Language, Inference, and Consciousness* (Cambridge: Cambridge University Press)

JORNET, ALFREDO, and WOLFF-MICHAEL ROTH. 2013. 'Situated Cognition', *Wiley Interdisciplinary Reviews: Cognitive Science*, 4: 463–78

KANEKAR, AARATI. 2013. 'Detours through Autonomy: Mismapping the *Divine Comedy*', *Perspecta*, 46: 262–83

KARNES, MICHELLE. 2011. *Imagination, Meditation, and Cognition in the Middle Ages* (Chicago: University of Chicago Press)

KEMP, SIMON. 1990. *Medieval Psychology* (New York: Greenwood Press)

—— 1998. 'Medieval Theories of Representation', *History of Psychology*, 1.4: 275–88

KENDON, ADAM. 2004. *Gesture: Visible Action as Utterance* (Cambridge: Cambridge University Press)

KIRKPATRICK, ROBIN. 1978. *Dante's 'Paradise' and the Limitations of Modern Criticism: A Study of Style and Poetic Theory* (Cambridge: Cambridge University Press)

—— 1987. *Dante's 'Inferno': Difficulty and Dead Poetry* (Cambridge: Cambridge University Press)

—— 2004. *Dante: The 'Divine Comedy'*, 2nd edn (Cambridge: Cambridge University Press)

—— 2010. 'Polemics of Praise: Theology as Text, Narrative, and Rhetoric in Dante's *Comedy*', in *Dante's 'Comedy': Theology as Poetry*, ed. by Vittorio Montemaggi and Matthew Treherne (Notre Dame: University of Notre Dame Press), pp. 14–35

—— 2019. 'Dante Translating', *Bibliotheca Dantesca: Journal of Dante Studies*, 2: 125–46

KLEINER, JOHN. 1989. 'Mismapping the Underworld', *Dante Studies*, 107: 1–31

KLINE, DANIEL T. 2014. 'Digital Gaming Re-imagines the Middle Ages', in *Digital Gaming Re-imagines the Middle Ages*, ed. by Daniel T. Kline (London; New York: Routledge), pp. 1–13

KOSSLYN, STEPHEN M. 1980. *Image and Mind* (Cambridge, MA: Harvard University Press)

KUKKONEN, KARIN, and MARCO CARACCIOLO. 2014. 'What is the "Second Generation?"', in *Cognitive Literary Study: Second Generation Approaches* (= *Style*, 48.3), pp. 261–74

LABOV, WILLIAM, and JOSHUA WALETZKY. 1967. 'Narrative Analysis: Oral Versions of Personal Experience', *Journal of Narrative and Life History*, 7.1–4: 3–38

LAKOFF, GEORGE, and MARK JOHNSON. 1980. *Metaphors We Live by* (Chicago: University of Chicago Press)

—— 1999. *Philosophy in the Flesh: The Embodied Mind and its Challenge to Western Thought* (New York: Basic Books)

LAMOTTE, SANDEE. 2017. 'The very Real Health Dangers of Virtual Reality', *cnn.com* <https://edition.cnn.com/2017/12/13/health/virtual-reality-vr-dangers-safety/index.html> [accessed 22 April 2020]

LANDY, JOSHUA. 2012. *How to Do Things with Fictions* (New York: Oxford University Press)

LANSING, RICHARD. 1977. *From Image to Idea: A Study of the Simile in Dante's 'Comedy'* (Ravenna: Longo)

LAUREL, BRENDA. 1993. 'Art and Activism in VR', *Wide Angle*, 15.4: 13–21

LECLERQ, J., ET AL. (eds). 1957–1977. *Sancti Bernardi opera*, 8 vols (Rome: Editiones Cistercienses)

LEE, KWAN MIN. 2004. 'Presence, Explicated', *Communication Theory*, 14.1: 27–50

LEWIS, CLIVE STAPLES. 1965. 'Dante's Similes', *Nottingham Medieval Studies*, 9: 32–41

living handbook of narratology <http://www.lhn.uni-hamburg.de> [accessed 15 June 2021]

LOMBARD, MATTHEW, and THERESA DITTON. 1997. 'At the Heart of It All: The Concept of Presence', *Journal of Computer-Mediated Communication*, 3.2: JCMC321

LOMBARDI, ELENA. 2010. 'Plurilingualism *sub specie aeternitatis* and the Strategies of a Minor Author', in *Dante's Plurilingualism: Authority, Knowledge, Subjectivity*, ed. by Sara Fortuna, Manuele Gragnolati, and Jürgen Trabant (London: Legenda), pp. 133–49

—— 2012. *The Wings of the Doves: Love and Desire in Dante and Medieval Culture* (Montreal: McGill-Queen's University Press)

—— 2016 [2007]. *The Syntax of Desire* (Toronto: University of Toronto Press)

LYNCH, KEVIN. 1960. *The Image of the City* (Cambridge, MA: MIT Press)

MACK, ARIEN, and IRVIN ROCK. 1998. *Inattentional Blindness* (Cambridge, MA: MIT Press)

MALDINA, NICOLÒ. 2008. 'Gli studi sulle similitudini di Dante. In margine alla ristampa de "Le similitudini dantesche" di Luigi Venturi', *L'Alighieri*, 32.49: 139–54

—— 2017. 'Le similitudini dantesche tra letteratura e predicazione: Il ruolo delle *artes*', in *Dante e la retorica*, ed. by Luca Marcozzi (Ravenna: Angelo Longo Editore), pp. 247–59

MALINA, DEBRA. 2002. *Breaking the Frame: Metalepsis and the Construction of the Subject* (Columbus: Ohio State University Press)

MALLIN, ERIC S. 1984. 'The False Simile in Dante's *Comedy*', *Dante Studies*, 102: 15–36

MANDLER, JEAN M., and NANCY S. JOHNSON. 1977. 'Remembrance of Things Parsed: Story Structure and Recall', *Cognitive Psychology*, 9.1: 111–51

MARCHESI, SIMONE. 2011. *Dante and Augustine: Linguistics, Poetics, Hermeneutics* (Toronto; New York: University of Toronto Press)

MARCOZZI, LUCA (ed.). 2017. *Dante e la retorica* (Ravenna: Longo Editore)

MARTÍNEZ, RONALD. 2015. 'Rhetoric, Literary Theory, and Practical Criticism', in *Dante in Context*, ed. by Zygmunt G. Barański and Lino Pertile (Cambridge: Cambridge University Press), pp. 277–96

MAZZEO, JOSEPH ANTHONY. 1958. *Structure and Thought in the 'Paradiso'* (New York: Cornell University Press)

McKOON, GAIL, and ROGER RATCLIFF. 1992. 'Inference during Reading', *Psychological Review*, 99.3: 440–66

McMAHAN, ALISON. 2003. 'Immersion, Engagement and Presence: A Method for Analysing 3-D Video Games', in *The Video Game Theory Reader*, ed. by Mark J. P. Wolf and Bernard Perron (New York: Routledge), pp. 67–86

McNAMER, SARAH. 2009. 'The Origins of the *Meditationes Vitae Christi*', *Speculum*, 84.4: 905–55

—— 2010. *Affective Meditation and the Invention of Medieval Compassion* (Philadelphia: University of Pennsylvania Press)

—— (ed.). 2018. *Meditations on the Life of Christ: The Short Italian Text* (Notre Dame: University of Notre Dame Press)

McNEILL, DAVID. 1996. *Hand and Mind: What Gestures Reveal about Thought* (Chicago: University of Chicago Press)

MENARY, RICHARD. 2010. 'Introduction to the Special Edition on 4E Cognition', *Phenomenology and the Cognitive Sciences*, 9.4: 459–63

MERLEAU-PONTY, MAURICE. 2002 [1945]. *Phenomenology of Perception*, trans. by Colin Smith (London: Routledge)

MILNER, STEPHEN J. 2015. ' "Bene comune e benessere": Rhetoric and the Affective Economy of Communal Life', in *Emotions, Passions, and Power in Renaissance Italy*, ed. by Fabrizio Ricciardelli and Andrea Zorzi (Amsterdam: Amsterdam University Press), pp. 237–51

MINNIS, ALASTAIR, and A. B. SCOTT. 1988. *Medieval Literary Theory and Criticism c.1100–c.1375* (Oxford: Oxford University Press)

MITCHELL, W. J. T. 1996. 'Word and Image', in *Critical Terms for Art History*, ed. by Robert S. Nelson and Richard Shiff (Chicago: University of Chicago Press), pp. 51–61

MOCAN, MIRA. 2012. 'Sulla "scala della contemplazione": I canti XXI–XXIII del *Paradiso*', in *L'arca della mente: Riccardo di San Vittore nella* Commedia *di Dante*. Saggi di lettere italiane, 68 (Florence: Olschki), pp. 191–231

MOEVS, CHRISTIAN. 2005. *The Metaphysics of Dante's 'Comedy'* (Oxford: Oxford University Press)

MONTEMAGGI, VITTORIO. 2014. 'Afterword: Forgiveness, Prayer, and the Meaning of Poetry', *Literature Compass*, 11.2: 138–47

MUNDY, PETER, and LISA NEWELL. 2007. 'Attention, Joint Attention, and Social Cognition', *Current Directions in Psychological Science*, 1.5: 269–74

NARDI, BRUNO. 1949. 'Dante profeta', in his *Dante e la cultura medievale*, 2nd edn (Bari: Laterza), pp. 336–416

NASTI, PAOLA, and CLAUDIA ROSSIGNOLI. 2013. 'Introduction', in *Interpreting Dante: Essays on the Traditions of Dante Commentary*, ed. by Paola Nasti and Claudia Rossignoli (Notre Dame: University of Notre Dame Press), pp. 1–16

O'NEILL, ROB. 2016. *Digital Character Development: Theory and Practice*, 2nd edn (Boca Raton, FL: CRC Press/Taylor & Francis)

PARKER, DEBORAH. 1997. 'Interpreting the Commentary Tradition to the *Comedy*', in *Dante: Contemporary Perspectives*, ed. by Amilcare A. Iannucci (Toronto: University of Toronto Press), pp. 240–58

PARKES, MALCOLM. 1976. 'Influence of the Concepts of *Ordinatio* and *Compilatio* in the Development of the Book', in *Medieval Learning and Literature: Essays Presented to R. W. Hunt*, ed. by Jonathan J. G. Alexander and Margaret T. Gibson (Oxford: Clarendon), pp. 35–70

PASNAU, ROBERT. 1997. *Theories of Cognition in the Later Middle Ages* (Cambridge: Cambridge University Press)

PEARCE, SPENCER. 1996. 'Dante and the Art of Memory', *The Italianist*, 16: 20–61

PERTILE, LINO. 2003. 'Does the *stilnovo* go to Heaven?', in *Dante for the New Millennium*, ed. by Teodolinda Barolini and H. Wayne Storey (New York: Fordham University Press), pp. 104–14

—— 2010. '"Trasmutabile per tutte guise": Dante in the *Comedy*', in *Dante's Plurilingualism: Authority, Knowledge, Subjectivity*, ed. by Sara Fortuna, Manuele Gragnolati, and Jürgen Trabant (London: Legenda), pp. 164–78

—— 2015. 'Works', in *Dante in Context*, ed. by Zygmunt G. Barański and Lino Pertile (Cambridge: Cambridge University Press), pp. 475–508

PERVIN, LAWRENCE A. 1978. 'Theoretical Approaches to the Analysis of Individual-Environment Interaction', in *Perspectives in International Psychology*, ed. by Lawrence A. Pervin (New York: Plenum Press), pp. 67–86

PETRONIO, GIUSEPPE. 1965. 'Appunti per uno studio di Dante e il pubblico', *Beiträge zur Romanischen Philologie*, 1–2: 98–108

PETRUCCI, ARMANDO. 1995. *Writers and Readers in Medieval Italy: Studies in the History of Written Culture* (New Haven: Yale University Press)

PFEIFFER, KERSTIN. 2012. 'Feeling the Passion: Neuropsychological Perspectives on Audience Response', *Postmedieval: A Journal of Medieval Culture Studies*, 3: 328–40

PHILLIPS-ROBINS, HELENA. 2016. '"Cantavan tutti insieme ad una voce": Singing and Community in the *Comedy*', *Italian Studies*, 71.1: 4–20

PINSENT, ANDREW. 2012. *The Second-Person Perspective in Aquinas's Ethics: Virtues and Gifts* (New York; London: Routledge)

PINT, KRIS. 2012. 'The Avatar as a Methodological Tool for the Embodied Exploration of Virtual Environments', *Comparative Literature and Culture*, 14.3: 1–9 <https://doi.org/10.7771/1481-4374.2037> [accessed 15 June 2021]

PLAMPER, JAN. 2017. *The History of Emotions*, trans. by Keith Tribe (Oxford: Oxford University Press)

POULET, GEORGES. 1969. 'Phenomenology of Reading', *New Literary History*, 1.1: 53–68

POWLESLAND, KATHERINE. 2017. 'Invitations to Participate: Bernard's Sign', *Le tre corone*, 4: 97–115

—— 2022. 'Dante and Video Games: The Unrealised Potential of the Virtual *Commedia*', in *Mediating Dante*, ed. by David Bowe and Federica Coluzzi (= *Italian Studies*, 77.2), 146–56

PROPP, VLADIMIR. 1968 [1928]. *Morphology of the Folktale*, 2nd edn, ed. by Louise A. Wagner (Austin: University of Texas Press)

PYLYSHYN, ZENON. 2003. *Seeing and Visualising: It's not What You Think* (Cambridge, MA: MIT Press)

REHAK, BOB. 2003. 'Playing at Being: Psychoanalysis and the Avatar', in *The Video Game Theory Reader*, ed. by Mark J. P. Wolf and Bernard Perron (New York: Routledge), pp. 103–28

REVONSUO, ANTTI. 2006. *Inner Presence: Consciousness as a Biological Phenomenon* (Cambridge, MA: MIT Press)

REYNOLDS, MATTHEW. 2020. 'Translating "I": Dante, Literariness, and the Inherent Multimodality of Language', in *Translation and Multimodality: Beyond Words*, ed. by Monica Boria, Ángeles Carreres, Maria Norlega-Sánchez, and Marcus Tomalin (Oxford: Routledge), pp. 117–33

REYNOLDS, SUZANNE. 1996. *Medieval Reading: Grammar, Rhetoric, and the Classical Text* (Cambridge: Cambridge University Press)

RICHARDS, I. A. 1965. *The Philosophy of Rhetoric* (London: Oxford University Press)

RITCHEY, SARA. 2012. 'Manual Thinking: John Mombaer's *Meditations*, the Neuroscience of the Imagination and the Future of the Humanities', *Postmedieval*, 3.3: 341–54

ROBERTSON, MARGARET. 2010. 'Can't Play, Won't Play', *Kotaku* <https://kotaku.com/5686393/cant-play-wont-play> [accessed 22 April 2020]

ROBIGLIO, ANDREA A. 2015. 'Philosophy and Theology', in *Dante in Context*, ed. by Zygmunt G. Barański and Lino Pertile (Cambridge: Cambridge University Press), pp. 137–58

RIZZOLATTI, GIACOMO, and LAILA CRAIGHERO. 2004. 'The Mirror-Neuron System', *Annual Review of Neuroscience*, 27: 169–92

ROSSIGNOLI, CLAUDIA. 2019. 'Playing the Afterlife: Dante's Otherworlds in the Gaming Age', *Games and Culture*, 15.7: 825–49

ROTH, WOLFF-MICHAEL. 2013. *Meaning and Mental Representation: A Pragmatic Approach* (Rotterdam: Sense)

RYAN, MARIE-LAURE. 2001. *Narrative as Virtual Reality: Immersion and Interactivity in Literature and Electronic Media* (Baltimore: Johns Hopkins University Press)

—— 2009. 'From Narrative Games to Playable Stories: Toward a Poetics of Interactive Narrative', *Storyworlds: A Journal of Narrative Studies*, 1: 43–59

—— 2015. *Narrative as Virtual Reality 2: Revisiting Immersion and Interactivity in Literature and Electronic Media*, 2nd edn (Baltimore: Johns Hopkins University Press)

RYAN, RICHARD M., and EDWARD L. DECI. 2000. 'Intrinsic and Extrinsic Motivations: Classic Definitions and New Directions', *Contemporary Educational Psychology*, 25.1: 54–67

SAENGER, PAUL. 1997. *Space Between Words: The Origins of Silent Reading* (Stanford: Stanford University Press)

SAUNDERS, CORINNE, and CHARLES FERNYHOUGH. 2016. 'The Medieval Mind', *The Psychologist*, 29: 880–83

SCARRY, ELAINE. 2001. *Dreaming by the Book* (Princeton: Princeton University Press)

SHAPIRO, LAWRENCE A. (ed.). 2011. *The Routledge Handbook of Embodied Cognition* (New York: Routledge)

SHAW, DAVID GARY. 2010. 'Embodiment and the Human from Dante through Tomorrow', *Postmedieval*, 1.1–2: 165–72

SHORT, JOHN, EDERYN WILLIAMS, and BRUCE CHRISTIE. 1976. *The Social Psychology of Telecommunications* (New York: Wiley)

SINDING, MICHAEL. 2014. *Body of Vision: Northrop Frye and the Poetics of Mind* (Toronto: University of Toronto Press)

SINGLETON, CHARLES S. 1954. 'Allegory', in *Dante Studies I: 'Comedy': Elements of Structure* (Cambridge, MA: Harvard University Press), pp. 1–17

—— 1957. 'The Irreducible Dove', *Comparative Literature*, 9: 129–35

—— 1977. *An Essay on the 'Vita Nuova'* (Baltimore: Johns Hopkins University Press)

SOBCHACK, VIVIAN. 1982. 'Toward Inhabited Space: The Semiotic Structure of Camera Movement in Cinema', *Journal of the International Association for Semiotic Studies*, 41.1/4: 317–35

SOWELL, MADISON U. 1983. 'A Bibliography of the Dantean Simile to 1981', *Dante Studies*, 101: 167–80

SPITZER, LEO. 1942. 'Speech and Language in *Inferno* XIII', *Italica*, 19.3: 81–104

—— 1955. 'The Addresses to the Reader in the *Comedy*', *Italica*, 32.3: 143–65

—— 1988. *Representative Essays*, ed. by Alban K. Forcione, Madeline Sutherland, and Herbert Lindenberger (Stanford: Stanford University Press)

SPOLSKY, ELLEN. 1993. *Gaps in Nature: Literary Interpretation and the Modular Mind* (Albany: State University of New York Press)

SPRUIT, LEEN. 1994. *Species Intelligibilis: From Perception to Knowledge, Vol. 1: Classical Roots and Medieval Discussions* (Leiden: Brill)

STANZEL, FRANZ K. 1984. *Theory of Narrative* (Cambridge: Cambridge University Press)

STEINBERG, JUSTIN. 2007. *Accounting for Dante: Urban Readers and Writers in Late Medieval Italy* (Notre Dame: University of Notre Dame Press)

STEVENSON, JILL. 2010. *Performance, Cognitive Theory, and Devotional Culture: Sensual Piety in Late Medieval York* (Basingstoke: Palgrave Macmillan)

STOCK, BRIAN. 1983. *The Implications of Literacy: Written Language and Models of Interpretation in the Eleventh and Twelfth Centuries* (Princeton: Princeton University Press)

—— 1996. *Augustine the Reader: Meditation, Self-Knowledge, and the Ethics of Interpretation* (Cambridge, MA: Harvard University Press)

—— 2001. *After Augustine: The Meditative Reader and the Text* (Philadelphia: University of Pennsylvania Press)

SUTTON, JOHN, and KELLIE WILLIAMSON. 2014. 'Embodied Remembering', in *The Routledge Handbook of Embodied Cognition*, ed. by Lawrence A. Shapiro (New York: Routledge), pp. 315–25

SWEETSER, PENNY. 2008. *Emergence in Games* (Boston, MA: Charles River Media)

TAMBLING, JEREMY. 1988. *Dante and Difference* (Cambridge: Cambridge University Press)

TAYLOR, ANDREW. 2002. *Textual Situations: Three Medieval Manuscripts and their Readers. Material Texts* (Philadelphia: University of Pennsylvania Press)

THOMAS, NIGEL J. T. 1999. 'Are Theories of Imagery Theories of Imagination? An Active Perception Approach to Conscious Mental Content', *Cognitive Science*, 23.2: 207–45

TOOK, JOHN. 2013. 'Style and Existence in Dante', in *Language and Style in Dante: Seven Essays*, ed. by John C. Barnes and Michelangelo Zaccarello (Dublin: Four Courts Press), pp. 197–222

TRONSTAD, RAGNHILD. 2014. 'Emergence', in *The Johns Hopkins Guide to Digital Media*, ed. by Marie-Laure Ryan, Lori Emerson, and Benjamin J. Robertson (Baltimore: Johns Hopkins University Press), pp. 180–81

TROSCIANKO, EMILY. 2013. 'Reading Imaginatively: The Imagination in Cognitive Science and Cognitive Literary Studies', *Journal of Literary Semantics*, 42.2: 181–98

—— 2014. *Kafka's Cognitive Realism* (New York: Routledge)

TURNER, DENYS. 2010. 'How to Do Things with Words: Poetry as Sacrament in Dante's *Comedy*', in *Dante's 'Comedy': Theology as Poetry*, ed. by Vittorio Montemaggi and Matthew Treherne (Notre Dame: University of Notre Dame Press), pp. 286–305

USHER, JONATHAN. 1982. 'Dante's Infernal Vision: How the Poet Saw in the Dark', *Journal of the Association of the Teachers of Italian*, 35: 24–30

VARELA, FRANCISCO, EVAN THOMPSON, and ELEANOR ROSCH. 1993 [1991]. *The Embodied Mind: Cognitive Science and Human Experience* (Cambridge, MA; London: MIT Press)

VIRGIL. 1995. *Aeneid*, trans. by E. McCrorie (Ann Arbor: University of Michigan Press)

WATERWORTH, JOHN A., and GIUSEPPE RIVA. 2014. *Feeling Present in the Physical World and in Computer-Mediated Environments* (Basingstoke: Palgrave Macmillan)

WEBB, HEATHER. 2013. 'Postures of Penitence in Dante's *Purgatory*', *Dante Studies*, 131: 219–36

—— 2016. *Dante's Persons: An Ethics of the Transhuman* (Oxford: Oxford University Press)

—— 2019. 'Botticelli's Illustrations of Dante's *Paradiso*: The Construction of Conjoined Vision', *I Tatti Studies in the Italian Renaissance*, 22.2: 187–208

WEINRICH, HARALD. 1994. 'La Mémoire linguistique de l'Europe', *Langages*, 114: 13–24

WELSH, TIMOTHY J., and JOHN SEBASTIAN. 2014. 'Shades of Dante. Virtual Bodies in Dante's *Inferno*', in *Digital Gaming Re-imagines the Middle Ages*, ed. by Daniel T. Kline (London: Routledge), pp. 162–74

WHATLING, STUART. 2010. 'Narrative Art in Northern Europe, c.1140–1300: A Narratological Re-appraisal' (unpublished doctoral thesis, Courtauld Institute of Art)

WILLIAMS, WILLIAM CARLOS. 1964. *Paterson, Books I-V* (London: McGibbon and Kee)

WILSON, MARGARET. 2002. 'Six Views of Embodied Cognition', *Psychonomic Bulletin and Review*, 9.4: 625–36

WITMER, BOB G., and MICHAEL J. SINGER. 1998. 'Measuring Presence in Virtual Environments: A Presence Questionnaire', *Presence: Teleoperators and Virtual Environments*, 7.3: 225–40

WOJCIEHOWSKI, HANNAH, and VITTORIO GALLESE. 2011. 'How Stories Make Us Feel: Toward an Embodied Narratology', *California Italian Studies*, 2.1

YATES, FRANCES A. 1984 [1966]. *The Art of Memory* (London: Ark Paperbacks)

ZOMPETTI, JOSEPH P. 2017. 'A Theory of Vernacular Rhetoric: Reading Dante's *De Vulgari Eloquentia*', *Inquiries Journal*, 9.4, <http://www.inquiriesjournal.com/a?id=1617> [accessed 15 June 2021]

Digital or non-textual works

Mirror's Edge, dir. by Senta Jakobsen, des. by Thomas Andersson. 2008. DICE/Electronic Arts, Playstation 3, Xbox 360, MS Windows <http://www.mirrorsedge.com/en_GB/>

TonyTCTN: TCTNGaming, Nenad Krstić's channel, YouTube, <https://www.youtube.com/user/TCTNGaming>

INDEX

❖

www.ingramcontent.com/pod-product-compliance
Lightning Source LLC
Chambersburg PA
CBHW050658110426
42739CB00035B/3448